ASSESSING STUDENT COMPETENCE
IN ACCREDITED DISCIPLINES

ASSESSING STUDENT COMPETENCE IN ACCREDITED DISCIPLINES

Pioneering Approaches to Assessment in Higher Education

EDITED BY *Catherine A. Palomba* and *Trudy W. Banta*

STERLING, VIRGINIA

Published in 2001 by

Stylus Publishing, LLC
22883 Quicksilver Drive
Sterling, Virginia 20166

Library of Congress Cataloging-in-Publication-Data

Assessing student competence in accredited disciplines : pioneering approaches to assessment in higher education / edited by Catherine A. Palomba and Trudy W. Banta.—1st ed.
    p. cm.
  Includes bibliographical references (p.) and index.
  ISBN 1-57922-034-7 (alk. paper)
    1. Professional education—Standards.   2. Education, Higher—Standards.   3. Educational tests and measurements.   I. Palomba, Catherine A., 1943– II. Banta, Trudy W.

LC1072.S73 A88 2001
378.1'66—dc21   2001032070

First edition, 2001
ISBN: hardcover 1-57922-034-7

Printed in Canada

All first editions printed on acid-free paper

This book is dedicated to:

Nancy, Neil, Nick, Mary Frances, and Maddie
Logan, Holly, and T.J.

CONTENTS

PREFACE

The past 15 years have been marked by a great deal of interest in assessment of student learning. Faculty in colleges and universities both in the United States and abroad have been asked to examine the competence of their graduates and to demonstrate that their educational programs are accomplishing their purposes. Pressures for assessment have come from several groups, including students and their parents, employers of graduates, state legislators, and the general public. In addition to these stakeholders, regional and disciplinary accreditors have played a particularly important role in fostering assessment of student learning within institutions and programs.

Since 1988, the U.S. Department of Education has required accrediting bodies to collect information about student learning as part of the accreditation process. The Council for Higher Education Accreditation (CHEA), created in 1996, expects accrediting organizations to have standards in place that emphasize high expectations for instruction and student achievement. CHEA's affiliate, the Association of Specialized and Professional Accreditors (ASPA), asks its member organizations to focus accreditation review on student development of knowledge and competence. In responding to these requirements and expectations, disciplinary accreditors have stimulated assessment activities on college campuses.

We have observed that faculty and staff in accredited fields are often campus leaders in assessing student learning. In addition to the impetus provided by disciplinary accrediting bodies, faculty in these fields have other advantages in conducting assessment. Peter Ewell (1997) has noted that the "assessment of individual students against clear, observable, criterion-based competency levels" has long been common in academic programs that are professionally focused. Hence, using these measures to examine group performance is "natural" for faculty in these disciplines (p. 369).

Because we believe that faculty in accredited programs have often been campus pioneers in assessment and thus have valuable experiences to share with their colleagues in other fields, we decided to create a volume of contributed chapters focused on assessment in disciplines that are subject to accreditation. To represent the universe of such disciplines, we selected teacher education, pharmacy, nursing, social work, business, computer science, engineering, and the visual arts. To identify campus assessment leaders in these areas, we contacted knowledgeable individuals in the central offices of the relevant disciplinary accrediting bodies. Then we invited these recommended campus leaders to tell the story of assessment in their disciplines.

We asked each contributor to pay close attention to the role that the specialized accreditor(s) played in fostering assessment of student learning in the discipline, to describe the current practice of assessment in that field on various campuses, and to identify assessment lessons for faculty in other fields. In addition, we commissioned a chapter written from a campus-wide perspective that describes how faculty in several accredited disciplines adapt a single tool—the Senior Assignment—to provide a comprehensive assessment of student learning in their major. Finally, we invited a well-known spokesperson from the United Kingdom to broaden the scope of this work by sharing information regarding the assessment of student competence in England.

Audience

We have observed that faculty often learn their most valuable lessons about assessment from educators in other fields, in addition to their own. Thus, we hope this book will appeal to faculty and staff who are interested in the current state of assessment, regardless of discipline. Faculty and staff who are engaged in or responsible for assessment of learning in the major, particularly those who are preparing students to work in professional fields, may be most likely to find the book of interest. Readers should gain an appreciation of the state of practice with respect to assessment, exposure to some new ideas about undertaking assessment, and familiarity with the contributions that specialized accrediting bodies have made to the process.

Overview of the Chapters

Chapter 1 explores the context for assessment of student competence in accredited programs. In this chapter, we consider what it means to declare a student competent and describe some of the pressures on faculty to examine student competence. In Chapter 2, we present our definition of *assessment* and identify several strategies that contribute to successful assessment of student competence. Chapter 3 through Chapter 10 focus on the implementation of assessment in particular disciplines. In Chapter 11, the focus is not on a single discipline but rather on a particular campus approach that has been adapted by faculty in several accredited disciplines to provide authentic assessment in the major field. Chapter 12 contains a description of the role of professional bodies in establishing expectations for student competence in England.

Chapter 13 provides an overview of the previous chapters and a review of the state of assessment in the eight disciplines treated in the book. In particular, we look at the effect of accreditation on assessment in these disciplines and the lessons and challenges that seem common among faculty who are practicing assessment in these fields. We conclude that with leadership and guidance from relevant accrediting bodies, faculty on many campuses have made significant progress in carrying out assessment. They have reached consensus about various competences expected of students in their programs, developed and implemented relevant assessment techniques, and used assessment results to improve student learning. We also conclude that specialized accrediting bodies have had noteworthy influence on the assessment of student learning within these disciplines, helping their members to understand and carry out meaningful assessment of student competence.

Acknowledgments

We are very grateful to the 13 knowledgeable authors who contributed to this volume, generously sharing their assessment expertise with our readers. We are also grateful to the leaders of the disciplinary accreditation organizations featured here. Every individual with whom we spoke in these organizations expressed support for our plan to create this volume and gave us valuable advice in identifying chapter authors. Jay Kridel at AACSB—The International Association for Management Education and Samuel Hope at the National Association of Schools of Art and Design were particularly helpful in sending assessment-related materials to us. The websites of the Council for Higher Education Accreditation, the Association of Specialized and Professional Accreditors, and several disciplinary accreditors also provided valuable information.

On our own campuses, we would like to thank Sherry Woosley, Brian Pickerill, Rebecca Costomiris, and Debra Atkinson at Ball State University and

Karen Black, Kim Kline, Peggy Wilkes, Linda Durr, Kathy Meredith, and Amy
Nichols at Indiana University–Purdue University Indianapolis.

Catherine A. Palomba
Ball State University
Muncie, Indiana

Trudy W. Banta
Indiana University–Purdue University Indianapolis
Indianapolis, Indiana

June 2001

Reference

Ewell, P. T. (1997). Strengthening assessment for academic quality improvement. In M. W. Peterson, D. D. Dill, L. A. Mets, & Associates (Eds.), *Planning and management for a changing environment: A handbook on redesigning postsecondary institutions*. San Francisco: Jossey-Bass.

THE AUTHORS

Catherine A. Palomba is director of institutional research and academic assessment at Ball State University (BSU). Previously, she was a research analyst at the Center for Naval Analyses in Alexandria, Virginia and an associate professor of economics at West Virginia University (WVU). While at WVU, she published referred articles in several journals and received two awards as an outstanding teacher. Recently, she has given presentations about assessment at several college campuses and assessment conferences. In 1998, the American Productivity and Quality Center recognized Ball State University's assessment program as a "best practice" institution for assessing learning outcomes. In 1999, Catherine co-authored *Assessment Essentials: Planning, Implementing, and Improving Assessment in Higher Education,* published by Jossey-Bass. Dr. Palomba earned a bachelor's degree from the Baruch School of the City College of New York (1965), a master's degree from the University of Minnesota (1966), and a Ph.D. from Iowa State University (1969), all in economics.

Trudy W. Banta is professor of higher education and vice chancellor for planning and institutional improvement at Indiana University–Purdue University Indianapolis. Prior to coming to Indianapolis in 1992, she was a professor of education and founding director of the Center for Assessment Research and Development at the University of Tennessee, Knoxville. Dr. Banta has edited seven previously published volumes on outcomes assessment in higher education and contributed more than 20 book chapters and 100 articles and reports to the literature of higher education. She is founding editor of the bimonthly *Assessment Update,* which has been published by Jossey-Bass since 1989. She has consulted with faculty in 42 states and made invited addresses in nine other countries on the subject of assessment. She has received awards for her work from the American Association for Higher Education, the National

Council on Measurement in Education, and the American Productivity and Quality Center. Dr. Banta received her baccalaureate and master's degrees from the University of Kentucky and her Ed.D. in educational psychology from the University of Tennessee.

Frank R. Baskind is dean of the School of Social Work at Virginia Commonwealth University and president of the Council on Social Work Education. He has served as a site-visitor for and chair of the Commission on Accreditation, Council on Social Work Education. His interest in assessment includes the development of social work education programs at the graduate and undergraduate levels. He earned the Master's of Social Work and the Ph.D. in curriculum and supervision from the University of Connecticut.

Donna L. Boland, R.N., is associate professor and associate dean for undergraduate programs at the Indiana University (IU) School of Nursing. Dr. Boland consults and publishes in the areas of curriculum design and evaluation and in outcomes assessment of student learning. She has presented on faculty evaluation, curriculum and teaching evaluation approaches, and assessment at a number of national nursing and higher education conferences. She is the recipient of the 1989 Utah State Nurses' Association Academic Education Award, the 1995 Midwest Alliance in Nursing Rozella Schlotfeldt Leadership Award, and the 2001 Honorary Alumna Award presented by the IU School of Nursing. She served on the National League for Nursing Council of Baccalaureate and Higher Degree's Accreditation and is currently a member of the Commission on Collegiate Nursing Education. Dr. Boland earned an A.A.S. at Corning Community College (1967), a B.S. at State University of New York Utica/Rome (1976), an M.S. at Russell Sage College, and a Ph.D. at the University of Utah (1986).

Mary E. Diez is professor of education and graduate dean at Alverno College in Milwaukee. A 1995 winner of the Harold W. McGraw, Jr. Prize in Education, she is former president of the American Association of Colleges for Teacher Education. She served for six years on the National Board for Professional Teaching Standards and is currently a member of the Board of Examiners of the National Council for the Accreditation of Teacher Education. She represents teacher education on a number of projects for the Interstate New Teacher Assessment and Support Consortium, a group sponsored by the Council of Chief State School Officers and charged with the design of prototype standards for initial teacher licensure. In her writing, she focuses on standards and assessment in both teacher education and K–12 school reform.

Dr. Diez received her B.A. at Alverno College, M.A. at the University of Nebraska–Lincoln, and Ph.D. at Michigan State University.

Douglas J. Eder is associate professor of neuroscience and director of undergraduate assessment and program review at Southern Illinois University Edwardsville (SIUE). Since 1993, Dr. Eder has led the construction of SIUE's assessment program, and consequently he has been a speaker at four dozen national and regional conferences, consulted on assessment with more than 60 institutions of higher learning from Canada to the Caribbean, and published numerous articles on various assessment topics, especially authentic assessment. SIUE's assessment program was cited in November 1998 by the American Association of State Colleges and Schools as a "best practice" site for academic quality assurance. He has twice received SIUE's Teaching Excellence Award and also received its Research Scholar Award. In 2000–2001, Dr. Eder served as the Emerson Visiting Distinguished Scholar at Hamilton College in New York. Dr. Eder holds an A.B. in religion from the College of Wooster (1966), and a M.S. in endocrinology (1969) and Ph.D. in physiology/biophysics (1973) from Florida State University.

Elaine K. Ferraro is chair of the Department of Human Relations at Columbia College and currently serves on the Council on Social Work Education (CSWE) Commission on Accreditation. As part of her Commission responsibilities, she chaired the Program Development Committee that developed training materials to assist programs in responding to the CSWE evaluative standard on program rationale and assessment. The committee has presented several training sessions at national social work education conferences. The main focus of Dr. Ferraro's assessment work has been developing and implementing assessment plans that provide helpful and useful data to the Human Relations Department and Social Work Program at Columbia College. She received her B.A. in sociology and psychology from Columbia College, her M.S.W. from Virginia Commonwealth University, and her Ph.D. in social work from the University of South Carolina.

Lee Harvey is professor and director of the Centre for Research into Quality (CRQ) at the University of Central England in Birmingham. His published books include: *Transforming Higher Education* (Open University Press), *Graduates' Work* (CRQ and Association for Graduate Recruiters); *Work Experience* (CRQ and Council for Industry and Higher Education); *Doing Sociology* (Macmillan); *Theories and Methods* (Hodder and Stoughton), and *Critical Social Research* (Routledge). He has many articles in referred journals and texts, including the widely cited *Defining Quality*. Dr. Harvey has wide experience in social research and is the editor of *Quality in Higher Education,* an international journal. He has also been a higher education quality advisor in New Zealand, Denmark, Australia, Brazil, Chile, Sweden, South Africa, Hong Kong and the United States. Dr. Harvey's current main research areas are employability and computer-supported learning. He holds a B.A. in economics from the University of East Anglia, a Postgraduate Certificate in education from Leeds University, an M.S. in information technology from Aston University, and a Ph.D. in sociology from the Open University.

Juanita M. Laidig, R.N., is associate professor and undergraduate coordinator in the Department of Adult Health at the Indiana University School of Nursing. She is most interested in assessment of the mathematical skills needed by students to be competent in dosage calculation for medication administration and she works with faculty in their design of plans to gather assessment data for measurement of achievement of course and program outcomes. Dr. Laidig holds a B.S. (1965), an M.S.N. (1977), and an Ed.D. (1995) from Indiana University.

Dr. John A. Muffo has been director of academic assessment at Virginia Polytechnic and State University (Virginia Tech) since 1990. Prior to that he held institutional research and related positions at Virginia Tech, the Indiana Commission for Higher Education, Cleveland State University, and the University of Illinois at Urbana-Champaign. Dr. Muffo serves as a reviewer for the Southern Association of Colleges and Schools, the Western Association for Schools and Colleges, and the Ohio Board of Regents. He has reviewed proposals for the Fund for the Improvement of Postsecondary Education (FIPSE), among other organizations, is a past-president of the Association for Institutional Research, and has served as a consultant on assessment and institutional effectiveness matters on every continent except Antarctica. He holds a B.A. from St. Francis College and an M.Ed. from Ohio University. His M.B.A. and Ph.D. in higher education administration are from the University of Denver.

Kristi Nelson is the vice provost for academic planning and professor of art history at the University of Cincinnati (UC) with responsibilities for the coordination of academic programs, collaboration initiatives, and new learning markets. She has been a faculty member at UC since 1979 and continues to teach both undergraduate and graduate courses in art history. Dr. Nelson currently serves on the Commission on Accreditation for the National Association of Schools of Art and Design (NASAD), and previously served a six-year term on NASAD's Executive Committee. She has reviewed many art and design colleges and universities through the country as an on-site evaluator for NASAD. She holds a B.A. from Florida State University and a Ph.D. in art history from the University of North Carolina at Chapel Hill.

Neil A. Palomba has been dean of the College of Business and professor of economics at Ball State University since 1984. Previously he was associate dean of the College of Business and Management at the University of Maryland. His main interests have been manpower economics issues, evaluation, and, more recently, assessment of student learning. He co-authored the text, *Manpower Economics* (Addison-Wesley Co.) and authored several articles that have appeared in referred journals such as the Journal of Political Economy, Journal of Law and Economics, and Southern Economic Journal. He has presented papers at several economics and assessment conferences. He received a B.B.A. in economics from the Baruch School of the City College of New York (1963) and a Ph.D. in economics from the University of Minnesota (1966).

Barbara W. Shank is professor and dean of the School of Social Work at the University of St. Thomas and the College of St. Catherine. She has chaired numerous accreditation site visits for the Council on Social Work Education and serves on the Commission on Accreditation. Dr. Shank has done extensive work on using student outcomes assessment for building curricula and program evaluation. She holds a Master's of Social Work and a Ph.D. in higher education administration from the University of Minnesota.

Gordon E. Stokes is a retired professor of computer science having taught at Brigham Young University for more than 30 years. He became interested in assessment during his doctoral work, focusing on the assessment of student achievement and the contribution of the assessment process to the learning environment. He has used various forms of mastery learning in his large introductory classes for more than 20 years. In addition to classroom experiences, Dr. Stokes has been involved with academic program accreditation in the computer science area for more than 25 years, serving as chairman of the Association for Computing Machinery's accreditation committee for 12 years. He is convinced that effective assessment of student learning is an absolutely essential part of quality education. Dr. Stokes holds a B.S. from Brigham Young University, an M.S. from the University of Idaho, both in physics, and an Ed.D. from Brigham Young University in curriculum design.

Thomas D. Zlatic is professor of English and director of the Writing Center at the St. Louis College of Pharmacy, where he has also served as director of the Division of Arts and Sciences and as director of the Assessment Center. Dr. Zlatic was principal investigator of a Grant Award for Pharmacy Schools grant for "Integrating Critical Thinking into the Pharmacy Curriculum" (1993–95) and was a local project coordinator for the three-college FIPSE Grant on "A Multi-Institutional Assessment Center Model to Facilitate Expansion of Ability-based Education in Schools of Pharmacy" (1993–96). He has served on the American Association of Colleges of Pharmacy (AACP) Focus Group for Liberalization of the Professional Curriculum and on the Center for the Advancement of Pharmaceutical Education (CAPE) Advisory Panel on Educational Outcomes. For 1999/2000, he was the chair of the AACP Academic Affairs Committee. He is author/editor of *Developing Thinking Abilities Within Pharmacy Education: A Sourcebook* (St. Louis College of Pharmacy, 1996). Dr. Zlatic received his B.A. in English from the University of Missouri–St. Louis (1969) and his Ph.D. in English from St. Louis University (1974).

I

ASSESSING COMPETENCE
IN HIGHER EDUCATION

Trudy W. Banta

What is competence?[1] A flippant response might be, "Competence, like quality, is in the eye of the beholder. Don't ask me to define it—I know it when I see it."

But educators with nearly two decades of experience in addressing external pressures to demonstrate accountability in higher education will not be satisfied with a flippant response. They recognize that institutions hoping to convince stakeholders of the value of their credentials and to compete successfully with for-profit and Internet providers of skills training and more advanced course work must define more precisely the knowledge, skills, and attitudes students are expected to develop as a result of their experiences at those institutions.

Defining Competence

So what is competence? Many have attempted to define it. For example, in their *Resource Handbook on Performance Assessment and Measurement*, Patricia Wheeler and Geneva Haertel define an area of competence as "a knowledge, skill, ability, personal quality, experience, or other characteristic that is applicable to learning and success in school or in work" (1993, p. 30). Similarly, in their assessment handbook for dieticians, Carolyn Haessig and Armand La Potin define core competences as the "set of knowledge, abilities, skills, capabilities, judgment, attitudes, and values that entry-level practitioners are expected to possess and apply for employment in dietetics" (2000, p. 48). Sue Otter (1995) notes in her discussion of student assessment in England that competence statements define "what learners are intended to achieve" rather than the courses or programs of learning that are used to develop them (p. 45). Otter points out that statements of competence also are used to describe "the underlying skills, qualities, and ways of working which characterize people who are good at it" (p. 49). These competences can be identified by studying people who are successful at their jobs. Chris Boys writes that in England vocational competence statements are used to specify clearly "what a candidate has to do in order to be judged competent to perform to the high standards required under real working conditions" (1995, p. 28). At King's College in the United States, competence growth plans for each student focus on assessment of "transferable skills of liberal learning" (Williams & Parsons, 1999, p. 4). In many cases, the term *competence* is used interchangeably with *skills, learning objectives,* or, more recently, with *expected learning outcomes.*

One recent attempt to answer the question concerning the definition of competence was undertaken by the Competency-Based Initiatives Working Group of the National Postsecondary Education Cooperative (NPEC), one of a series of panels appointed to advise the National Center on Education Statistics on the ramifications of collecting various kinds of data on the postsecondary education enterprise. After lengthy debate, the Working Group concluded that competence may be viewed as sitting "atop the apex of a hierarchy of experiences that have currency for the learner" (Jones & Voorhees, 2000, p. 8). At the base of the hierarchy, *traits and characteristics* provide the foundation for learning; they are the innate qualities on which learning experiences help to build *skills, abilities, and knowledge*—the next level of the hierarchy. At the third level, *competence* is "the result of integrative learning experiences in which skills, abilities, and knowledge interact to form bundles" (p. 8) that are relevant to the task for which they are assembled. The Working Group conceived of *demonstrations* as the results of applying competence and the bases for assessing performance. To ensure that a student has attained competence, three items of information are needed: a description of the competence, a means of measuring the competence, and a standard by which the student may be judged as competent.

The NPEC Working Group developed a classification structure based on timing and context for assessing competence in postsecondary education. That is, assessment of the competence of individual students can take place at entry, within, and/or just prior to exit from postsecondary education. In addition, overall assessments of the competence of groups of students can be used to determine program and institutional effectiveness and provide direction for improvements as well as evidence of accountability to external stakeholders. The Working Group used this classification framework for selecting case studies that would illustrate good practice in competence-based education.

The Working Group sought programs in which faculty first introduce students to the types of competence they are expected to develop, then provide clear opportunities throughout the curriculum for students to learn and practice various levels of the specified knowledge and skills and be tested on them, and finally assess and certify competence at or near the end of the program. In addition, Working Group members hoped to locate programs that are making continuous progress in refining the definitions of competence at various levels, improving the technical quality of the measuring instruments used to assess competence, and adjusting instructional methods to ensure the development of competence.

Over a period of some 18 months, Working Group members and a consultant attempted to locate colleges and universities employing competence-based initiatives in one or more disciplines. Ultimately, about two dozen such institutions nationwide were identified and five were selected to serve as sites for case studies. But very few institutions in this group were sufficiently advanced in their work to demonstrate all the characteristics outlined in the previous paragraph.

Why is competence so difficult to define and assess? What can we learn from those who have attempted these tasks? These are two of the questions that motivated the authors to compile the chapters in this book, which are based primarily on the experiences of faculty in professional fields, presumably those most likely to find it appropriate and comfortable to define and assess student competence.

Who Cares About Competence?

If we define competence as the integration of skills, abilities, and knowledge as focused on a particular task (Jones & Voorhees, 2000), it means that competence outside the classroom will most often be associated with job performance. Thus, the people who care most about the development of competence are employers of graduates—particularly those who serve as trustees for public and private colleges and universities and those who influence the policies established for higher education by governors and legislators, both state and national.

The globalization of the world economy and the growth of information technology have brought numerous changes in the way employers conduct business. One of these changes has involved setting higher expectations for the performances of college graduates who enter the workforce (American Council on Education, 1997). Because education is increasingly important to their economic success, American corporations "are evaluating ever more critically whether college and university graduates are meeting their needs" (Broad, 1998, p. vi). Although various businesses differ in their specific requirements, nearly all seek employees who can think critically, communicate effectively, solve applied problems, manage their time, and work with others. Knowledge about information technologies and the global environment is essential as well (Gardner, 1998; Broad, 1998).

Basing their findings on interviews with thousands of employers, staff from the National Center for Higher Education Management Systems (NCHEMS, 2000) concluded recently that to be successful in the 21st century workforce, students need appropriate attitudes such as adaptability and dependability, essential skills such as computing and writing, and interpretive-applied skills such as critical thinking and information processing. In addition, they need to be exposed not only to solving problems but also to "identifying real world messy problems that defy neat solutions" (NCHEMS, 2000, p. 3).

National and state surveys suggest that employers would like colleges and universities to incorporate in curricula more emphasis on transferable skills such as leadership, communication, quantification, adaptability to change, and interpersonal relations. Nevertheless, employers are generally satisfied with the specialized knowledge graduates acquire in their majors (Van Horn, 1995; Rodriguez & Ruppert, 1996). A review of findings from several studies led Gardner to conclude that "College students show strength in their content or academic skill base but lack competencies to handle successfully the principal complex issues of work: interpersonal communication, teamwork, applied problem solving, time management, setting priorities, and taking initiative" (1998, p. 61).

To produce graduates who are prepared to work and function as responsible citizens, educators at all levels must understand society's needs. Criticisms of workforce preparation focused initially on high-school graduates, and by 1991 the Secretary of Labor's Commission on Achieving Necessary Skills (SCANS) had identified five competences that high-school graduates need whether they go to work, apprenticeship, the armed services, or college. These include abilities to identify, organize, plan, and allocate resources; work with others, including those with diverse backgrounds; acquire and use information; understand complex technological and organizational systems; and select and work with a variety of technologies to accomplish various tasks. A three-part foundation of skills and personal qualities is necessary as well. The foundation includes basic skills such as reading, writing, and mathematical ability; thinking skills including creativity, decision making, and problem solving; and personal qualities such as self-esteem, integrity, and honesty (pp. xvii and xviii). Based on their conviction that "We are failing to develop the full academic abilities of most students and utterly failing the majority of poor, disadvantaged, and minority students" (p. vi), the writers of the SCANS report urged educators to infuse the competences and foundation into "every nook and cranny of the school curriculum" (p. ix).

As attention has turned to the preparation of postsecondary students, the federal government has commissioned studies of the skills college graduates need in the workplace. With funding from the National Center for Education Statistics (NCES), faculty at the National Center on Postsecondary Teaching, Learning, and Assessment at the Pennsylvania State University began in 1994 to conduct surveys of faculty, employers, and state policymakers that focused on essential skills in writing, speaking and listening, reading, critical thinking, and problem solving. Rather than providing definitions, these studies were designed to determine if stakeholders could agree on necessary college outcomes and to stimulate discussion among college faculty about the learning goals that are most appropriate for their own undergraduates.

The NCES-sponsored studies actually found substantial agreement among participants about many of the skills college graduates need to develop. However, the studies also uncovered some differences among the groups in how broad skills such as communication and critical thinking are defined. Survey results dealing with written communication skills revealed that, compared to employers, faculty were more interested in the process of writing. Hence, faculty stressed the need for time to develop, draft, and revise ideas. Employers, concerned with time constraints, were more interested in the final products of writing, including the effective use of tables, graphs, and other visual aids in completed documents. Employers and policymakers indicated that basic writing skills, such as using correct grammar and accurately quoting sources, were extremely important and often lacking in new employees. Some faculty thought that students should already have mastered basic skills; therefore, these skills were too elementary to be addressed at the college level. With respect to speech communication skills, faculty placed importance on both interpersonal communication and public speaking. In contrast, many employers were concerned primarily with interpersonal communication and placed little importance on public speaking. The NCES studies make clear that while there is widespread agreement among stakeholders about the importance of communication and other broad skills, achieving agreement about how these skills translate into specific expectations is still some distance away (Jones, 1996a, 1996b).

Canadian observers have also commented on the tendency of educational institutions and employer organizations to operate as "isolated spheres" (Evers, Rush, & Berdrow, 1998, p. xviii). Drawing on their comprehensive study of corporate managers, undergraduate students from five Ontario universities, and college graduates employed in twenty Canadian organizations, Evers, Rush, and Berdrow identify a "skill gulf between education and employment," particularly for skills that are used in dealing with people and coping with change (p. 16). In their recent book, *The Bases of Competence,* the authors argue for a "competency-based approach in teaching and learning" (p. xvii). Reflecting their conviction that higher education curricula need "a fundamental shift toward an emphasis on general skills," the authors describe four competences that graduates should possess to complement the specialist skills they typically develop in college (p. 12). These include managing self, communicating, managing people and tasks, and mobilizing for innovation and change. Each represents a grouping of nontechnical skills as "salient and enduring as reading and writing" (p. 16).

Although various observers identify somewhat different sets of competences that should be emphasized across college and university curricula, most come to the same general conclusion: educators must invest additional energy if they are to produce graduates who are "ready to work." In the view of Oblinger and Verville (1998), authors of *What Business Wants From Higher Education,* quality in the academy will occur only "when graduates are prepared for the world of work and a balanced life." They recommend that educators apply the industrial concept of "fitness for use" to the readiness of graduates (p. 125).

Why Assess Competence?

Competence lies dormant and unidentified until it is applied or demonstrated, according to the NPEC Working Group. The act of demonstrating competence provides an opportunity to measure or assess it, and today there are many compelling reasons to assess the competence of college students and graduates.

For most of its long history, higher education maintained a status that made it seem immune from the intense public scrutiny that was so often focused on elementary and secondary education and other social services. But, in the early 1980s, a number of reports that were critical of various aspects of American higher education began to appear. One of the most influential was *Involvement in Learning,* compiled by a distinguished group of educators working under the auspices of the National Institute of Education (NIE Study Group, 1984). After calling into question what college students were actually learning, the NIE Study Group made three recommendations based on current research on learning. They urged their colleagues in higher education to set high expectations for student learning, engage students actively in learning, and provide frequent assessment of learning accompanied by prompt feedback to students about their performance.

The NIE had planned to follow the release of *Involvement in Learning* with a national conference a year later to call attention to examples of good practice in the areas defined by the report's three recommendations. But, by the time that conference was held in late 1985, the attention riveted on assessment had so far outstripped that on high expectations and active learning that the national conference was on assessment, not on the report in its entirety. The American Association for Higher Education assumed responsibility for the annual assessment conference; and, over the past 15 years, this event has grown to attract 1,200 to 1,500 educators annually. By 1995, the American Council on Education's annual *Campus Trends* survey of college and university provosts revealed that the interest in assessment in higher education had become so pervasive that more than 90 percent of institutions in the United States were conducting assessment initiatives or planning to do so (El-Khawas, 1995).

Additional pressures for assessing student learning have come from outside the academy. While educators have been looking at assessment with feedback as a way to increase learning for individual students and at the result of assessing groups of students as a source of guidance for improving instruction, stakeholders in the external community have called for assessment to provide evidence of accountability.

In 1979, Tennessee became the first state to base a portion of state funding for its public colleges and universities on the assessment of student competence (Banta, Rudolph, Van Dyke, & Fisher 1996). Graduating students are required to take tests in general education and in the major, and an institution receives an increase in its budget for instruction if cumulative test scores are above the national average on standardized exams or if continuous improvement on locally developed tests can be demonstrated. Though few other programs are as prescriptive as Tennessee's performance funding initiative, many governors, legislatures, and boards of trustees have followed Tennessee's lead in issuing mandates for assessing competence. A 1998 survey of state higher education finance officers revealed that performance—often in the realm of student learning—was linked to budgeting for public institutions in 42% of the 50 states and that this figure was likely to grow to 62% within five years of the survey date (Burke, 1998).

While state and trustee mandates have been compelling influences for public colleges and universities to assess and improve student competence, governors, legislators, and trustees come and go, often taking with them their policies and priorities. In some states, performance criteria have been changed periodically (Ewell, 2000); and, in others, performance budgeting has been introduced, then withdrawn for a few years, and finally reinstated using a new set of measures. Moreover, state mandates may have little or no impact on private institutions. Regional and disciplinary accrediting agencies that regulate both public and private institutions and maintain approval criteria with little modification for more than a decade may be the most stable and thus powerful external sources of pressure for assessment. In the next section, we describe accreditation and its growing influence on the assessment of competence.

Accreditors' Responses to Pressures to Assess Competence

Between 1870 and 1925, six regional associations of postsecondary institutions were formed in the United States, initially for the purpose of facilitating college entry by imposing some uniformity on entrance requirements. These six voluntary associations (by order of founding: New England, Middle States, Southern, North Central, Northwest, and Western), which eventually encompassed all 50 states, established their own criteria for institutional membership. According to Harcleroad (1999), ". . . at the same time that the federal government instituted regulatory commissions to control similar problems (the Interstate Commerce Commission in 1887, the Federal Trade Commission in 1914, and the Federal Power Commission in 1920), these nongovernmental voluntary membership groups sprang up to provide yardsticks for student achievement and institutional operations" (p. 251).

Regional accrediting associations have always been concerned with postsecondary institutions as a whole, focusing in particular on ensuring that these institutions are doing what their mission statements say they should be doing. Beginning with the American Medical Association in 1847, practitioners and faculty in professional fields began to form their own voluntary associations, and, by the early 1900s, the concept of reviewing and approving member programs in academic disciplines emerged—first in medicine (Harcleroad, 1999).

Disciplinary accreditation, like regional accreditation, has traditionally focused more on input and processes than on outcomes. Typical questions asked by visiting teams include the following: Is there an appropriate mission statement, and are there governance structures to support it? Are admissions criteria clearly stated and faithfully applied? Is there a general education program to impart basic skills and understandings? Do the faculty have appropriate credentials to carry out the mission? Is the library collection adequate? Does the curriculum in each discipline contain course work and other experiences that will prepare professionals with qualifications for work in their chosen field?

Where accreditors have addressed student learning, their questions have been: What courses are students taking? and, Are appropriate grading procedures in place? rather than, What are students actually learning? With the current emphases on accountability and continuous improvement, there is a need to aggregate measures of individual student learning to obtain information for assessing course and program effectiveness and providing direction for improving curriculum and methods of instruction. Neither regional nor disciplinary accrediting bodies were positioned to provide much help in these areas to their member institutions and departments, respectively, when governors, legislators, and trustees began clamoring for more evidence of program quality and performance in the early 1980s.

This situation has changed dramatically since 1988. In that year, then Secretary of Education William Bennett issued an executive order that required accrediting agencies to include in their criteria provisions for documenting the educational achievements of students and verifying "that institutions or programs confer degrees only on those students who have demonstrated educational achievement as assessed and documented through appropriate measures" (U.S. Department of Education, 1988, p. 25098). The threat of losing approval from the Department of Education and with it access to federal funds caused most accrediting organizations to revise their criteria to include a focus on program outcomes, particularly student learning. However, the ability to define and enforce the new criteria has been developed far more rapidly by some agencies than by others.

In 1998, amendments to the Higher Education Act gave the force of law to the intent of the 1988 Executive Order. New accrediting agencies seeking recognition from the Department of Education must evaluate the ability of a program or institution to maintain and achieve clearly specified educational objectives and assess the quality of education provided, as well as efforts to improve that quality (Higher Education Amendments, 1998). Any accrediting associations that may have been reluctant to take action to define and enforce assessment criteria previously must certainly pay attention to these matters now.

In addition to writing an emphasis on outcomes into criteria for self-study and for continued attention following the accreditation decision, many accreditors have taken steps to assist their members in addressing the new standards. Some have drafted reference materials on outcomes assessment. Others, like the New England Association of Schools and Colleges and AACSB—The International Association for Management Education (formerly the American Assembly of Collegiate Schools of Business), have conducted assessment conferences and workshops to enable members to learn from each other. Virtually all have committed sessions or entire tracks at their annual meetings to papers and panel presentations on assessment.

Not every faculty offering a college major is subject to disciplinary accreditation. For instance, while there are voluntary associations for humanities, social science, and science faculties, these associations do not accredit fields like English, philosophy, political science, or biology. We have chosen to focus on professional fields in this volume in large part because they are subject to accreditation. In our experience, this external influence has made professional fields like nursing, medicine, and social work early adopters of outcomes assessment on campuses across the country.

Professional programs also have other characteristics that have enabled them to become exemplars in conducting assessment for internal improvement and external accountability. These fields are populated by practitioners who have a keen interest in hiring co-workers who are well prepared to add value to their organizations. These practitioners often work with educators in their national disciplinary associations to set learning expectations for college graduates; many also serve on local advisory boards that help faculty keep curricula current. Thus, professional fields are more likely than humanities and science fields to have statements of expected competences for students that can guide curriculum development and instruction.

Professional programs are also more likely to include internships and capstone experiences, like student teaching, in which students must apply the skills and knowledge acquired in the curriculum. Such settings afford faculty unique opportunities to assess student learning from a variety of perspectives.

In short, our thesis is that outcomes assessment in higher education has been shaped fundamentally by regional and disciplinary accrediting associations; thus, approaches to assessment in accredited fields are likely to be more mature and more fully developed than is the case elsewhere in the academy. We have enlisted the assistance of well-informed colleagues in a variety of settings to explore the influences of accreditation on campuses, including faculty reactions to the externally imposed requirements and the kinds of assessment methods to which these requirements have given rise.

Note

1. The authors prefer the term *competence,* with the plural spelled *competences.* However, colleagues in the United States often substitute *competency* and *competencies* for these terms. We use the preferred terms throughout except in direct quotations or references to published works or established groups that include the latter terms in their titles.

References

American Council on Education. (1997). *Spanning the chasm: Corporate and academic cooperation to improve work-force preparation.* Washington, DC: Author.

Banta, T. W., Rudolph, L. B., Van Dyke, J., & Fisher, H. S. (1996). Performance funding comes of age in Tennessee. *Journal of Higher Education, 67,* 23–45.

Boys, C. (1995). National vocational qualifications: The outcomes-plus model of assessment. In A. Edwards & P. Knight (Eds.), *Assessing competence in higher education.* London: Kogan Page.

Broad, M. C. (1998). Foreword in D. G. Oblinger & A. Verville. *What business wants from higher education.* American Council on Education/Oryx Press series on higher education. Phoenix, AZ: The Oryx Press.

Burke, J. C. (1998). Performance budgeting and funding: Making results count where it matters. *Assessment Update, 10*(6), 1–2, 10–11.

El-Khawas, E. (1995). *Campus trends* (Higher Education Panel Rep. No. 85). Washington, DC: American Council on Education.

Evers, T. E., Rush, J. C., & Berdrow, I. (1998). *The bases of competence: Skills for lifelong learning and employability.* San Francisco: Jossey-Bass.

Ewell, P. T. (2000) Accountability with a vengeance: New mandates in Colorado. *Assessment Update, 12*(5), 3, 13, 16.

Gardner, P. D. (1998). Are college seniors prepared to work? In J. N. Gardner, G. Van Der Veer, and Associates (Eds.), *The senior year experience: Facilitating integration, reflection, closure, and transition.* San Francisco: Jossey-Boss.

Haessig, C. J., & La Potin, A. S. (2000). *Outcomes assessment for dietetics educators.* Chicago, IL: Commission on Accreditation for Dietetics Education, The American Dietetics Association.

Harcleroad, F. F. (1999). The hidden hand: External constituencies and their impact. In P. G. Altbach, R. O. Berdahl, & P. J. Gumport (Eds.), *American higher education in the twenty-first century: Social, political, and economic challenges.* Baltimore: Johns Hopkins University Press.

Higher Education Amendments of 1998, Pub. L. No. 105–244.

Jones, E. A. (1996a). Communication outcomes expected by faculty, employers, and policymakers. *Assessment Update, 8*(6), 7–8, 15.

Jones, E. A. (1996b). Editor's notes. In E. A. Jones (Ed.), *Preparing competent college graduates: Setting new and higher expectations for student learning* (New Directions for Higher Education, No. 96). San Francisco: Jossey-Bass.

Jones, E., & Voorhees, R. (2000). *Defining and assessing competencies: Exploring data ramifications of competency-based initiatives. (Draft) Final report of the Working Group on Competency-Based Initiatives.* Washington DC: National Postsecondary Education Cooperative.

National Center for Higher Education Management Systems. (2000, June). Knowledge and skills needed to succeed in the 21st century workforce. *NCHEMS News, 16,* 2–3.

National Institute of Education Study Group. (1984). *Involvement in learning: Realizing the potential of American higher education.* Washington, DC: Author.

Oblinger, D. G., & Verville, A. (1998). *What business wants from higher education.* American Council on Education/Oryx Press series on higher education. Phoenix, AZ: The Oryx Press.

Otter, S. (1995). Assessing competence—The experience of the enterprise in higher education. In A. Edwards & P. Knight. (Eds.), *Assessing competence in higher education.* London: Kogan Page.

Rodriquez, E. M., & Ruppert, S. S. (1996). *Postsecondary education and the new workforce.* Washington, DC: U.S. Department of Education, Office of Educational Research and Improvement.

The Secretary's Commission on Achieving Necessary Skills. (1991). *What work requires of schools: A SCANS report for America 2000.* Washington, DC: U.S. Department of Labor.

U.S. Department of Education. (1988). *Focus on Educational Effectiveness,* Federal Register 53:127, 602.17, p. 25098.

Van Horn, C. E. (1995). *Enhancing the connection between higher education and the workforce: A survey of employers.* Denver, CO: State Higher Education Executive Officers and Education Commission of the States.

Wheeler, P., & Haertel, G. D. (1993). *Resource handbook on performance assessment and measurement: A tool for students, practitioners, and policymakers.* Berkeley, CA: The Owl Press.

Williams, B. H., & Parsons, A. L. (1999, February). *Assessment program essentials: Designs for data collection.* Paper presented at the AACSB Outcome Assessment Seminar, Clearwater Beach, FL.

2

IMPLEMENTING EFFECTIVE ASSESSMENT

Catherine A. Palomba

We define assessment as "the systematic collection, review, and use of information about educational programs undertaken for the purpose of improving student learning and development" (Palomba & Banta, 1999, p. 4). Assessment helps faculty determine whether or not students are acquiring the knowledge, skills, and values that faculty collectively have determined are important. However, assessment involves more than merely documenting the competence of individual students. It requires faculty to focus on the collective impact their programs are having on student learning, to ask not only "How are our students doing?" but also "How are we doing?" Assessment encourages educators to examine whether their programs make sense as a whole and whether students, as a result of all their experiences, are well prepared for the world of work or further education. The goal of assessment is to examine the qualitative and quantitative evidence generated about student competence and to use that evidence to improve the learning of current and future students.

Assessment is a comprehensive process that typically begins when faculty come together to develop statements of what graduates should know, be able to do, and value. These statements capture the expectations that faculty have for student learning and are often called "expected learning outcomes" or "expected competences." Next, faculty may develop their assessment plans, including the selection or design of data collection approaches that will provide evidence of learning. Additional steps in assessment occur when faculty examine, share, and act on their assessment findings and when they reexamine the assessment process itself. Widespread involvement from faculty, current students, alumni, employers, and other key players is necessary as assessment unfolds. Each of the strategies mentioned here is important to the assessment process, whether at the institutional level or the program level, and each is described in the following sections of this chapter.

Developing Statements of Expected Learning Outcomes/Competences

Faculty often find that discussions with colleagues about expected learning outcomes are the most valuable part of the assessment process, even if the conversations are sometimes difficult. These discussions can reveal important assumptions, break down barriers, and sharpen the collective view of faculty about intentions for their graduates. As Elizabeth Jones notes, "structured, ongoing dialogues among faculty about educational goals, objectives, and criteria create cultures with an emphasis on learning outcomes" (1996, p. 1).

Statements of intended learning outcomes, or competences, provide the foundation for assessment. They capture what is important for learning and guide choices for data collection. But equally important, these statements guide decisions about instruction. Diamond believes that, without well-stated learning objectives, "a good instructional program cannot be developed, and assessment lacks a basis on which to collect data or make decisions" (1998, p. 128). In Diamond's view, successful assessment depends on "the match between the objectives and the assessment instruments" and "the match between the objectives and the instructional methods selected" (p. 127). Objectives, instruction, and assessment must be aligned for assessment to improve learning.

Because they are public, statements of expected learning outcomes play additional roles. They provide information to employers about the likely competence of program graduates, helping them make choices about whom to employ. They also inform students about the aims of higher education, helping them make choices about where and what they want to study. These statements direct the attention of students to what is important, clarify what is expected of students, and help students develop skills of self- and peer-evaluation (Diamond, 1998; Huba & Freed, 2000).

In applied fields, the development of expected competences is often facilitated by guidance from professional associations or accrediting bodies. Most have issued statements of expectations about the knowledge, skills, and values that graduates in the field should possess. Usually, these statements are developed collaboratively by faculty and professionals in the discipline and are credible to others in the field. Rather than adopting these statements verbatim, in most cases faculty can adapt them to reflect the characteristics of their own programs. Other materials, such as information from alumni, suggestions from employers of graduates, textbook materials, and classroom assignments, also can be used by faculty as they create their own statements about what the graduates of their program will accomplish.

To be useful in guiding assessment, statements of expected competences need to describe student learning rather than teacher behavior or subject matter coverage. The statement that "graduates of this program will be able to use multimedia to prepare presentations" is an effective way to express an expected competence. The statement that "the program will include instruction in multimedia techniques" is not. The latter describes what teachers will do. To turn statements about teacher behavior into expected learning outcomes, faculty must ask: As a result of this instruction, what will students know, be able to do, or value?

When describing expected learning outcomes for the major, faculty should consider institutional expectations about learning. These expectations, which may appear in the institution's mission statement or in materials describing the general education program, capture the knowledge, skills, and values that graduates of an institution have in common. Typically, these expectations address the transferable skills that are of increasing concern to employers. Departments and programs may be called upon to reinforce these expectations in their own curricula. If so, disciplinary faculty may be able to restate institutional outcomes in language that is specific to their program. For example, a psychology department may restate a broad communication outcome in the following manner: Students will be able to explain the concepts of learning and cognition to a lay audience, using language that is free of jargon.

To reinforce learning, program outcomes need to be reflected in course outcomes. The ability of faculty to translate broad program goals into course specific goals is another assessment success factor identified by Diamond (1998). In practice, some faculty are more comfortable articulating course outcomes first, then reviewing these collectively to decide on program level outcomes. Regardless of the starting point, once program outcomes have been determined, a good practice is to ask course instructors to state explicitly in each course syllabus the program level objectives addressed in that course.

Planning for Assessment

Because all regional accreditors require assessment, many public and private colleges and universities now have functioning assessment plans and activities in place. Institutional assessment requirements often shape assessment at the division, department, and/or program level. Institutional plans may require units to take specific actions such as developing a unit assessment plan, conducting specific assessment activities, or submitting regular reports of assessment progress. In those institutions that include separate divisions or colleges, the division or college assessment plan also may influence what happens in departments or programs.

To be successful at the unit level, assessment requires both leadership and organization. In some cases, disciplinary accreditation standards have an impact on how assessment is organized. For example, the standards of the Commission on Accreditation for Dietetics Education (CADE) of the American Dietetics Association specifically state that "The responsibilities of the Program Director shall include assessment, planning, implementation, and evaluation critical to an effective program" (2000, p. 42). In other cases, it is the department chair who takes leadership or he/she may appoint a respected faculty member to act as an assessment coordinator. To involve faculty, the chair or assessment coordinator may create an assessment committee or add assessment responsibilities to those of an already existing curriculum, strategic planning, or other committee. Any of these approaches can work as long as responsibilities are clearly assigned and faculty have an opportunity to participate in designing and carrying out the assessment program.

Even if there is no institutional requirement, units can benefit from creating assessment plans. Such a plan provides direction for actions and gives faculty a blueprint to determine if they are making progress. Creating a plan encourages faculty to be explicit about what matters in the assessment process. For example, the plan may begin with a statement about the purposes for undertaking assessment. Although accreditors generally argue that their purpose in requiring assessment is to help their members improve instruction and programs, faculty at the unit level can benefit from spending some time discussing their own motives as they proceed with assessment. If faculty agree that assessment will focus on improving programs as well as meeting accreditors' standards, this motive for assessment should be included in the statement of purposes.

Rather than preparing a long written document, faculty agreements can be captured in a simple matrix or time line. For each expected learning outcome, a planning matrix might include the types of assessment activities that will be used, the schedule for these activities, and the intended audiences for the information. In the *Outcomes Assessment for Dietetics Educators* handbook published by the CADE, the authors indicate that a programmatic assessment plan is critical to the assessment process. They recommend that faculty develop a matrix with a separate row for each expected competence and columns that show the data needed for assessment, the group that will be assessed, the assessment method, the individual(s) responsible for conducting the assessment, and the time line. This kind of matrix helps ensure that the assessment process will be systematic rather than haphazard (Haessig & La Potin, 2000).

Selecting and Applying Assessment Methods

The ability of assessment to improve student learning depends on the relevance and usefulness of the information that is generated. To be useful, assessment methods must gather evidence that is closely related to the expected learning outcomes selected by faculty. Gary Pike urges faculty to select techniques that are "sensitive to educational effects" (1998, p. 8). Without this quality, it is difficult for either qualitative or quantitative approaches to detect whether or not improvements are having the desired impact. One of the best initial steps that faculty can take when selecting assessment techniques is to discuss thoughtfully the characteristics of methods that matter to them. Issues of technical quality, convenience, timeliness, and cost will likely dominate that discussion. The value that an assessment activity has for students also is important.

Over time, assessment practitioners have come to realize that the best assessment activities are those that make their own contribution to learning. A number of reports and studies have identified aspects of "good practice" in undergraduate education (Association of American Colleges, 1985; National Institute of Education Study Group, 1984; Chickering & Gamson, 1987). Ewell and Jones (1991) describe several attributes that can serve as effective indicators of campus practice, including setting high expectations for students, creating synthesizing experiences, promoting active learning and ongoing practice of learned skills, encouraging collaborative learning, and providing assessment with prompt feedback. If assessment is to contribute to learning, it makes sense to choose techniques that capture these elements of "good practice." Huba and Freed make this case persuasively in their new book, *Learner-Centered Assessment on College Campuses* (2000). They urge faculty to consider the characteristics mentioned here (along with several others) when selecting assessment methods. Faculty who are teaching in professionally oriented disciplines have many opportunities to apply these principles. For example, these programs can conclude with capstone projects that require students to synthesize their knowledge and skills, allowing students to engage in the kind of experiences they likely will encounter in their first jobs.

Assessment methods can be categorized as either direct or indirect in the evidence they produce about learning. Direct assessment methods, such as performance measures and objective tests, actually demonstrate learning. In contrast, indirect assessment methods, such as questionnaires, interviews, and focus groups, provide reflections about learning. Graduates of programs in nursing, teacher education, dietetics, accounting, and engineering are required to pass a licensing examination in order to enter certain jobs in their fields. Thus, faculty in these disciplines are likely to monitor examination passage rates as one element of their assessment program. In some cases, the accreditor insists that the faculty track these statistics. For example, the accreditation standards for dietetics explicitly state that "One outcome measure shall be the pass rate of first-time test takers on the Registration Examination" (CADE, 2000, p. 43). Programs with a passage rate of less than 80 percent are required to develop an action plan for improvement. In the absence of licensing examinations, faculty may develop their own objective test or they may choose to use a commercially available instrument as part of their assessment program. The Educational Testing Service (ETS) Major Field Tests are available in several disciplines, including economics, English, chemistry, biology, psychology, and political science, as well as business and education. The ETS tests appeal to many faculty because the test developers provide information about reliability and validity, as well as comparative results from test users.

During the past several years, faculty have recognized the limitations of objective tests. These include the tendency of items to focus on factual knowledge rather than higher-order thinking skills, the lack of connection to what professionals do in the real world, and the subtle message that problems always have "right" answers (Diamond, 1998; Huba & Freed, 2000). To overcome these limitations, faculty have shown increasing interest in using performance measures to evaluate their students and programs. Performance assessment allows students to demonstrate their skills through activities such as essays, presentations, demonstrations, and exhibits. As part of the assessment process, these activities or products are rated or scored by faculty and the results are shared with students. For these methods to be successful, faculty must develop and use appropriate scoring guides. The process of performance assessment can be described as "good grading applied to active learning." Performance assessment that is closely aligned with the kind of work students will do as professionals is described as "authentic" (Wiggins, 1998, p. 141).

Performance assessment captures many aspects of educational "good practice" and has a number of important advantages (Palomba & Banta, 1999). First, because performance assessment is often integrated into ongoing course content, the processes of instruction and assessment are no longer seen as disconnected activities. The thoughtful development of performance assessment encourages faculty to align expected learning outcomes, instructional activities, and assessment. A further advantage is that performance assessment draws on the interrelated skills and abilities of students, often asking them to synthesize and integrate what they are learning. The process of performance assessment requires faculty to make their criteria for evaluation explicit and public. Because public criteria "assist students in visualizing the skilled performance expected of them" (Doherty, Chenevert, Miller, Roth, & Truchan, 1997, p. 186), these criteria enhance opportunities for students to develop skills of self- and peer-evaluation. The feedback that accompanies performance assessment also enhances these skills, particularly if the work is publicly displayed and evaluated, perhaps by judges who are external to the program (Wright, 1997). Performance assessment allows students to rethink, revise, and reflect on their work and provides choices for students in the ways they demonstrate their competence.

The process of performance assessment is not without possible limitations, however, particularly with respect to issues of reliability and validity. For example, the fact that student performances are not usually standardized decreases the reliability of assigned scores. In addition, the issue of generalizability, the degree to which performance on one task can be generalized to other tasks, is a major concern (Linn & Baker, 1996). Portfolios (a type of performance assessment in which students reflect on examples of their own work that they have collected over time) provide rich information for faculty to evaluate the achievements of students. Shulman notes, "You don't get higher-order thinking in an hour." Portfolios "have the virtue of permitting students to display, think about, and engage in the kind of intellectual work that takes time to unfold . . ." (1998, p. 36). But, if not done well, portfolios can be cumbersome collections of material that are not worthy of student or faculty reflection (Shulman, 1998).

Indirect assessment measures provide valuable opportunities to collect information from groups such as alumni, internship supervisors, recruiters, and employers who often have explicit expectations about educational programs. Faculty who teach in professionally oriented disciplines can gain useful information about the skills needed in the workplace and the workforce preparation of graduates through surveys or focus groups conducted with these groups. Advisory boards also can be helpful in providing and collecting information about program strengths and weaknesses. AACSB—The International Association for Management Education explicitly recommends the use of feedback from such stakeholders (AACSB, 2000). Indirect assessment methods also work well with current students. Faculty in a number of disciplines interview graduating seniors about program effectiveness and use focus groups to gather students' reflections on their learning and experiences.

The effective use of assessment techniques requires faculty to consider practical questions such as when, where, and from whom assessment information will be collected. For example, once faculty have decided they want to gather opinions about work preparation from alumni, they must select a specific target group. Studies of both recent and long-term alumni are common. Faculty who have not conducted a previous survey may decide to mail questionnaires to every alumnus who graduated from their program in the past five or ten years and then to follow up every year or two with studies of recent graduates. Faculty also may be able to draw on information collected at the institutional level. A number of campuses provide extracts of surveys of alumni and other groups to units.

Several options exist when deciding how to collect information from current students. One of the most effective approaches is to embed the collection of assessment information into normal classroom activities. Faculty can make use of the materials that already are generated through regular course work or create new assignments for this purpose (Wright, 1997; Ewell, 1997). In addition to using these materials to evaluate individual students, faculty can take a "second look" to gather evidence about the overall program. This approach is transparent to students and minimally intrusive for faculty. As Wright points out, course-embedded assessment "makes sense in the individual discipline," respecting its definition of knowledge and traditions of inquiry (p. 547). The emergence of technology-driven self-paced courses that directly embed the assessment of mastery into the delivery of instruction will further blur the lines between instruction and assessment (Ewell, 1997). Still other approaches for collecting information do exist. For example, some faculty make use of specially designed assessment days during which students undertake performance assessments before a panel of judges. And other faculty take advantage of existing contact points with students, such as orientation, advising, and graduation, to collect or share assessment information.

Although we have used the expression "expected outcomes" throughout this chapter, in practice, faculty need information about much more than just the competences of students at the time they leave the program. The Council of Arts Accrediting Associations explicitly states that "It is important not to allow a focus on outcomes to diminish the importance of resources and processes in education" (1990, p. 4). And Ewell notes that, "after finding end-point results essentially uninterpretable" (1997, p. 367), many of those engaged in assessment have realized the value of longitudinal designs and of collecting information about student perceptions, experiences, and course-taking patterns. Among other possibilities, faculty in applied disciplines can conduct surveys about student participation in out-of-class activities, ask students to create journals describing their internship experiences, and/or study student transcripts showing the selection and sequencing of courses they have taken. These approaches help faculty determine "which paths and patterns appear to work best" (p. 372) as students move toward completion of their programs.

Reporting and Using Assessment Results

The ultimate goal of assessment is to generate qualitative and quantitative evidence that can be used to improve student learning. Whether or not assessment will be successful in this regard is not determined at the time evidence is generated; it is determined early in the process when the groundwork for assessment is being put in place. Thus, care must be taken to develop a meaningful assessment plan that identifies not only what information will be collected but who will use it. Ewell (1994) suggests explicitly asking questions such as these: Who will see assessment results? Who will make recommendations based on these results? Who will take action based on the recommendations? Answering these questions clarifies the role of the assessment committee in relationship to other committees. It also clarifies the role of the assessment process in relationship to planning, budgeting, and other processes. One strategy that maximizes the use of assessment information is to require that such information be presented in requests for curriculum changes, budget allocations, or planning initiatives. Ewell argues that assessment should be deemphasized as a "distinct and visible activity" and, instead, educators should focus on making information about academic effectiveness "an integral part of academic planning and pedagogical design" (1997, p. 370). Marchese also has argued that accreditors and institutions should focus on improvement rather than assessment (2000).

Discussion among faculty is a key to the usefulness of assessment and should include more individuals than just those serving on the assessment committee. Planned conversations can occur at regularly scheduled meetings or at special events such as retreats or brown bag sessions. In their discussions, faculty can consider such things as strengths and weaknesses of individuals who were assessed, the collective performance of the group, differences in results across demographic groups or by class level, trends in results, and implications for improvement (Ewell, 1994; Wright, 1997). These conversations can be challenging. College of Business faculty at Ball State University found that as difficult as it was to develop objective statements and assessment plans, "it was infinitely more difficult to take the collected data and make sense of it" (Replogle, 1997, p. 1).

Faculty conversations should occur before reports are written or recommendations are submitted and should include anyone who is likely to be affected by the assessment results. Although assessment reports need to include negative as well as positive findings, they should be written in such a way as to respect the identity of individual participants, both students and faculty. This generally means that written reports will include group rather than individual results. Reports themselves can vary in format, perhaps including the findings from a particular project or bringing together qualitative and quantitative evidence about a particular theme such as critical thinking, writing, or out-of-class experiences. Faculty at the department level may need to provide reports according to an outline prepared at the division or institutional level; and, in accredited disciplines, specific report requirements, such as tables and outlines, may be required by the accreditor.

Dennis Jones, president of NCHEMS, notes that clients are seeking "responsiveness" from higher education, yet, "most institutions would argue they are already delivering" what employers need (2000, p. 1). Educators who do have evidence that they are responding to the workforce requirements of employers may need to find better ways to share this information. Ewell urges faculty to report assessment evidence in ways that are "far more focused on results" and more in line with the "balance sheet" model available in industry (Ewell, 1997, p. 375). In Chapter 5, Donna Boland and Juanita Laidig point out that faculty in some nursing programs have adopted the idea of a report card as a way to share what they are doing with various publics.

Assessing Assessment

A final step in the assessment process is to take time to reflect on how it is working. Some accreditors have explicitly recognized the importance of this action. For example, the outcomes manual published several years ago by the American Association of Dental Schools notes that "Continual evaluation of the plan needs to be built into it. . . . The outcomes assessment system itself should be sensitive to measures of effectiveness and be subject to change as a result of the findings of assessment activities." According to the manual, areas that should be considered when evaluating the effectiveness of the assessment program include cost/benefit analysis, the ability of outcomes measures to detect the need for change, the adequacy of resources allocated to assessment, and the utility of the process (Romberg, 1990, p. 21).

Any discussions of assessment results should include reflection on the activities that generated them. But focused discussion about assessment processes and methods is also important. A particularly good strategy is to set aside at least one meeting per year specifically for the purpose of critiquing the assessment program. Although there is some evidence that faculty neglect this aspect of the assessment process (Patton, Dasher-Alston, Ratteray, & Kait 1996), in their study of institutional assessment, Peterson and his colleagues found that "modifying student assessment plans, policies, and processes" was the most frequently reported action taken on the basis of assessment information (Peterson, Augustine, & Einarson, 2000, p. 8). Indeed, there is always the danger that when assessment evidence causes discomfort, the reaction will be to change the assessment instruments rather than the curriculum or other practices. Faculty who start with a clear notion of what their assessment program is about, why they are doing it, and how it should proceed have the best chance of moving it forward. Even at the program level, faculty can benefit from a clear statement of assessment philosophy or guidelines. This statement can then be used as a yardstick in evaluating the success of the program.

Involving Stakeholders in Assessment

Although campus assessment efforts may be "doomed without strong administrative support" (Wright, 1997, p. 571), another critical factor in their success is the involvement of faculty and other stakeholders. Faculty need to participate in all aspects of the assessment process, including the development of objectives, the selection of assessment techniques, and the review of assessment results. One of the great benefits of designing rather than purchasing assessment instruments is the opportunity this gives for faculty to become deeply engaged in assessment.

The first prerequisite to successful involvement of faculty in assessment is the appropriate delegation of responsibility and the delineation of clear roles for all participants. But success in assessment necessitates that faculty have the familiarity and understanding to carry out their roles. In many cases, assessment leaders recognize that faculty development is a key ingredient if involvement in assessment is to be widespread and effective. Faculty in various programs may be able to take advantage of workshops or assessment materials that are available at the institution or division level. In other cases, program faculty undertake their own initiatives. When faculty in Ball State University's School of Nursing wanted to develop portfolios for their students, they invited colleagues from across campus to come to an afternoon workshop and share information about what they already were doing with portfolios. Materials such as workbooks, question and answer guides, and newsletters can also help. Committees that are requesting plans and reports from faculty can assist the process by providing outlines or examples of what they expect.

What faculty learn about assessment can have implications beyond their assessment responsibilities, perhaps helping them become better educators overall. Banta has argued that "when faculty become fully involved in assessment, they create, and become active participants in their own program of professional growth and development" (1996, p. 367). And Ewell notes that, at some institutions, assessment has gradually become "an indistinguishable part of curricular and faculty development" (1997, p. 370).

A third important element of meaningful faculty involvement is the recognition of faculty efforts with respect to assessment. Some campuses have been successful using poster sessions or campus newsletters to report about the assessment work of faculty. Release time, summer grant programs, and funding for assessment-related travel often are used to support faculty assessment efforts. Still, if assessment is to be considered an important aspect of campus culture, it needs to be recognized in the traditional reward structure. One possibility is to request information about assessment activities in annual reports about faculty activities and to consider this information when assigning faculty rewards and recognition (Palomba & Banta, 1999).

Student involvement in assessment presents other issues and opportunities. An important challenge here is whether or not students will take seriously their responsibilities to participate in assessment activities. One of the advantages of course-embedded assessment is that it draws on the natural motivation of students to do well in their courses. In addition to participating in assessment projects, students can play other roles in assessment. These include: serving on program assessment committees, participating in design of portfolio or other assessment projects, critiquing existing techniques through focus groups or other approaches, and assisting in conducting assessment projects. As one example, students act as assessors themselves when they complete peer- and self-evaluations. Students, too, need training and materials that can help them be effective participants in assessment. Faculty in some programs have used workshops, brochures, and pamphlets to help students learn about assessment. In addition, some faculty devote time in their introductory courses to building a foundation for assessment, perhaps explaining its purposes, establishing expectations, and collecting initial information (Palomba & Banta, 1999).

Students should garner rewards from their participation in assessment. Occasionally, students are given small incentives for participating in surveys or testing projects. But the real payoff to students for their involvement in assessment should be the opportunity to learn more than they would have learned without it. The effective use of feedback from faculty and professionals in the field and the opportunities for self-reflection and self-evaluation seem to hold the most promise for improving the learning of individual students through assessment. Good assessment helps students learn their own strengths and weaknesses and thus become competent at self-assessment. Doherty and her coauthors believe that faculty should provide "opportunities for self-assessment in every assessment situation" (1997, p. 185). Wiggins argues that feedback should occur along with assessment activities, rather than between them, so that students have the opportunity to adjust their performances as they take place. To be effective, feedback should be highly specific, descriptive of what resulted, clear to the student, and related to precise targets or standards. The best feedback is "information about how a person did in light of what he or she attempted" (1998, p. 46). It is "purely descriptive" rather than an expression of approval or disapproval (p. 47). Students may be pleased to hear that they did a good job, but this expression alone does not help them improve their learning. According to Mentkowski and her coauthors, feedback serves the important function of helping students "learn to evaluate their own level of performance and focus their efforts to improve their skills" (2000, p. 88).

In addition to faculty and students, a number of external stakeholders should be involved in assessment. Providing roles for alumni, employers, and community members seems particularly prudent for assessment of the major. Staff from the National Center for Higher Education Management Systems (NCHEMS) suggest involving employers in assessing student projects as one way to help institutions become more responsive to employer needs. "The 'outside' view employers bring enriches what students, as well as faculty, learn in this process" (NCHEMS, 2000, p. 3).

The strategies reviewed here can help assessment meet its full potential to engage faculty, students, and other stakeholders in a systematic effort to improve higher education. Compared to those in other programs, faculty in applied disciplines have some advantages in implementing these strategies. Professional programs typically have coherent requirements with minimal electives, structured course sequences, capstone courses, and, sometimes, orientation courses. This creates opportunities for faculty to design and administer performance assessments as students move through the program. In addition, related programs in the arts, engineering, or business may be housed together in colleges or divisions, allowing economies of scale for surveys and other projects. Generally, faculty in applied programs have more information about the likely paths of graduates and more access to employers, recruiters, and supervisors of internships in gathering information about the necessary workforce skills required of graduates. This information can help faculty in formulating expected outcomes for their programs. Faculty in accredited programs also can look to accrediting bodies for guidance in selecting outcomes and, perhaps, for materials to help them learn about assessment. Accreditors must be cautious, however, in how much structure they impose. Faculty need to be able to decide for themselves what it means to be a graduate of their program. If they merely adopt the accreditor's view, they miss many of the substantial benefits of assessment.

References

AACSB—The International Association for Management Education. (2000, April). *Achieving quality and continuous improvement through self-evaluation and peer review: Standards for accreditation.* St. Louis, MO: Author.

Association of American Colleges. (1985). *Integrity in the college curriculum: A report to the academic community.* Washington, DC: Author.

Banta, T. W. (1996). Using assessment to improve instruction. In R. J. Menges & M. Weimer (Eds.), *Teaching on solid ground: Using scholarship to improve practice.* San Francisco: Jossey-Bass.

Chickering, A. W., & Gamson, Z. F. (1987). Seven principles for good practice in undergraduate education. *AAHE Bulletin, 39*(7), 3–7.

Commission on Accreditation for Dietetics Education (CADE). (2000). *Standards of education.* Chicago, IL: The American Dietetic Association.

Council of Arts Accrediting Associations. (1990, April). *Outcomes assessment and arts programs in higher education.* Briefing Paper. Reston, VA: Author.

Diamond, R. M. (1998). *Designing and assessing courses and curricula: A practical guide.* San Francisco: Jossey-Bass.

Doherty, A., Chenevert, J., Miller, R. R., Roth, J. L., & Truchan, L. C. (1997). Developing intellectual skills. In J. G. Gaff, J. L. Ratcliff, & Associates (Eds.), *Handbook of the undergraduate curriculum: A comprehensive guide to purposes, structures, practices, and change.* A publication of the Association of American Colleges and Universities. San Francisco: Jossey-Bass.

Ewell, P. T. (1994). *A policy guide for assessment: Making good use of tasks in critical thinking.* Princeton, NJ: Educational Testing Service.

Ewell, P. T. (1997). Strengthening assessment for academic quality improvement. In M. W. Peterson, D. D. Dill, L. A. Mets, & Associates (Eds.), *Planning and management for a changing environment: A handbook on redesigning postsecondary institutions.* San Francisco: Jossey-Bass.

Ewell, P. T., & Jones, D. P. (1991). *Indicators of "good practice" in undergraduate education: A handbook for development and implementation.* Boulder, CO: National Center for Higher Education Management Systems (NCHEMS).

Haessig, C. J., & La Potin, A. S. (2000). *Outcomes assessment for dietetics educators.* Chicago, IL: Commission on Accreditation for Dietetics Education, The American Dietetics Association.

Huba, M. E., & Freed, J. E. (2000). *Learner-centered assessment on college campuses: Shifting the focus from teaching to learning.* Boston, MA: Allyn and Bacon.

Jones, D. (2000, June). From the President. National Center for Higher Education Management Systems. *NCHEMS News, 16,* 1.

Jones, E. A. (1996). Editor's notes. In E. A. Jones (Ed.), *Preparing competent college graduates: Setting new and higher expectations for student learning* (New Directions for Higher Education, No. 96). San Francisco: Jossey-Bass.

Linn, R. L., & Baker, E. L. (1996). Can performance-based student assessments be psychometrically sound? In J. B. Baron and D. P. Wolf (Eds.), *Performance-based student assessment: Challenges and possibilities, ninety-fifth yearbook of the National Society for the Study of Education, Part 1.* Chicago, IL: University of Chicago Press.

Marchese, T. J. (2000, April). *Assessment: The national scene.* Paper presented at the North Central Association of College and Schools Annual Meeting, Chicago, IL.

Mentkowski, M., & Associates (2000). *Learning that lasts: Integrating learning, development, and performance in college and beyond.* San Francisco: Jossey-Bass.

National Center for Higher Education Management Systems. (2000, June). Knowledge and skills needed to succeed in the 21st century workforce. *NCHEMS News, 16,* 2–3.

National Institute of Education Study Group. (1984). *Involvement in learning: Realizing the potential of American higher education.* Washington, DC: Author.

Palomba, C. A., & Banta, T. W. (1999). *Assessment essentials: Planning, implementing, and improving assessment in higher education.* San Francisco: Jossey-Bass.

Patton, G. W., Dasher-Alston, R., Ratteray, O. M. T., & Kait, M. B. (1996). *Outcomes assessment in the middle states region: A report on the 1995 outcomes assessment survey.* Philadelphia, PA: Commission on Higher Education of the Middle States Association of Colleges and Schools.

Peterson, M. W., Augustine, C. H., & Einarson, M. K. (2000, May). *Organizational practices enhancing the influence of student assessment information in academic decisions.* Paper presented at the annual meeting of the Association for Institutional Research, Cincinnati, OH.

Pike, G. R. (1998, November–December). Assessment measures: Looking back at assessment measures. *Assessment Update, 10* (6), 8–9.

Replogle, J. C. (1997). *Review of assessment progress.* Muncie, IN: Ball State University College of Business.

Romberg, E. (Ed.). (1990). *Outcomes assessment: A resource book.* Washington, D.C.: American Association of Dental Schools.

Shulman, L. (1998). Teacher portfolios: A theoretical activity. In N. Lyons (Ed.), *With portfolio in hand: Validating the new teacher professionalism.* New York: Teachers College Press.

Wiggins, G. (1998). *Educative assessment: Designing assessments to inform and improve student performance.* San Francisco: Jossey-Bass.

Wright, B. D. (1997). Evaluating learning in individual courses. In J. G. Gaff, J. L. Ratcliff, & Associates (Eds.), *Handbook of the undergraduate curriculum: A comprehensive guide to purposes, structures, practices, and change.* A publication of the Association of American Colleges and Universities. San Francisco: Jossey-Bass.

3

ASSESSING STUDENT COMPETENCE IN TEACHER EDUCATION PROGRAMS

Mary E. Diez

At the beginning of the 21st century, teacher education in the United States is in an unprecedented position in relationship to assessment. Governed for most of the last century by bureaucratic rules that specified course requirements and other program inputs, both states and the national accreditation body for teacher education are moving to a focus on the demonstration of outcomes, although the types of measures for these outcomes vary widely. Most significant, perhaps, is a focus on linking the performance of teachers and education candidates to the learning of their students, although again the specification of appropriate measures for this outcome is in dispute. This chapter addresses three central questions: How did teacher education come to focus on assessment of performance outcomes? What does a focus on assessment of performance mean for the practice of teacher education? What emerging issues must be addressed?

Sources of Change in Teacher Education Accreditation

The shift in accreditation requirements has its roots in the merging of two agendas; both are related to education reform and both emerged in their current form in the last 15 to 20 years of the 20th century. In 1986, *A Nation Prepared* called for the professionalization of teaching as a new approach to addressing the quality of America's schools. Among other proposals, *A Nation Prepared* called for the creation of " . . . a National Board for Professional Teaching Standards, organized with regional and state membership structure, to establish high standards for what teachers need to know and be able to do, and to certify teachers who meet that standard" (Carnegie Forum on Education and the Economy, 1986, p. 55). The *professionalization of teaching agenda* was embraced by the leaders of the two national teachers unions, which supported the establishment of the board the next year. At the same time, the National Council for the Accreditation of Teacher Education (NCATE) inaugurated a set of "redesigned" standards, which required that institutions build their programs on conceptual frameworks, spelling out critical knowledge bases, as well as philosophy and purpose, to guide the design of all aspects of the program (NCATE, 1987).

Less tied to specific documents, a second agenda nonetheless has also influenced teacher education in roughly the same period. An *agenda focused on the improvement of teaching and learning* has actually emerged and reemerged several times in the last century, often in response to the threat of a foreign power (the Sputnik crisis of the late 1950s), the need to make education a national priority (GOALS 2000 in the 1990s), or a sense of diminishing superiority (fueled by international comparisons like the Third International Mathematics and Science Study reports published by the U.S. National Research Center for TIMSS in 1996).

While the National Board for Professional Teaching Standards began as a proposal centered in the professionalization agenda, the work undertaken to develop standards and assessments for accomplished teachers can also be seen as supporting the improvement of teaching and learning agenda. Today, the National Board clearly sees itself as not only recognizing accomplished teachers and supporting the development of incentives and rewards for teachers to undertake the process of certification but also contributing to the improvement of teaching and learning through the articulation of its standards and the development of an assessment process based on those standards (National Board for Professional Teaching Standards, 1989; Castor, 2000).

The work of the National Board has influenced the development of accreditation policy in two ways. The first is an indirect influence. As the National Board began its work to define standards for accomplished teaching, interest grew in the development of a set of normative standards for beginning teacher practice. The Interstate New Teacher Assessment and Support Consortium (INTASC), which began as a small group of states joined together to share resources being developed for beginning teacher assessment and support, has grown to a consortium of more than 30 states (Ambach, 1996). In 1992,

INTASC published a set of model standards for beginning teacher licensure, designed to be compatible with the standards of the National Board. INTASC's work focuses on both the professionalization agenda (in recognizing that beginning teachers need to demonstrate standards of knowledge and practice), as well as the improvement of teaching and learning agenda (in a focus on demonstration of practice with K-12 learners during the first two years of teaching). The changes that INTASC promotes in beginning teacher licensure also raise questions for the step that comes before licensure—teacher preparation programs. Hence, the National Board's influence on INTASC constituted an indirect influence on teacher education accreditation.

A second, direct influence emerges in NCATE's second major redesign: NCATE 2000. Both the National Board and INTASC have developed standards that are linked to subject area standards for K–12 students and to developmental levels of learners. Both have designed performance assessment instruments that bring together subject area knowledge, pedagogical knowledge, and practice in the classroom. Following their lead, NCATE 2000 requires links between standards and performance-based assessment.

The mid-80s version of NCATE (1987), while guided by knowledge bases and conceptual frameworks, had still maintained an "input focused" approach typical of specialized accreditation. NCATE 2000 represents a major shift to performance assessment of outcomes. For example, the new Standard I requires demonstration that

> Candidates[1] preparing to work in schools as teachers or other school personnel know the content of their fields and demonstrate professional and pedagogical knowledge, skills, and dispositions, and *apply them so that students learn* [emphasis added]. The unit's assessments indicate that candidates meet professional, state, and institutional standards. (NCATE, 2000, p. 1)

NCATE 2000 spells out two levels of expectation about assessment as evidence of performance. First, teacher education faculty must assess candidates over time, using multiple methods and approaches and using assessment data to improve teaching and learning. Second, teacher education programs must have some way of showing that candidates and graduates influence the learning of the K–12 students they teach.

Showing impact on the learning of teacher education candidates is a critical new expectation, and it calls for new forms of assessment. No longer is it acceptable simply to sort the learners into those who passed and those who failed. Rather, the use of assessment information diagnostically becomes forefronted, with the goal of improving teaching (by gearing instruction to the needs identified) and improving learning (by providing multiple experiences to master knowledge and its application in practice).

Contrasts in Assessment for Different Purposes

To understand fully the influence of accreditation on assessment, the next sections of this paper look in depth at a critical aspect—the influence of *purpose* on the *nature* of the assessment in the National Board for Professional Teaching Standards, INTASC, and NCATE. To what degree is each focused on a high stakes decision? To what degree is each intended to move the profession forward? How does support of candidates fit into the picture?

High Stakes Assessments

Over nearly 15 years, with an investment of millions of dollars, the National Board and INTASC, respectively, have developed legally defensible processes to determine a candidate's certification as an accomplished teacher or eligibility for a regular teaching license. The assessments of both the National Board and INTASC are, by definition, high stakes assessments (see Figure 3.1), subject to very stringent psychometric requirements to ensure accuracy and fairness of judgment (Pearlman, 2000).

For example, in the National Board process, each candidate for a specific Board certificate completes the same portfolio entries, with the same page limits; they complete the same assessment center exercises, with the same time

---

- Aspects of the standards are selected based both on what is judged to be important and what can be measured most effectively.
- The assessment takes place under prescribed conditions.
- The prompts and modes of response are standardized, having been developed through a rigorous process of development, pilot testing, and field testing.
- Prompts and modes may need to be "secure" (e.g., in the Assessment Center Exercises of the National Board).
- The assessment is a one-time event.
- The assessment is "summative," with a cut score that determines whether the candidate is certified or licensed.
- Cut scores are determined through a process for which assessors are trained and care is taken to assure reliability of assessors.
- No detailed feedback is provided to the candidate.

FIGURE 3.1   Characteristics of high stakes assessments

constraints. Given everything that the standards call for, the portfolio, of necessity, focuses on a narrow range of performance if one contrasts it with everything that a teacher does in the course of a year's work with students or, indeed, with all aspects of the standards for the certificate. The INTASC Portfolio, which asks candidates to develop portfolio entries across 10 days of instruction, has a similarly limited range in relationship to the whole of the standards.

While the Board now allows unsuccessful candidates to bank scores of 2.75 or more and to redo exercises with scores below that number, the assessment, like other high stakes measures, is essentially a one-time event. Retakes are another one-time event. Moreover, a candidate's scores and a generalized description of levels of performance across candidates are the only feedback provided. The Board has recognized in recent years the importance of support for teachers who are preparing for standing for certification; it now holds a series of facilitator workshops for those who support candidates. In addition, it is beginning to market a set of "remote preparation" materials designed to help teachers develop the critical analysis and reflection skills necessary to document accomplished teaching practice.

The INTASC support process for new teachers is intended to provide ongoing formative feedback to teachers; from the beginning, the use of the word "Support" in INTASC's title made this a key aspect of the overall design for state policy and practice. This support, however, is kept separate from the assessment process itself; those who serve as mentors to new teachers are not part of those teachers' teams. The INTASC portfolio will not provide detailed feedback to candidates. The characteristics of high stakes assessment, appropriate for the purpose, have some limitations from the perspective of support. In the next section, I suggest alternatives for another kind of assessment focused on support.

Assessment for Development

While assessment and support are separate entities for the National Board and INTASC, NCATE 2000 suggests using assessment itself as a kind of support, promoting development over time in a teacher education program. Assessment for development, while becoming more common in K–12 settings, is fairly rare in higher education. Related to concepts like classroom assessment (Borko, 1997; Bryant & Driscoll, 1998), local assessment (Roberts, 1997), course- or curriculum-embedded assessment (Swisher, Green, & Tollefson, 1999), and assessment as learning (Alverno College Faculty, 1994), *assessment for development* provides several contrasts to high stakes assessment practice (see Figure 3.2).

- A wide range of aspects of the standards can be addressed, not only because there is time to do so but also because multiple modes of assessment over time can be applied.
- Conditions can vary from candidate to candidate and for the same candidate over time.
- The prompts and modes of response need not be standardized; faculty continuously develop assessments to meet the needs of candidates and refine them as they learn from their use.
- An assessment can take place over time and can be revised.
- The assessment process is "cumulative," with the body of work developing an ever-richer picture of the candidate's performance.
- Faculty who work with candidates develop a community of professional judgment through which they share understanding and apply criteria; this community of professional judgment is the source of reliability of judgment.
- Feedback is a central means for improving candidate performance.
- Self-assessment is a critical process for candidate learning.

FIGURE 3.2   Characteristics of assessment for development

While assessment for development also relates to standards—for example, from the state, the learned societies, and an institution's own conceptual framework, the amount of time available in a teacher education program (often two or three years) allows for the assessment plan of a program to address many more aspects of the standards, including some aspects of standards that are not likely to be addressed in high stakes assessments. Indeed, some aspects of standards would be assessed best in an ongoing way. For example, the INTASC expectation that candidates for licensure would develop certain "dispositions" for teachers does not seem amenable to high stakes testing. But consider dispositions like showing "enthusiasm for the discipline(s) s/he teaches" (INTASC, 1992, p. 11) or valuing "planning as a collegial activity" (p. 23). These can be assessed over time, using videotaped discussions, class presentations, and reflective writings to look for consistent engagement in learning settings and appropriate, professional interaction in work with colleagues.

Depending upon candidates' developmental needs and also upon their choices based upon interest, individual work in assessment for development is not constrained by a standardized set of prompts or made to fit into a standardized set of modes; thus, one candidate's total set of assessments would not be exactly like the set completed by others. In a learning mode, it makes sense for candidates to try out approaches that may look different from another candidate's or even to have a choice among a number of possible demonstrations rather than doing the same tasks as everyone else (Rogers, 1994).

Choice of subject matter or theoretical approach allows candidates to demonstrate their knowledge and skill in unique ways, while also providing evidence over time related to a common set of standards. Moreover, the faculty can use assessment diagnostically and tailor work to individual candidate needs. Time constraints are more fluid, and assessments may be refined after feedback. In a developmental mode, it makes sense for candidates to revise their work in response to feedback.

Feedback and self-assessment are critical factors in assessment for development. Because assessments tied to learning do not need to be "secure," faculty can provide detailed feedback in relationship to the criteria for an assessment. Moreover, making the criteria public in advance of completing the assessment allows candidates to grow in their ability to critique their own work as well.

NCATE 2000 calls for teacher preparation to incorporate assessment over time, using multiple methods, with ongoing feedback to individual candidates. The use of terms like "formative" and "summative" suggests a major break between practice and the "real thing." That is why my colleagues at Alverno College have chosen to use "cumulative" as a characteristic of our assessment process (1994, pp. 22–23). Underlying the distinction between formative and summative is the assumption that highly controlled and standardized settings are necessary for validity and reliability of fine-tuned judgments of candidate knowledge. But the proponents of assessment for development argue that the rich body of evidence of a candidate's performance over time, across multiple assessments, using varied methods, is a different, but also valid, picture of the candidate's level of performance (Alverno College Faculty, 1994; Borko, 1997; Bryant & Driscoll, 1998; Loacker, 1991; Mentkowski & Loacker, 1985; Mentkowski, 1998; Mentkowski & Associates, 2000; Roberts, 1997; Swisher et al., 1999).

Thus, assessment for development is more in keeping with the NCATE vision for what should happen in a teacher education program than are the high stakes assessments of either the National Board or INTASC. In assessment for development, reliability depends upon the consistent application of criteria by faculty who have developed a community of professional judgment and, by sharing the criteria with candidates, invite them into that community (Loacker, 1991; Loacker & Mentkowski, 1993). Longitudinal research at Alverno illustrates the aspects of the process of establishing a community of professional judgment, including identifying outcomes, "creating processes for specifying criteria, training assessors, making expert judgments, interpreting results, and discussing applications" (Loacker, 1991, p. 40).

Of course, NCATE 2000 does not rule out the use of some high stakes decisions in the course of a teacher education program. Many programs have points at which candidates are reviewed for readiness to move into the next stage of the program (Lowe & Banker, 1994; Diez, 1996). In the case of the Alverno program, the decision for advancement to the next stage of development is made on the basis of both specific demonstrations (e.g., of communication performance meeting a particular level of criteria) and the cumulative picture of performance (e.g., across assessments in multiple courses); these demonstrations serve both as assessment for development and cumulative information on which to make an advancement decision.

What Does a Focus on Assessment Mean for Teacher Education?

While NCATE 2000 is just being implemented, teacher educators at some institutions have already begun to develop the kinds of programs that NCATE 2000 will require. As illustrated here, these institutions provide some answers to the question of what a focus on assessment will mean in teacher education. In this section, the discussion uses a set of characteristics of assessments and assessment systems drawn from the work of faculty at Alverno College (1994), a pioneer in performance assessment in higher education. These characteristics provide a framework for redeveloping programs to meet NCATE 2000 standards.

Explicit Outcomes

NCATE specifies national, state, and institutional standards, which may be seen as another term for outcomes or competences. Whatever the name, teacher educators need to provide a clear picture of the expectations of a candidate's knowledge and performance in teacher education and in the disciplinary areas through the outcomes that guide course and program development and through the assessments that candidates complete in their courses and in the field. NCATE has made the development of a conceptual framework a necessary precondition for accreditation; typically, the outcomes for a program are incorporated in this framework. For example, Schnug and Converse (1998) describe the work of faculty at Ashland University (Ohio) in "distilling the essence" of their program, outlining eight tenets describing the knowledge and skills of the professional educator:

1. Works cooperatively and collaboratively with all members of the educational community

2. Communicates clearly and effectively through a variety of means

3. Demonstrates understanding of human development, cultural diversity, socioeconomic influences, and learning differences, thereby enabling all children to learn and contribute

4. Employs research in areas such as learning theory and instructional methodology

5. Uses a variety of appropriate assessment techniques to enhance learning

6. Masters appropriate disciplines so as to engage students in meaningful, active academic study

7. Integrates educational technology in the teaching and learning process

8. Assumes the lifelong responsibility to grow academically, professionally, and personally (p. 65)

Nelms and Thomas (1998) from Clayton College and State University (Georgia) explain six learning outcomes that guided the development of their program, including

1. Diagnoses learning needs

2. Plans for student learning

3. Facilitates student learning

4. Demonstrates appropriate knowledge

5. Fosters student well-being to support learning

6. Assumes the role of professional educator (p. 83)

Faculty at Alverno College have documented their development of five education "abilities" that serve as the conceptual framework for teacher education programs:

1. Conceptualization—integrating content knowledge with educational frameworks and a broadly based understanding of the liberal arts in order to plan and implement instruction

2. Diagnosis—relating observed behavior to relevant frameworks in order to determine and implement learning prescriptions

3. Coordination—managing resources effectively to support learning goals

4. Communication—using verbal, nonverbal, and media modes of communication to establish the environment of the classroom and to structure and reinforce learning

5. Integrative interaction—acting with professional values as a situational decision maker in order to develop students as learners (Diez, 1990, pp. 9–10)

A focus on broad outcomes protects against the problem that emerged in competence-based education in the 1970s, where hundreds of discrete "bits" prevented candidates (and teacher educators) from having a sense of the teacher as a whole and functioning professional. Like the INTASC standards, such broad outcomes are larger than any one performance and so need to be assessed in many ways over time.

Performance

NCATE requires that teacher education programs provide data over time to show that candidates demonstrate the outcomes. Assessment of candidate performance allows the faculty to have a sense not only of what candidates know but also what they can do with what they know. Alverno faculty (Diez, in press; Diez, Lake, & Rickards, 1994) work to create projects that make *visible* the teacher education outcomes. For example, across methods courses and field experiences, Alverno faculty develop experiences that give candidates practice with the outcome ability of *diagnosis*—"the ability to use conceptual frameworks to look at student work in order to make decisions for the next step in the teaching-learning process" (Alverno College Faculty, 1996, p. 2). Demonstrations build from one-on-one interactions with K–12 students (e.g., a miscue analysis with a beginning reader) to small group projects (e.g., tutoring a group of learners in mathematics) to management of diagnostic data for a whole class. Thus, the program produces multiple samples of performance for each candidate over time.

Similarly, the Western Oregon Teacher Work Sampling Model (TWSM) described by Schalock, Schalock, and Myton (1998) requires that candidates demonstrate the impact of their teaching on student performance, using a pretest, posttest approach and analyzing the performance both of individual learners and subgroups of learners.

Public, Explicit Criteria

Implicit in NCATE's requirement of assessment is that faculty develop agreements about "what counts" as acceptable performance. Criteria describe the expected quality of performance that must be met. As Loacker, Cromwell, and O'Brien (1986) explain,

> criteria are standards external to the object of judgment, used to identify those characteristics of the object that indicate its worth. Thus, they are one of the components of assessment that distinguish it as learning. The picture sketched by criteria should be sufficient to enable the assessor to judge the presence of an ability. It also needs to

be clear enough for the beginning learner to imagine a performance that would match the criteria. (p. 51)

Criteria need to capture the knowledge and skills related to disciplinary content, as well as to reinforce pedagogical skills. Through criteria, candidates learn to examine their planning and decision making against the expectation, for example, that they link decisions to theoretical frameworks and show the relationships between the evidence they present and the conclusions they draw. Durden and Hunt (1998) describe a process in which they ask candidates to create a mathematics lesson using Sketchpad® and employing instructional strategies related to the van Hiele theory of how students learn geometry. They then involve candidates in articulating appropriate criteria, building the candidates' understanding of the outcomes and giving them practice for their own work with middle school students. When candidates contribute criteria like "promotes exploration," "serves differing ability levels," or "incorporates the van Hiele theory" (p. 92), they give evidence of understanding key concepts expected by the faculty.

Feedback

Feedback is a powerful tool in supporting candidate growth. Diez and her coauthors (1994) describe how faculty carefully examine the candidate's performance, highlighting evidence of strengths and weaknesses in relationship to the criteria. Research on the Alverno program (Mentkowski & Associates, 2000) details how feedback assists candidates to understand the outcomes and criteria, as well as provides a basis for goal setting for future performance. The focus on feedback is a key difference between assessment for development and high stakes assessment. The message of feedback is that the assessment is a learning opportunity.

Self-Assessment

As powerful as feedback from teachers and peers may be, self-assessment may be even more powerful, once the learner has gained an understanding of the criteria (Mentkowski & Associates, 2000). With developed skill in self-assessment, the candidate can, in effect, become his or her own coach and critic. For many programs with a focus on the teacher as a reflective practitioner, guiding candidates in self-assessment is an important way to build ongoing reflective skill. And, as Blackwell and Diez (1999) point out, key abilities necessary for successful performance on assessments of the National Board for Professional Teaching Standards are related to self-assessment—the teacher's ability to reflect on his/her own practice and to engage in inquiry into that practice.

Multiplicity

Lowe and Banker (1998) describe the importance of multiple measures of performance in their program at Asbury College (Kentucky); they describe their use of a "Continuous Assessment Model" that incorporates on-demand performance tasks, projects, exhibitions, and portfolios as promoting "fair, flexible, and creative evaluation" (p. 54). Mihalevich and Carr (1998) from Central Missouri State University note that the mode of assessments should be consistent with instructional methods, arguing that active learning, for example, requires a greater focus on performance assessment. Because they encourage multiple methods of instruction, faculty at Central Missouri also employ multiple modes of assessment.

Alverno College faculty (1994) argue that multiplicity should include multiple *times* to practice using knowledge, multiple *methods* and *modes* of assessment, and multiple *contexts*. Multiple times provide support for learning; too often candidates bring stories from high school or other colleges, recounting how they had only one chance to learn something before the teacher moved on. Multiple methods and modes are important for two reasons—every candidate gets chances to express him/herself in a preferred mode and every candidate is stretched in trying out new modes of expression. Using multiple contexts helps candidates see the range of ways what they are learning can be applied. And multiple times to practice means that candidates have the chance to build strength and consistency of performance.

Externality

As a concept, externality may be seen, first, as important to having candidates see the relevance of their work by trying it out in real K–12 classroom settings. Weisenbach, Mack, Scannell, and Steffel (1998) describe the importance of grounding candidate performance assessment in authentic situations. They identify as key types of assessments the use of lesson plans, videotapes, and reflective statements, as well as portfolios made up of multiple samples across types of classrooms. Second, faculty can also gain perspective through externality, for example, by looking across a number of performances from a variety of contexts or by bringing in others not usually involved with the class to provide feedback, as when principals and teachers participate in reviewing candidates' portfolios at Alverno College (Diez et al., 1994) or when faculty at the University of Indianapolis involve teachers from their professional development school sites in the design of assessments (Weisenbach, 2000).

A third aspect of externality is seen when a group of faculty members create an assessment that will be used across candidates in their own (and others') classes. Weisenbach (2000) points out that shared responsibility and accountability require externality, with a focus on pronouns like "we" and "ours" rather than "I" and "mine."

Developmental in Nature

Assessments need to fit the level of candidates' development of ability and knowledge. Asbury's continuous assessment model identifies developmental expectations for candidate growth, using four "gates" to review candidate performance at key points in the curriculum (Lowe & Banker, 1998). While the "gates" represent decision points, the identification of expectations allows for the preparation for each "gate" to promote assessment for development. Similarly, at Alverno, early course work and field work build critical frameworks from developmental and learning theories, as well as from subject area study. Through developmentally appropriate assessments, candidates focus, initially, on work with individual students. They gradually put more aspects of teaching together, in the ways they occur in classrooms, both in terms of more complex tasks and in terms of working with groups of learners, including a whole class (Diez, in press).

Cumulative in Nature

Two principles call for assessment to be cumulative in nature. First, the standards that guide the teacher education program are always larger than any one assessment or set of assessments (Alverno College Faculty, 1994). Because no one assessment can tell the whole story about a candidate's knowledge and skill or readiness to teach, faculty need to look across multiple performances for a picture of a candidate. Second, because candidates learn and grow over time, assessment must take into account the emerging picture of a candidate's growth. In addition, assessments need to create a balance between challenge and encouragement—building on candidates' current strengths and moving them forward into areas that need development (Diez, in press).

Expansive in Nature

Alverno faculty recognize that teacher educators need to work with candidates with the standards in mind. Developmentally, a candidate in an early field experience may be at the beginning of understanding how to craft learning experiences, but the faculty member's sense of *where the candidate will eventually be*—as pictured in the standards—guides his/her work. Faculty members develop assessments, then, to elicit from candidates the most advanced performance of which each is capable. Such a design not only provides them with good diagnostic information, but it also allows candidates to go as far as they are ready to go (Alverno College Faculty, 1994). These same principles can guide candidates in learning how to assess student learning in K–12 settings, serving as part of the knowledge base that beginning teachers bring to their work with students.

Emerging Issues for Teacher Education Practice

While the preceding characteristics may be helpful to teacher educators work- ing to meet NCATE accreditation requirements or, indeed, to faculty involved in assessment in other disciplines, a number of issues make the effort chal- lenging. Two are discussed here—the impact of public policy and the danger of reductionism.

The Impact of Public Policy

Public policy at the state level and under Title II of the federal education statutes suggests that we will not do away with the kinds of standardized high stakes tests that allow for comparisons (American Council on Education, 2000). If teacher education institutions provide ongoing cumulative assessment—across broader ranges of knowledge, performance, and disposition than are possible to address in the high stakes mode—and if states maintain measures that give some assurance to the public that candidates endorsed by a teacher education pro- gram can meet an objective test of performance, then having both kinds of assessment is probably a strength. As I argue subsequently, that would be true *only* if the standardized exams survive the danger of reductionism.

There are critical moral consequences, perhaps unintended, of ranking institutions on standardized measures. When the Title II regulations requiring states to rank their teacher education programs began to emerge, some insti- tutions moved quickly to figuring out how to maintain an acceptable ranking. High, if not always first, on the list of approaches was screening potential can- didates to see which can already do well on the types of measures that will "count." It is easier to sort candidates than to teach them, but teacher educa- tors need to address the moral issue of excluding persons who are motivated to make a difference in the lives of children and who might become wonder- fully effective teachers, both knowledgeable and caring, if provided with learn- ing experiences to release their potential. Diversification of the teaching force (based on the evidence that middle to upper class learners come to college already skilled in ways that help them succeed on standardized tests) would be made more difficult. This issue highlights the importance of NCATE's requir- ing teacher education programs to show the impact of teaching on *candidates* as well as the impact of those candidates on learners. As this chapter is being written, a second accreditation body is likely to be recognized for teacher education. While the Teacher Education Accreditation Council (TEAC) differs in several ways from NCATE, it has a similar focus on providing solid evidence that the teacher education program's students have learned what was expected of them, that the system of measuring the learning was valid, and that there is convincing evidence that the program has a sound quality control system in place that addresses all aspects of the evidence for the quality of the program (Murray, in press).

Assessment for development has the potential to support and nurture the learning of diverse candidates for teaching. Equally important, among *all* candidates, assessment for development is necessary for bringing novices into the professional community by developing their conceptual understanding, ethical principles, and patterns of judgment in practice. Because high stakes standardized measures necessarily focus on a limited range of what the standards describe, thinking of these as the only valid measures creates a serious danger that the critical aspects of professional community will be ignored.

If curriculum and teaching can have powerful effects on candidate learning, then how might teacher educators address the appropriate places of assessment for development and high stakes assessment? Clearly, within the two or three years of a teacher education program, the use of assessment for development provides the opportunity for candidates to develop the knowledge, skills, and dispositions required by the standards of NCATE and INTASC for beginning teachers and, more long range, of the National Board for Professional Teaching Standards for accomplished teaching. Equally clearly, high stakes assessments will continue to be used by state licensing bodies and by the National Board as a certifying body. The ideal situation is for the two approaches to assessment to work together, with a clear sense of purpose guiding the application of each. Thus, it is critical to develop state policy that recognizes the benefit of both approaches.

Reductionism

As previously alluded to, there are dangers in an exclusive focus on high stakes testing. In relation to standards-based reform, a major concern is with reductionism, which suggests that if high stakes assessments only look at a part of practice, only a part of practice is necessary for the teacher candidate to know. I was dismayed in 1998—the first summer of the INTASC Academies (designed to provide training for potential assessors and mentors in the INTASC Portfolio process)—when some of the teacher educators in attendance took a reductionist perspective. After being introduced to the items required in the portfolio, they remarked that if this portfolio is what INTASC wants in the first year of teaching, then those tasks must be what we need to prepare candidates to do in our programs.

Reductionism, simply put, is the failure to see that a standard is always larger than any one assessment of it. Teacher educators do need to create tasks to elicit performances from candidates so that they can see their progress, give them feedback, and prepare the next set of learning experiences. *But the tasks themselves are not the goal.* The standards—richly describing the range of knowledge, performance, and dispositions needed to practice effectively in the classroom—are the critical outcomes.

Thus, whatever INTASC portfolios include and whatever test is selected by a state for compliance with Title II, much more evidence is available in the whole of a candidate's cumulative record of performance than might be captured by a single assessment, no matter how complex.

In working with teacher educators around the country, I have recognized this kind of reductionism in the use of the term "portfolio." Portfolios have become "trendy," a quick and easy answer to the call for new modes of assessment. But simply putting materials between the covers of a notebook does not an assessment make.

Again, there are two dangers. The first is to change nothing about the way we teach and make assignments, and ask the candidates to put everything in a folder or notebook. The result is often a "scrapbook" from which one can make few observations about a candidate's growth and development. This kind of portfolio is often not examined until the end of a program and so has no real influence on growth (Zeichner, 2000). Missing are these key characteristics of assessment systems: public, explicit criteria; developmental feedback; self-assessment; and externality.

The second is to specify a set of "things," putting the focus on discrete tasks rather than on the gradual building of a complex and rich picture of knowledge in action. This approach to portfolios tends to look more like "competency-based teacher education" from the 1970s in its lack of connection, that is, where candidates completed a task, checked it off, and moved on. Not only does such an approach take away a candidate's choice of meaningful tasks, but it is often missing other key characteristics of assessment-systems: for example, the focus on broad outcomes and performance across multiple contexts; qualitative, public, and explicit criteria; developmental feedback; self-assessment; and expansiveness.

In truth, the "portfolio" as a technology for assessment requires all of the characteristics of assessment systems described in this chapter. Without clear focus on outcomes and without pedagogy that leads, developmentally, to those outcomes, a portfolio will not have impact. Portfolio technology requires, above all, multiple assessments that contribute to the development of the learner even as they document the evidence of learning.

Conclusion

Assessing candidate competence in education has clearly been a central focus of the reform efforts of the past 15 years. The growing focus on assessment has not only driven the development of standards and outcomes, clarifying the expectations of what teachers need to know and be able to do, but it has also sparked the beginnings of substantial change in how teacher education candidates are assessed in the course of their programs. Teacher education, however, perhaps more than any other discipline or profession in higher education, will continue to be challenged by an accountability movement that seems to be motivated neither by the professionalization agenda nor the improvement of teaching and learning agenda. Moreover, it will continue to be challenged by policy makers and a public with little awareness of the nuances of measurement, assessment, and meaningful data. The dangers of applying high stakes measures inappropriately or falling into reductionistic approaches can be offset, somewhat, by the requirements of NCATE 2000. These requirements make clear that teacher educators must use multiple measures over time to assure that candidates meet the range of knowledge, skills, and dispositions necessary for effective classroom practice and "apply them so that students learn."

Note

1. To prevent confusion, this text uses "candidate" when referring to teacher education students and teachers participating in licensure or certification assessments and reserves "student" for K–12 learners.

References

Alverno College Faculty. (1994). *Student assessment-as-learning at Alverno College.* Milwaukee, WI: Alverno Institute.

Alverno College Faculty. (1996). *Ability-based learning program: Teacher education.* Milwaukee, WI: Alverno Institute.

Ambach, G. (1996). Standards for teachers: Potential for improving practice. *Phi Delta Kappan, 78* (3), 207–210.

American Council on Education. (2000). Teacher ed pass-rate guidelines published. *Higher Education and National Affairs, 49* (8), 3–4.

Blackwell, P. J., & Diez, M. E. (1999). *Achieving the new vision of master's education for teachers.* Washington, DC: National Council for the Accreditation of Teacher Education.

Borko, H. (1997). New forms of classroom assessment: Implications for staff development. *Theory Into Practice, 36* (4), 231–238.

Bryant, D., & Driscoll, M. (1998). *Exploring classroom assessment in mathematics: A guide for professional development.* Reston, VA: National Council of Teachers of Mathematics.

Carnegie Forum on Education and the Economy. (1986). *A nation prepared: Teachers for the 21st century—The report of the Task Force on Teaching as a Profession.* New York: Author.

Castor, B. (2000). *Kappa Delta Pi Lecture.* Paper presented at the American Association of Colleges for Teacher Education Annual Meeting, Chicago.

Diez, M. E. (1990). A thrust from within: Reconceptualizing teacher education at Alverno College. *Peabody Journal of Education, 65* (2), 4–18.

Diez, M. E. (1996). *Admission and advancement in teacher education programs at Alverno College.* Unpublished department chart, Alverno College, Milwaukee, WI.

Diez, M. E. (in press). Assessment's future in teacher education: An assessment scenario from the future. In R. W. Lissitz & W. D. Schafer (Eds.), *Assessments in educational reform.* Needham Heights, MA: Allyn & Bacon.

Diez, M. E., Lake, K., & Rickards, W. (1994). Performance assessment in teacher education at Alverno College. In T. Warren (Ed.), *Promising practices: Teacher education in liberal arts colleges* (pp. 9–18). Landham, MD: University Press of America, Inc., and Association of Independent Liberal Arts Colleges for Teacher Education.

Durden, D., & Hunt, A. (1998). Outcomes and assessment in language arts and mathematics. In M. E. Diez (Ed.), *Changing the practice of teacher education: Standards and assessment as a lever for change* (pp. 89–97). Washington, DC: American Association of Colleges for Teacher Education.

Interstate New Teacher Assessment and Support Consortium (INTASC). (1992). *Model standards for beginning teacher licensing and development: A resource for state dialogue.* Washington, DC: Council of Chief State School Officers.

Loacker, G. (1991). *Designing a national assessment system: Alverno's institutional perspective.* Washington, DC: U.S. Department of Education, National Center for Education Statistics.

Loacker, G., Cromwell, L., & O'Brien, K. (1986). Assessment in higher education: To serve the learners. In C. Adelman (Ed.), *Assessment in American higher education.* Washington, DC: Office of Educational Research and Improvement, U.S. Department of Education.

Loacker, G., & Mentkowski, M. (1993). Creating a culture where assessment improves learning. In T. W. Banta & Associates (Eds.), *Making a difference: Outcomes of a decade of assessment in higher education.* San Francisco: Jossey-Bass.

Lowe, V. J., & Banker, B. J. (1994). Preparing teachers at college: Restructuring for the 21st century. In Diez, M. E. (Ed.), *Changing the practice of teacher education: Standards and assessment as a lever for change* (pp. 51–59). Washington, DC: American Association of Colleges for Teacher Education.

Mentkowski, M. (1998). Higher education assessment and national goals for education: Issues, assumptions, and principles. In N. M. Lambert & B. L. McCombs (Eds.), *How students learn: Reforming schools through learner-centered education* (pp. 259–310). Washington, DC: American Psychological Association.

Mentkowski, M., & Associates (2000). *Learning that lasts: Integrating learning, development, and performance in college and beyond.* San Francisco: Jossey-Bass.

Mentkowski, M., & Loacker, G. (1985). Assessing and validating the outcomes of college. In P. T. Ewell (Ed.), *Assessing educational outcomes.* (New Directions for Institutional Research No. 47). San Francisco: Jossey-Bass.

Mihalevich, C. D., & Carr, K. S. (1998). One university's journey toward teacher education restructuring. In M.E. Diez (Ed.), *Changing the practice of teacher education: Standards and assessment as a lever for change* (pp. 71–79). Washington, DC: American Association of Colleges for Teacher Education.

Murray, F. B. (in press). The over-reliance of accreditors on consensus standards. *Journal of Teacher Education.*

National Board for Professional Teaching Standards. (1989). *What teachers should know and be able to do.* Detroit, MI: Author.

National Council for the Accreditation of Teacher Education (NCATE). (1987). *NCATE standards for the accreditation of professional education units.* Washington, DC: Author.

National Council for the Accreditation of Teacher Education (NCATE). (2000). *NCATE 2000 unit standards.* Washington, DC: Author.

Nelms, V., & Thomas, M. (1998). Assessment: A process. In M. E. Diez (Ed.), *Changing the practice of teacher education: Standards and assessment as a lever for change* (pp. 81–88). Washington, DC: American Association of Colleges for Teacher Education.

Pearlman, M. (2000). *Using standards as the foundation for assessment of beginning teachers: Issues and implications.* Paper presented at the American Educational Research Association Annual Meeting, New Orleans, LA.

Roberts, L. (1997). *Evaluating teacher professional development: Local assessment moderation and the challenge of multi-site evaluation.* Paper presented at the Annual Meeting of the National Evaluation Institute, Indianapolis, IN.

Rogers, G. (1994). Measurement and judgment in curriculum assessment systems. *Assessment Update, 6,* 1, 6–7.

Schalock, H. D., Schalock, M. D., & Myton, D. (1998). Effectiveness along with quality should be the focus. *Phi Delta Kappan, 79* (6), 468–470.

Schnug, J., & Converse, S. A. (1998). Mission: Possible. In M. E. Diez (Ed.), *Changing the practice of teacher education: Standards and assessment as a lever for change* (pp. 61–69). Washington, DC: American Association of Colleges for Teacher Education.

Swisher, J. D., Green, S. B., & Tollefson, N. (1999). *Using curriculum-embedded assessment for making educational decisions: An empirical study with implications for including students with disabilities in accountability.* Paper presented at the Annual Meeting of the American Educational Research Association, Montreal.

U.S. National Research Center for TIMSS. (1996). *A splintered vision: An investigation of U.S. mathematics and science education.* East Lansing: Michigan State University.

Weisenbach, E. L. (2000). *Standards based accountability as a tool for making a difference in student learning.* Paper presented at the American Association of Colleges for Teacher Education Annual Meeting, Chicago, IL.

Weisenbach, E. L., Mack, K., Scannell, M., & Steffel, N. (1998). *Multiple voices: A shared vision.* Paper presented at the American Association of Colleges for Teacher Education Annual Meeting, New Orleans, LA.

Zeichner, K. (2000). *The teaching portfolio as a vehicle for student teacher development.* Paper presented at the American Educational Research Association Annual Meeting, New Orleans, LA.

4

REDEFINING A PROFESSION

Assessment in Pharmacy Education

Thomas D. Zlatic

One of the striking things about the responses to our survey was **how much attention was given to assessment of learning outcomes and how little to teaching students how to achieve them.**

Riordan and Doherty, Alverno College
Institute, "Student Learning Outcomes"

Pharmacy is a profession that is redefining itself. Traditionally, the mission of pharmacy has been to prepare and dispense medications. In the performance of these roles, pharmacists have had close interactions with customers, so much so that for a number of years pharmacists have been ranked in national polls as one of the nation's most trusted group of professionals. Nonetheless, pharmacy, much more so than any other health-related profession, has been based upon a product-oriented ethos, and, as late as the 1950s, national law regulated the type of interactions pharmacists could have with their customers.

Over the last decade or two, a new mission has been emerging for the profession of pharmacy: pharmaceutical care. In this patient-centered ethos, the pharmacist takes responsibility for patient outcomes related to drug therapy.[1] The pharmacist's "social object" is no longer a product but a patient. This new mission intensifies the fiduciary responsibilities that a professional has for the people he or she serves. Pharmacists still must be firmly grounded in biology, chemistry, and pharmacology, but increasingly important are their abilities to think critically, solve problems, communicate, and resolve ethical dilemmas. This new mission of pharmacy practice necessitates a corresponding new mission for pharmacy education: to prepare practitioners to provide pharmaceu tical care. The challenge of pharmacy education today is to design, ir and assess curricula that integrate the general and professional ab: will enable practitioners to be responsible for drug therapy outcome well-being of patients.

Two highly palpable results of this evolving sense of mission ar: in the amount of education and the degree required for someone w enter pharmacy. Since the 1950s, pharmacy had been a five-year pro minating in a bachelor of science degree, though some programs also as an alternative the doctor of pharmacy (Pharm.D.) degree normally re ing a minimum of four years of professional education preceded by two y of general education. By 2001, all pharmacy schools will admit only Pharm students—the B.S. will no longer be an option for incoming students. Anot change involved what learning occurred during those years of professic education. Pharmacy has been a content-driven discipline; most common pe agogical practices were large class lectures and objective testing. Over the pas 15 years, leaders have urged educational reform through the implementation of competence- or outcome-based curricula in which desired student outcomes determine content, teaching methods, and assessment strategies.

The development of a new mission of pharmacy practice and the identifi- cation of abilities needed for graduates to practice pharmaceutical care have shaped the evolution of assessment in pharmacy education. Assessment of course is a multifaceted process, involving institutions, programs, faculty, and students. It can be formative or summative in nature, and it can take the forms of objective data (such as attrition rates, employment figures, board examina- tion success rates); attitudinal and opinion surveys (including exit interviews, focus groups, course evaluations, employer interviews); and performance measures (such as tests, simulations, projects). The emphasis here, however, is on assessment and improvement of student learning—specifically, students learning to master the abilities required to provide pharmaceutical care.[2] In short, the focus of this chapter is assessment as a method to help create a new type of pharmacy practice.

Creating an Assessment Culture

Pharmacy as a profession has methodically attempted to provide a framework and enabling strategies for colleges of pharmacy to develop assessment as a tool both for accountability and for improved student learning. A climate of assessment has been engendered by the activities of professional associations; by the guidelines provided by pharmacy's accrediting body, the American Council on Pharmaceutical Education (ACPE); and by the efforts of pharmacy institutions to implement curricula and assessment plans consistent with those guidelines.

Pharmacy's response to internal and external pressures to document success in higher education has been abetted by strong leadership from the American Association of Colleges of Pharmacy (AACP). Through a variety of committees, commissions, grant projects, and development programs, AACP has attempted to provide a vision and process for ensuring that pharmacy schools meet their educational goals.[3]

Particularly significant in spurring pharmacy education toward curricular development was the AACP Commission to Implement Change in Pharmaceutical Education, appointed in 1989. In a series of background papers, the Commission affirmed pharmaceutical care as the new mission of pharmacy practice and argued that pharmaceutical care should be the basis for strategic planning regarding educational outcomes, curricular content, and pedagogical processes within pharmacy education (AACP, 1993a). Recognizing the importance of developing outcomes by which to assess student achievement, the Commission endorsed for pharmacy education the four professional competences that had been identified by The University of Michigan Professional Preparation Network (Stark & Lowther, 1988)—conceptual competence, technical competence, integrative competence, and career marketability—and then listed both general outcomes/competences and professional outcomes that would be needed for graduates to practice pharmaceutical care:

General: Thinking, communication, values and ethics, personal awareness and social responsibility, self-learning, social interaction, and citizenship

Professional: Solve problems and make decisions, manage, learn, communicate/teach/educate/collaborate, participate in policy formation/professional development

Insightful was the Commission's realization that the content and educational processes for pharmacy education would be dictated by the outcomes that had been selected.

The year following the creation of the Commission, AACP appointed a Focus Group on Liberalization of the Professional Curriculum to provide examples of a pharmacy curriculum and of teaching strategies that would prepare students to render pharmaceutical care and to function as responsible citizens in a free society (Chalmers et al., 1992; Chalmers et al., 1994). The Focus Group opted to illustrate the benefits of an ability-based curricular plan, thus bringing assessment issues to the forefront; their task was to illustrate "the effective use of outcome measures in designing curriculums and assessing student learning." A foundational concept was that "Outcome-based education necessitates understanding the term 'curriculum' to mean an educational plan that is designed to assure that each student achieves well-defined performance-based abilities" (1992 p. 304). The principles that underlay the Focus Group's ability-based curricular plan were:

1. It will focus on the ability-based outcomes described in Commission Background Paper II as being important to the educated professional and citizen (irrespective of immediate career goals).

2. The outcome goals will be further described in terms of measurable, performance abilities so that identified components of the abilities can be taught, modeled, practiced, and assessed. Further, to help students and faculty visualize the goals for progressive development and achievement of outcome abilities, each outcome ability will be described as a set of expectations at three levels of progress through the curriculum (e.g., entering level, developing level, outcome level).

3. The plan will provide descriptions of a number of learning experiences in different types of courses to develop specific ability components. . . .

4. The plan will identify examples of assessment methods that are designed to assess the component elements of the abilities and that provide feedback to the student to help him/her gauge his/her progress and focus efforts for continuing development.

Georgine Loacker, Chair of the Council for Student Assessment at Alverno College, was a consultant to the Focus Group. Accordingly, the Focus Group reflected the assessment-as-learning principles and practices that Alverno had pioneered over the previous thirty years.[4] Assessment at Alverno is not primarily an after-the-fact measurement of student learning but an intrinsic part of the learning process whereby students are given specific feedback on how to improve their performance of ability outcomes, feedback that is anchored to clearly enunciated performance criteria. These early Focus Group efforts at assessment did not ignore institutional effectiveness, but clearly the emphasis was on the types of assessment that led to enhanced student learning. Or, more accurately, institutional effectiveness was gauged in terms of student achievement of ability outcomes.

Another AACP initiative important for the assessment effort was the formulation of educational outcomes for pharmacy education by the Center for the Advancement of Pharmaceutical Education (CAPE) Advisory Panel on Educational Outcomes. This broad-based group from pharmacy education and practice studied the findings of the Commission, the Focus Group, and a Scope of Practice Project survey in order to propose six professional and six general ability outcomes required for the practice of pharmaceutical care:

General: (1) Thinking, (2) communication, (3) valuing and ethical decision making, (4) social awareness and social responsibility, (5) self-learning, and (6) social interaction and citizenship

Professional: (1) Provide pharmaceutical care, (2) develop and manage medication distribution and control systems, (3) manage the pharmacy, (4) manage medication use systems, (5) promote public health, and (6) provide drug information and education[5]

Once again, the intention was not for colleges of pharmacy to adopt these educational outcomes intact but to use them as a resource as they created curricular and assessment plans that were appropriate to their institutions.

The work of the CAPE Advisory Panel and the Focus Group was reinvigorated when the chair of the Focus Group, Robert Chalmers, became principal investigator for a project supported by the U.S. Department of Education Fund for the Improvement of Postsecondary Education (FIPSE): "A Multi-Institutional Assessment Center Model to Facilitate Expansion of Ability-based Education in Schools of Pharmacy." The intent of this three-year grant (1993–96) was to extend and make concrete the principles and strategies recommended by the Focus Group by applying them at three colleges of pharmacy (Purdue, University of Maryland, and St. Louis), each of which had had at least one representative on the Focus Group. The project goal was to enable students to progress toward the achievement of performance-based outcome abilities; the project strategies were to develop among the three schools a common approach to the student assessment process and then for each school to implement and evaluate an assessment center model as a coordinating resource to facilitate expansion of ability-based education within pharmacy.

Each institution selected pilot courses through which to develop a common approach to assessment. For each course, the instructors identified two to seven course ability outcomes (such as thinking, self-learning, group interaction) and then restructured their teaching methods so that practice of the abilities became the focus of course activities. Faculty from different disciplines and colleges provided cross-fertilization in the development of exercises and assessment tools that would allow students to progress in their performance of course ability outcomes. An assessment-as-learning philosophy was adopted, and assessment tools were constructed to provide to students clear and specific feedback regarding their performance so that they could improve. Faculty of these pilot courses pooled their experiences to form an assessment center to assist other faculty in developing courses following this model. Ideally, as the common assessment approach was integrated across the college, faculty would construct a curriculum in which ability outcomes were sequenced over a four-year professional program so that students could repetitively practice them at increasingly more complex levels and within expanding contexts. To assess program effectiveness, the schools employed college outcomes surveys, post-graduation surveys, interviews, performance testing, and student portfolios.

The tremendous amount of faculty time devoted to this FIPSE assessment project generated valuable lessons that were shared with other schools through presentations and articles, but more systematic dissemination was undertaken between 1996 and 1998 when AACP was awarded a follow-up FIPSE grant to assist other colleges and schools of pharmacy in curricular development and assessment. Selected faculty from the three colleges involved in the original assessment grant served as consultants to eight "adapter" schools (Auburn, Drake, Houston, Illinois at Chicago, Mercer, Mississippi, Philadelphia, and Wilkes) who were designing curricula based upon ability outcomes, active learning, and formative assessment.

Another innovative dissemination strategy for pedagogical and curricular reform within pharmacy education has been the AACP Institute on Pedagogical and Curricular Change. This five-day development conference has been offered annually every summer since 1996 to promote academic leadership and the development of strategies to enhance institutional effectiveness regarding teaching and learning. What is unique about the Institute is that each of 20 to 25 schools of pharmacy selects five of its faculty to participate as a team, usually faculty who play key leadership roles at their institutions. Each Institute offers a series of pedagogical workshops, but a significant amount of time is allotted for the faculty teams to develop "take-home plans" to use to initiate more broad-based, strategic educational planning at their institutions. At these Institutes, assessment is presented as a crucial factor in curricular reform. School teams are encouraged to develop or adapt general and professional ability outcomes that give coherence to their programs.[6]

In summary, changes in the health care environment and in the practice of pharmacy happily have coincided with the omnipresent call for accountability that has sparked the assessment movement. The need to reorient pharmacy education because of the evolving mission of pharmacy practice has motivated a greater openness to new teaching philosophies, pedagogical strategies, and assessment methods. With an increasing need for pharmacists to demonstrate interpersonal communication skills, problem solving, ethical decision making, and other professional competences, ability-based assessment has been found to be a useful tool for refocusing what is taught, when and where it is taught, and how it is taught. Or, even more radically, ability-based assessment has influenced what is to be learned, when and where it is to be learned, and how it is to be learned. The vision and models for assessment promulgated through a number of councils, committees, workshops, grants, and presentations have been codified by the accrediting institution.

Accreditation Guidelines

The American Council on Pharmaceutical Education's (ACPE's) *Accreditation Standards and Guidelines for the Professional Program in Pharmacy Leading to the Doctor of Pharmacy Degree* adopted June 14, 1997, put ACPE's imprimatur on many of the innovative efforts that had been percolating within pharmacy education. Although the term "assessment" seldom appeared in earlier ACPE accreditation standards and guidelines, in the new standards (Standards 2000), specific guidelines were promulgated for the assessment of learning processes, student achievement, and curricular effectiveness.[7]

First of all, ACPE in Standard 1 of the standards and guidelines acknowledged pharmaceutical care to be the mission of pharmacy practice and thereby gave direction to the type of education required to prepare future practitioners: "The professional program in pharmacy should promote the knowledge, skills, abilities, attitudes, and values necessary to the provision of pharmaceutical care for the general practice of pharmacy in any setting." By referencing "knowledge, skills, abilities, attitudes, and values" as the focus of pharmacy education, ACPE set a foundation for ability-based assessment, though of course other approaches are left open. The measurement for program success is student performance of competences, and the measures are not merely posterior assessments of what students have learned but strategies by which students can improve their abilities.

> The College or School of Pharmacy should establish principles and methods for the formative and summative evaluation of student achievement. A variety of evaluation measures should be systematically and sequentially applied throughout the professional program in pharmacy. Assessments should measure cognitive learning, mastery of

essential practice skills, and the abilities to communicate effectively
and to use data in the critical thinking and problem solving processes.
Evaluation processes should measure student performance in all of the
professional competencies in accord with outcome expectations.
(Standard No. 13)

The focus on outcomes also determines the pedagogical strategies that
should be employed to prepare practitioners for pharmaceutical care. Faculty
must "adapt teaching methods to the attainment of student abilities and [the
Standard] requires that schools provide evidence that those teaching methods
are producing self-directed learners capable of performing the required capabilities" (Standard No. 12).

The Standards and Guidelines document requires schools and colleges to
be systematic and rigorous in their assessments and to show evidence that
findings have been used for program enhancements: "A system of outcome
assessment should be developed which fosters data-driven continuous
improvement of curricular structure, content, process, and outcomes" (Guideline 14.1). Evidence for student achievement should be gathered "systematically from sources such as students, alumni, state boards of pharmacy and
other publics, professional staff of affiliated practice facilities, and a variety of
other practitioners, . . . student exit interviews, preceptor evaluations, alumni
surveys, and standardized licensure examinations" (Guideline 3.1). However,
performance assessments should also be conducted both to encourage and
measure learning: "Evaluation should extend beyond the acquisition of
knowledge by students to the application of knowledge and skills in the care
of patients in improving medication use" (Standard 3); and "Testing procedures should condition students for the integration and application of principles, critical thinking, and problem solving rather than for short-term retention or memorization of specific details or isolated facts" (Guideline 13.1).

The expectations, strategies, and even language of the ACPE accrediting
body are consonant with the educational theory and practice that had been
evolving for a dozen years within pharmacy education. This degree of harmony probably has facilitated the preparation of some pharmacy schools for
the accreditation process.

Institutional Examples

In 1999, Alverno College published *Student Learning Outcomes in Baccalaureate Education*, a synthesis of responses by 140 baccalaureate institutions to
a survey on assessment (Riordan & Doherty). In my observations, the findings
in that report are representative of what is occurring in pharmacy schools.

Almost all pharmacy schools have articulated a set of learning outcomes, most commonly (following AACP initiatives) *ability* outcomes; most have learning outcomes for both the general and professional curriculum. Some learning outcomes are developed from the department level upward; others, probably more commonly, are developed downward from published lists of ability outcomes, such as the CAPE outcomes. Some schools have created criteria to flesh out the abilities, and fewer have done so for different developmental levels.

However, generally speaking, it is as unfortunately true in pharmacy as in many baccalaureate institutions:

> One of the difficulties that institutions have encountered once they articulated learning outcomes is **how to teach and assess for outcomes in a developmental way. . . .**[T]he connection between program and individual assessment is often obscure. This disconnect means that efforts at assessment in general are not operating at their maximum benefit for each student or for program improvement. **While assessments as sources for data on the success of programs provide critical information, it appears that learning outcomes per se are not yet an integral dimension of the degree for the person for whom it most matters—the student.** (Riordan & Doherty, 1999, p. 3)

To be fair, within pharmacy education, new accreditation standards have been only recently approved, and it will take some time for schools to excel. At this time, ACPE appears content if institutions can point to an assessment plan in development; in another five or six years, the agency will begin to look for evidence that assessment improves student learning. Nonetheless, even now a number of schools of pharmacy can provide examples of some assessment strategies that have the potential to enhance student learning.

Sometimes one of the most challenging questions regarding assessment is where to start. Thomas Angelo implies one answer when he identifies four "pillars of transformative assessment" (1999, p. 5): shared trust, shared visions and goals, shared language and concepts, and identification of research-based guidelines. Faculty consensus and community underlie most efforts at successful assessment.

The building of an ability-based learning and assessment program upon these pillars was undertaken by the Division of Pharmacy Practice at the St. Louis College of Pharmacy.[8] At Division meetings, development workshops, and retreats, faculty reported on pharmacy documents and educational literature to understand better the rationale for curricular reform in pharmacy education. Particularly helpful was that each summer since 1995, teams of faculty were sent to the week-long assessment workshops at Alverno College, with each person being assigned specific tasks that related to improvement of the division's program. Applying what they learned, Division faculty created seven divisional abilities for all didactic and experiential courses within Pharmacy Practice. For each of the seven ability outcomes, ability subcommittees were formed to develop over a twelve-month period criteria for three levels of student performance, with each level being correlated with performance expectations for each course in the pharmacy practice curriculum. Groups of faculty painstakingly developed, shared, and revised self-, peer-, and expert-assessment forms used both to provide formative feedback to students and to serve as the basis for summative assessment. Then the faculty mapped the abilities across courses in the pharmacy practice curriculum to ensure that sufficient and appropriate practice opportunities existed to allow students to progress in each ability. For curriculum committee review, each pharmacy practice course's syllabus was clearly structured along ability-based lines, with outcomes, practice, criteria, and feedback systematically laid out. Because of this lengthy process, faculty created a culture of assessment and felt ownership of the program. Just as importantly, they achieved the shared trust, language, and vision that Angelo identifies as essential for assessment to bloom into learning.

A productive tool for promoting assessment as learning is the assessment center, which is not so much a place but a function, or a set of related functions. Assessment centers are groups of teaching faculty who assist in developing curriculum centered on ability outcomes, who help other faculty design courses whose practice experiences and assessments enhance student development of ability outcomes, and who collect data that can document student progress and that eventually can be used for program improvement. One of the earliest adaptations of the assessment center concept in pharmacy was at Purdue, whose explorations into assessment center operationalization and the implementation of integrated courses have influenced assessment strategies at other schools (Purkerson, Mason, Chalmers, Popovich, & Scott, 1996, 1997).

Assessment centers are particularly helpful in developing performance activities and assessments. Pharmacy faculty at the University of Colorado, for instance, have developed "Professional Skills Development," a six-semester sequence of related courses taught over three years (D. Hammer, personal communication, May 2000; R. Altiere, personal communication, April 2000). During modules mapped to course outcomes, students practice such activities as patient consultation skills, consulting with standardized patients who assess students according to instructor-defined criteria. As students peer- and self-assess, they are required to provide evidence that they understand what constitutes good performance—that is, assessment is used for learning. Similarly, in the self-assessment of achievement of professional development goals, students at the beginning of the semester write a two- or three-page essay on areas they seek to improve and at the end of the semester write another short essay reflecting upon their progress. Along the same lines, performance assessment in Drake University's pre-pharmacy program is tied to self-learning. Students self-assess using a SOAP (i.e., subjective, objective, assessment, planning) note process common to clinical problem solving and enter the information onto a database located on the Web so that students and faculty have easy access (R. Chestnut, personal communication, May 2000; Rospond & Dirks, 1999a, 1999b). The entries include students' perceptions of strengths/weaknesses, their pharmacy major, a career in pharmacy, and class activities (subjective); GPAs, their ongoing activities, and learning styles (objective); goals relating to their personal, academic, and professional lives (assessment); and detailed plans to accomplish their goals, including timetables (planning). At the end of the semester, students reflect upon their progress toward goal completion. At both Drake and Colorado, assessment initially is formative, with much feedback being given to students. The advanced experiential program at Drake is competence based, so to be successful, students upon completion of 36 semesters of rotations must have achieved a "4" ranking (on a five-point scale) in each of the competences. However, at the end of every rotation except for the last, students may score lower than a "4" and still progress. Through a system of midterm and final assessments, students, preceptors, and faculty identify student weaknesses and then construct learning experiences that will help students improve their competence. In other words, high standards are set, but there are many nonpunitive opportunities for remediation. Similarly, at Colorado, mastery learning and assessment as learning guide the courses: students have many opportunities to practice and receive feedback regarding ability outcomes so that their grades are not based upon one or two major summative assessments.

A number of pharmacy schools are developing end-of-the-year formative and summative assessments of students' abilities, often adapting an assessment tool common in medical education: the Objective Structured Clinical Examination (OSCE). An OSCE is a simulation that often utilizes standardized patients to evaluate the effectiveness of medical students in a variety of clinical experiences.

For instance, in response to ACPE recommendations that "clinical evaluation [should] measure cognitive learning, mastery of essential practice skills, and the ability to use data in realistic problem solving" (ACPE, 1993, p. 21), faculty from the pharmacy schools at Creighton University, the University of Arkansas, and Shenandoah University developed a Pharmaceutical Care Encounters Program (PCEP) to determine if students can perform practice-based competences expected of pharmacists (Monaghan, Gardner, Schneider, Grady, & McKay, 1997). The PCEP was determined to be a valid and reliable indicator of the quality of ability-based performances that involved problem solving, critical thinking, communication, and application of pharmacologic knowledge. Auburn University's "Milestone Examinations" (MEs) are more comprehensive than OSCEs in that they assess not only patient interactions but also other abilities such as scientific reasoning (D. Beck, 1999, personal communication, May 2000). At the end of each curricular year, each student takes a four-hour exam, rotating through sixteen stations at which he or she is required to solve problems while interacting with Standardized Role Players (SRPs) recruited from the community. The SRPs evaluate student performance using a checklist, and students' performances are also videotaped for review by the school's Outcomes Assessment Committee. Currently, the MEs are used to provide feedback regarding student and program performance, but once they are sufficiently validated, they may be used to determine whether or not students can advance in the curriculum.[9]

Moving in the direction of "high stakes" testing is the University of Mississippi School of Pharmacy, where a significant departure from traditional teaching and assessments is represented by Pharmaceutical Care I–IV, a four-course sequence taught in the students' fifth professional year (B. Crabtree, personal communication, May 2000). The course is a student-centered problem-based learning (PBL) educational experience structured to help students develop an extensive knowledge base, clinical reasoning skills, self-directed learning, motivation to learn, awareness of the ambiguities and ethical dilemmas embodied in professional practice, and collaboration skills. Instead of attending lectures, students in small group sessions are expected to analyze "progressive disclosure cases" with a faculty member serving as a facilitator. Three methods of assessment are employed. (1) "Assessment of Performance in Group" is an extensive biweekly program that uses specific criteria for self-, peer-, and expert-assessment of knowledge, clinical reasoning, self-directed learning, and interpersonal and group skills. At the end of the semester, the assessments are formalized in writing and saved to a disk, with the instructor's assessment also being contained therein. These assessments constitute a proportion of the course grade. (2) Near the end of the semester, students' clinical reasoning and self-learning are assessed through a novel case they are assigned to complete over a weekend without guidance from faculty. (3) At course end, a "core knowledge" exam is given. The course is truly ability-based in that, in order to pass, students must demonstrate a minimum acceptable performance on all three assessments. Initially, the program has elicited high stress, but the faculty are confident that this program of instruction and assessment prepares students to assume entry-level positions in pharmacy. The measurement instruments used revealed a dramatic increase in abilities as the course progressed.

Faculty from the Bernard J. Dunn School of Pharmacy at Shenandoah University also require students to pass annual progression exams (A. McKay, personal communication, May 2000). In a technologically rich environment that includes a suite of rooms with closed televison, standardized patients assist in assessing students according to predefined criteria sheets. Students cannot advance without passing, but because 80 percent of instruction is modular and available on the Internet, students who do not pass can remediate over the summer by completing the appropriate modules at their own pace, free of charge. Feedback has been very positive. A downside is program expense, but this may be offset somewhat as Shenandoah markets the system to other schools. Faculty from the College of Pharmacy at the University of Houston plan to prepare students for high stakes testing over a three-year period. At the end of year one, students are asked to study over the summer material from a list of topics they should know. The next fall, they are given a formative exam over the previous year's material. As an incentive to learn, prizes are awarded to top performers. At the beginning of the third year, another formative exam is given over the previous two years' material. Then, at the beginning of the fourth year, a summative exam is given, and only those who pass are allowed to go on rotations (T. Lemke, personal communication, May 2000).

Student portfolios are another assessment tool that can be employed to enhance learning, though too frequently they are used in other ways: "While their form and use does vary significantly across institutions, it is most often the case that **portfolios tend to be used to document student performance in aggregate, not to evaluate and assist the students in their development as learners**" (Riordan & Doherty, 1999, p. 4). Pharmacy education offers some notable exceptions. At St. Louis, for instance, Sheldon Holstad and others developed an Electronic Student Portfolio (ESP) to support ability-based education within the clinical environment. Into this Web-based portfolio are placed samples and assessments of students' work—self- and expert-assessments tied to clearly delineated performance criteria. As students pass through a number of clinical rotations with different preceptors at various sites, the ESP allows each preceptor and student to access the portfolio from any location. Since the rotations are ability-based and criteria-referenced, the preceptor can consult the ESP to identify student deficiencies in such abilities as select/recommend drug therapy, or collaborate with health care professionals, then create learning experiences that allow students to improve.

It should be clear by now that collecting data is a necessary step for assessment but not its primary purpose; improved student learning is the ultimate goal. The use of data to improve a curriculum is demonstrated by the University of Georgia College of Pharmacy, which collects three types of data (self, direct observation, and peer review) for both teaching and learning (G. Francisco, personal communication, May 2000). For the assessment of teaching, the instruments used are teaching portfolios, teaching evaluations, and promotion/tenure peer reports. In assessment of student learning, "direct observation" consists of grades and laboratory and clinical experiences, and the "peer" data consist of surveys to employers and alumni regarding strengths and weaknesses. For "self-assessment" of their learning, surveys are given to students at the end of each semester to determine which of the announced learning objectives were met during the year. Administrators then discuss the results with the instructor to identify whether or not changes in instruction are needed. Midpoint evaluations of each course have also been conducted, whereby students listed positive aspects of each course and suggestions for change. Faculty sometimes did not value the quality of feedback and questioned the validity of surveys, so now a focus group of 10 students meets with the Curriculum Committee at the midpoint of the semester and provides feedback about each course. Using similar procedures, the University of Houston assesses individual courses every semester based upon student perceptions of achievement of the course's proficiency statements. The Assessment Task Force's discussions with instructors have been very collegial, with instructors generally agreeing that student perceptions are "right on target." The same form with 34 terminal outcomes is also used for exit interviews and to survey alumni, who are asked how they use the competences in practice. All the data are reviewed to suggest program changes (T. Lemke, personal communication, May 2000).

A novel way to integrate student and curriculum assessment is to ask students to analyze their learning experiences. The College of Pharmacy at Western University has implemented a "Discovery Map Project" in which students identify when and where in the curriculum they learned the knowledge, skills, and attitudes to practice professional abilities. First- and second-year students in groups report on their findings by preparing a poster presentation and by writing a 14-page document. The project thus requires students to reflect upon their learning but also provides evidence with which to evaluate the curriculum (K. Franson, personal communication, May 2000).

Another approach for achieving a "picture" of the curriculum in practice is the University of North Carolina's "The Lecture Outcome—CAPE Outcome Review" (LOCOR) project, designed to (1) provide public expectations for learning outcomes for each course, (2) identify curricular content gaps or redundancies, and (3) help establish integrated course work that supports achievement of defined learning outcomes across the curriculum (K. Deloatch, personal communication, May 2000). Instructors in each core course in years 1 to 3 of the professional curriculum each class day are sent an E-mail from the LOCOR coordinators, asking them to define the primary learning objectives or outcomes for that day's class. Instructor responses are posted on a website and made accessible on-line for both faculty and students. At the end of each semester, the LOCOR coordinators analyze the responses to determine whether or not the desired abilities and competences are being addressed in the classroom. This information, along with review of course syllabi and course evaluation data, provide the basis for proposing course revisions.

In summary, pharmacy has experimented with innovations in assessment and some schools have implemented innovative and coherent assessment plans, but many, if not most, institutions are still experimenting and sometimes struggling. On almost all campuses, there is activity to develop assessment plans, and on many there is excitement regarding innovative ideas and practices. It will take time to formalize and systematize these innovations, and it will take longer to gather and interpret data that can lead to improvements in programs and student learning. However, with the assistance of professional organizations and the helpful pressure of accrediting bodies, pharmacy schools generally are moving toward meaningful assessment of students' ability to provide pharmaceutical care.

Lessons Learned and Ongoing Issues

This brief overview of assessment in pharmacy education is probably both overstated and underreported: self-reports can be inflationary, and it is likely that many worthy efforts are not widely known. However, some generalizations can be made.

Probably the single most important criterion for success in meaningful assessment is that it be a faculty-driven process. Externally driven assessment programs that impose structure and accountability upon a college faculty produce "compliance rather than commitment" (Riordan & Doherty, 1999, p. 5) and sometimes not even compliance but a resistant backlash. Successful programs require faculty initiative and ownership. If faculty do not understand and agree with the purposes and methods of assessment, the efforts will become moribund.

But although assessment almost assuredly will falter unless it flames up from within the faculty, leadership is essential to fan the enthusiasm and perhaps ignite the fire in the first place. Fear of accountability and a common preconception that assessment and learning are inimical are powerful opposing forces to assessment. Required is a leadership with courage and charisma to educate faculty and to draw forth from them the commitment to student learning that resides at the heart of most educators. Messianic proponents or inflexible adherents to a single approach to assessment, however, are not the solution; regardless of intentions or insights, all they will produce is resistance. However, it is also naive to think that productive assessment will flourish if academic leaders do not create an environment and a rewards system that encourage innovators and discourage malcontents. Persons who fall from trees whose branches have been cut off with them in them are unlikely to climb trees again; those who watch the falls are lucky enough to learn their lessons vicariously—but just as deeply.

"Paper assessment" is a recurring danger. Recognizing the need to satisfy accrediting bodies, some colleges are tempted to create assessment plans that are addressed more to the immediate problem of getting accredited than to the purpose for accreditation in the first place: enhancement of student learning. Faculty become cynical when asked to collaborate on assessment efforts that merely justify what has always been done or that create pro forma plans that are wasted effort for the accomplishment of any goal other than accreditation itself. In some schools, frustrated assessment-oriented faculty privately hope that accrediting agencies will probe below the veneer to force substantive changes that will make assessment more meaningful. Accrediting teams that confuse paper with reality will slow the assessment movement.

Administrators and faculty intent on satisfying not just the letter but also the spirit of accreditation guidelines are handicapped by blurred visions of what needs to be accomplished and how to accomplish it. Some schools are confused by theories and definitions, caught up in politics, buried in many other activities, and uncertain about what direction to take; one rational solution is "let's wait until evaluators come and tell us what to do." More sharing needs to be established between schools, honest sharing that extends beyond public relations documents. Accrediting agencies can assist by identifying and publicizing model assessment programs and approaches and models that they have encountered. ACPE and AACP are discussing possibilities for collaborating on such efforts.

Of course there is the ongoing need for faculty development to acquaint instructors with reasons and strategies for assessment and to motivate them to spend the time performing extra tasks that they may originally perceive as bureaucratic intrusions into academic life. Faculty reservations are both philosophical and temperamental. There are fears that assessment will undermine faculty autonomy and academic freedom; that an emphasis on abilities undercuts content; that assessment will create a "teaching toward tests" environment; that assessment is too expensive and diverts funds from instruction; that insufficient data exist to warrant an assessment-driven curriculum. Once they are convinced of the value of a meaningful assessment effort, faculty require assistance to develop the knowledge and skills needed to bring it to reality.

Coaxing established faculty to reconsider teaching strategies and assessment methods can be challenging, but unfortunately new faculty often imitate the teaching methods and styles they encountered during their own education. Some schools are recognizing the need to educate pharmacy students contemplating teaching careers regarding the centrality of assessment in the learning process and the merits of the "learning paradigm" advocated by Barr and Tagg (1995). Each fall in St. Louis, pharmacy residents participate in nine two-hour teaching seminars in which they learn and practice the principles of ability-based education. After extensive practice and formative feedback, each resident, individually or in pairs, completes (1) a script for one two-hour module for a course in Antimicrobial Pharmacotherapy and (2) a detailed content-based homework assignment for students to complete prior to class so that the two-hour module can minimize lecture and focus instead on active learning. In the spring semester, the residents practice what they have learned in the seminars by teaching an Antimicrobial Pharmacotherapy course. Upon completion of the residency, residents who accept faculty appointments walk into their positions with a better grasp of the intimate connection between learning and assessment, and in some cases they have been able to contribute to the promulgation of the assessment-as-learning philosophy within their new institutions.

Within pharmacy, the profession's innovative efforts to develop general and professional ability outcomes have provided colleges with a head start on assessment planning. However, a drawback is the tendency at times to isolate the general and professional outcomes—in the curriculum and in instruction. Students learn critical thinking in the early or even pre-pharmacy curriculum and then later learn how to select and recommend drug therapy, as if there were no continuity between the two. More attention needs to be given to the *integration* of general and professional ability outcomes.[10] As pharmacy practice becomes more patient-centered, as pharmacy continues to evolve from training to education, general abilities must be taught in professional contexts. In the booming herbal products market, for instance, it will be essential for future professionals not only to know toxicity, side effects, efficacy, and mechanisms of action of herbals; they also will need critical analysis to evaluate scientific and popular data, communication skills to counsel misinformed and sometimes desperate patients, and ethical decision making to navigate in the expanding alternative therapies area of medicine[11] (Zlatic, Nowak, & Sylvester, 2000). ACPE's guideline that the pharmacy curriculum include early practice experiences could promote this integration of general and professional outcomes.

Along related lines, abilities, or competences are integrations of three components: (1) knowledge; (2) skills; (3) attitudes, habits, and values. Pharmacy education has always been adept at assessing knowledge and is becoming increasingly sophisticated in assessing skills, but still elusive is the assessment of attitudes, habits, and values within such abilities as problem solving, selection of drug therapies, or patient education. It is difficult enough to "teach" such values as lifelong learning, truth seeking, and caring, but it is even more challenging to assess them. Attitudinal surveys, standardized tests such as the California Critical Thinking Dispositions Inventory, and preceptor evaluations are being used with some degree of success, but perhaps even more effective would be a more conscious integration of attitudes, habits, and values within the practice opportunities for each ability within the curriculum. Modeling by faculty of course is essential, but students can also be made more conscious of professional values and attitudes through criterion-based assessments by experts, peers, and self. A particularly encouraging trend is the growing number of schools of pharmacy that require service learning experiences to promote in students a "caring" attitude and a habit of service (Nickman, 1998). Portfolios, reflection essays, site evaluations, and exit interviews often call attention to the effectiveness of such a strategy. As pharmacy continues to move in the direction of pharmaceutical care, it will be crucial to provide and assess curricular and cocurricular experiences that encourage professionalism, service, and care.

Future socioeconomic trends and health care environments are unpredictable. In some cases, pharmacy students are being prepared for a practice that does not yet exist. Even now, not all pharmacy educators are convinced that a six-year doctor of pharmacy degree should be required for all new graduates wishing to enter pharmacy. Others believe that education should not only follow practice but should take initiatives to help to define and create practice. For those espousing this agenda of self-definition, assessment is a powerful tool.

Notes

1. See Hepler and Strand (1989); Sleath and Campbell (1998); and Zellmer (1996).

2. Eric Boyce, currently an AACP Scholar in Residence, is preparing a comprehensive Web page of resources dealing with assessment within pharmacy education.

3. A summary can be found in Zlatic, Alkana, et al. (2000).

4. For an explanation of ability-based education, see Alverno College (1994) and Zlatic (2000a).

5. The Cape Outcomes were updated in 1998: *Professional:* (1) Provide pharmaceutical care, (2) manage the practice, (3) manage medication use systems, (4) promote public health, (5) provide drug information and education; *General:* (1) Thinking, (2) communication, (3) valuing and ethical decision making, (4) social and contextual awareness, (5) social responsibility, (6) social interaction, (7) self-learning abilities (Educational Outcomes 1998).

6. Assessment continues to be an important topic within AACP. See Hollenbeck (1999) and Beck et al. (1998).

7. See also American Council on Pharmaceutical Education's *Standards 2000 Self-Study* (1996).

8. See Loacker and Mentkowski (1993); Vrahnos et al. (1998); and Maddux (2000).

9. For another approach at the University of North Carolina, see Brock, Ellis-Nielsen, Deloatch, Joyner, and Raasch (1999); and at the University of Arkansas, see Grady and Vanderbush (1998).

10. See Smith (1999); Zlatic, Alkana, et al. (2000); and Zlatic (2000c).

11. See also Zlatic (2000b). Guideposts for future work in this area can be found in Mentkowski and Associates (2000).

References

Alverno College. (1994). *Ability-based learning program* (Rev. ed.). Milwaukee, WI: Alverno Institute.

American Association of Colleges of Pharmacy (AACP). (1993a). Background Paper I: What is the mission of pharmaceutical education? *American Journal of Pharmaceutical Education, 57,* 374–376.

American Association of Colleges of Pharmacy. (1993b). Background Paper II: Entry-level, curricular outcomes, curricular content and educational process. *American Journal of Pharmaceutical Education, 57,* 377–385.

American Association of Colleges of Pharmacy. (1993; rev. 1998). *Educational outcomes.* Alexandria, VA: Center for the Advancement of Pharmaceutical Education, Author.

American Council on Pharmaceutical Education. (1993). *The proposed revision of accreditation standards and guidelines for the professional program in pharmacy leading to the Doctor of Pharmacy Degree.* Chicago, IL: Author.

American Council on Pharmaceutical Education. (1996). *Standards 2000 self-study.* Chicago, IL: Author.

American Council on Pharmaceutical Education. (1997). *Accreditation standards and guidelines for the professional program in pharmacy leading to the Doctor of Pharmacy Degree.* Chicago, IL: Author.

Angelo, T.A. (1999, May). Doing assessment as if learning matters most. *AAHE Bulletin,* 3–6.

Barr, R. B., & Tagg, J. (1995). From teaching to learning: A new paradigm for undergraduate education. *Change, 27,* 12–25.

Beck, D. (1999). Implementation of a pharmacy school continuous quality improvement program: Phase III—curricula outcomes assessment using milestone exams, Abstract. *American Journal of Pharmaceutical Education, 63,* 82S.

Beck, D., Brandt, B., Broedel-Zaugg, K., Coffman, R., Marshall, L., Robbins, M., Swaffar, D., & Tipton, D. (1998). Teaching and outcomes assessment committee report. Council of Faculties, American Association of Colleges of Pharmacy.

Brock, T. P., Ellis-Nielsen, A. D., Deloatch, K. H., Joyner, P.U., & Raasch, R. H. (1999). Objective structured clinical exams (OSCE) as evaluative tools in pharmacy curricula. *American Journal of Pharmaceutical Education, 63,* 86S.

Chalmers, R.K. (1993). A multi-institutional assessment center model to facilitate expansion of ability-based education in schools of pharmacy, Grant Application, Foundation for the Improvement of Postsecondary Education (FIPSE).

Chalmers, R. K., Grotpeter, J. J., Hollenbeck, R. G., Nickman, N. A., Sommi, R. W., Zlatic, T. D., Loacker, G., & Meyer, S. M. (1994). Changing to an outcome-based, assessment-guided curriculum: A report of the Focus Group on Liberalization of the Professional Curriculum. *American Journal of Pharmaceutical Education, 58,* 304–309.

Chalmers, R. K., Grotpeter, J. J., Hollenbeck, R. G., Nickman, N. A., Wincor, M. Z., Loacker, G., & Meyer, S.M. (1992). Ability-based outcome goals for the professional curriculum: A report of the Focus Group on Liberalization of the Professional Curriculum. *American Journal of Pharmaceutical Education, 56,* 304–309.

Grady, A. R., & Vanderbush, R. (1998). Evaluation of student performance feedback in staged scenario encounters with standardized patients (Sps), Abstract. *American Journal of Pharmaceutical Education, 63,* 109S.

Hepler, C. D., & Strand, L. M. (1989). Opportunities and responsibilities in pharmaceutical care. *American Journal of Pharmaceutical Education, 53,* 7S–15S.

Hollenbeck, R.G. (1999). Chair report of the 1998/99 Academic Affairs Committee. *American Journal of Pharmaceutical Education, 63,* 7S–13S.

Loacker, G., & Mentkowski, M. (1993). Creating a culture where assessment improves learning. In T. W. Banta & Associates (Eds.), *Making a difference: Outcomes of a decade of assessment in higher education.* San Francisco: Jossey-Bass.

Maddux, M.S. (2000). Using assessment as learning within an ability-based program. *Journal of Pharmacy Teaching, 7,* 141–160.

Mentkowski, M., & Associates. (2000). *Learning that lasts: Integrating learning, development, and performance in college and beyond.* San Francisco: Jossey-Bass.

Monaghan, M., Gardner, S., Schneider. E., Grady, A. , & McKay, A. (1997). Standardized patients: An ability-based outcomes assessment for the evaluation of clinical skills in traditional and nontraditional education. *American Journal of Pharmaceutical Education, 61,* 337–344.

Nickman, N.A. (1998). (Re-)learning to care: Use of service-learning as an early professionalization experience. *American Journal of Pharmaceutical Education, 62,* 380–387.

Purkerson, D., Mason, H., Chalmers, R., Popovich, G., & Scott, S. (1996). Evaluating pharmacy students' ability-based educational outcomes using an assessment center approach. *American Journal of Pharmaceutical Education, 60,* 239–248.

Purkerson, D., Mason, H., Chalmers, R., Popovich, G., & Scott, S. (1997). Expansion of ability-based education using an assessment center approach with pharmacists as assessors. *American Journal of Pharmaceutical Education, 61,* 241–248.

Riordan, T., & Doherty, A. (1999). Student learning outcomes in baccalaureate education, Report of the Alverno College Institute. Milwaukee, WI: Alverno College Institute

Rospond, R. M., & Dirks, S.J. (1999a). Assessment of reflective problem solving skills in an integrated introductory practice experience, Abstract. *American Journal of Pharmaceutical Education, 63,* 78S.

Rospond, R. M., & Dirks, S. J. (1999b). Integrated introductory pharmacy practice experience model, Abstract. *American Journal of Pharmaceutical Education, 63,* 78S.

Sleath, B., & Campbell, W. (1998). American pharmacy: A profession in the final stage of dividing? *Journal of Social and Administrative Pharmacy, 15,* 225–240.

Smith, R. E. (1999). Unleash the greatness. *American Journal of Pharmaceutical Education, 63,* 436–441.

Stark, J. S., & Lowther, M. A. (1988). *Report of the professional preparation network: Strengthening the ties that bind—Integrating undergraduate liberal and professional study.* Ann Arbor, MI: University of Michigan Center for the Study of Higher and Postsecondary Education.

Vrahnos, D., Dahdal, W. Y., Wallace, C. S., Burke, J. M., Holstad, S. G., Zlatic, T. D., & Maddux, M. S. (1998). Developing ability outcomes across the clinical curriculum, Abstract. *American Journal of Pharmaceutical Education, 62,* 109S.

Zellmer, W. A. (1996). Searching for the soul of pharmacy. *American Journal of Health-Syst Pharm, 53,* 1911–1916.

Zlatic, T. D. (2000a). Ability-based assessment within pharmacy education: Preparing students for practice of pharmaceutical care. *Journal of Pharmacy Teaching, 7,* 5–27.

Zlatic, T. D. (2000b). Integrating general and professional outcomes through writing. *Journal of Pharmacy Teaching, 8*(2), 3–23.

Zlatic, T. D. (2000c). Liberalizing professional education: Integrating general and professional ability outcomes. *Journal of Pharmacy Practice, 13*(5), 365–372.

Zlatic, T. D., Alkana, R. L., Bradberry, J. C., Boyce, E., Chalmers, R. K., Crabtree, B. L., Polli, J. E., Wadelin, J. W. (Liaison ACPE), & Meyer, S. M. (AACP staff). (2000). Integrating education: Chair report of the 1999/2000 Academic Affairs Committee, American Association of Colleges of Pharmacy. Forthcoming in *American Journal of Pharmaceutical Education, 2001, 65.*

Zlatic, T. D., Nowak, D. M., & Sylvester, D. (2000). Integrating general and professional education through a study of herbal products: An intercollegiate collaboration. *American Journal of Pharmaceutical Education, 64,* 83–94.

5

ASSESSMENT OF STUDENT LEARNING IN THE DISCIPLINE OF NURSING

Donna L. Boland and Juanita Laidig

Nursing Education's Heritage

Western or modern nursing is relatively young, having a history that spans only the last century. Nursing as an academic discipline has an even shorter history. Early training of nurses, like that for physicians, followed an established pedagogical path of apprenticeship. The apprentice model of nurse training dealt with defined content related to basic science concepts of the day and a set of housekeeping skills. This knowledge was incorporated into a curricular blueprint for training refined "ladies" who were called into service to alleviate suffering and support the implementation of the medical prescription of the day.

Florence Nightingale, the recognized visionary of modern nursing, believed that the training of nurses must focus not only on what nurses should be doing but also on how it should be done (Baly, 1991). The integration of learning and doing remains the hallmark of nursing education. As nursing education moved from a proprietary relationship with hospitals to a collegiate affiliation with institutions of higher education, there continued to be a commitment to the philosophy that the utility or applicability of knowledge remains critical to the practice of nursing. Performance expectations are part of nursing's heritage as well as nursing's future. As consistent with expectations of professional practice-oriented disciplines, knowledge generation, application, and dissemination must reach well beyond the axiom of knowledge for knowledge's sake alone. Nurse educators therefore have had little trouble in supporting the current emphasis on assessment of student learning.

Modern Nursing Education

The migration of nursing education from hospital-based training programs to two- and four-year college and university settings has taken more than 50 years to accomplish. Moreover, this transition occurred without a grand plan or time frame. The lack of planning resulted in the development of nursing education models that followed a multiplicity of educational paths. These divergent educational paths created unique challenges for both nurse educators and those engaged in the practice of nursing.

The nursing discipline now supports the education of nurses at the associate, bachelor, master's, and doctoral levels. Each level of educational preparation has different student learning expectations and outcomes. However, the nursing collective has yet to agree on how these various educational levels should be used in differentiating the practice of nursing. The diversity of educational models, educational outcomes, and orientation to the discipline of nursing has proven to be a challenge for those educating nurses, those hiring nurses, and those practicing nursing. Educators and practitioners grapple with common language to explain what comprises discipline-specific nursing knowledge and how nurses apply this knowledge in practice to affect the health of individuals positively. The challenge for educators and practitioners to identify the knowledge and skill mix nurses need to know and put into practice is being reshaped continually by the explosion of new knowledge and technology affecting health care of people, their communities, and the world. In addition, these challenges are embedded in a social environment that is calling for increasing objective evidence to verify that nursing educational programs are preparing beginning and advanced practitioners with the necessary competences to affect care outcomes positively within an economically minded health care system (Hill, 1999).

The Impact of External Forces on the Practice of Nursing

The practice of nursing experienced enormous changes during the last century. As the profession of nursing carried on arduous discourse in an effort to characterize the practice and education of nursing, external forces helped mold these conversations. These external forces include

1. Changing population demographics and population diversity

2. Reformulating of health care by the technological explosion

3. Expanding the view of health to include societal globalization

4. Dealing with educated consumers of the health care systems, both traditional and nontraditional

5. Moving from individual-based care orientation to population-based care orientation

6. Increasing costs of health care and the challenges of dealing with systems created to manage these increases

7. Dealing with issues related to health care regulation and policy

8. Growing emphasis on and need for interdisciplinary collaborative practice models

9. Decreasing nursing workforce equipped with the tools to affect patient care outcomes

10. Increasing need for a more learned workforce (Heller, Osos, & Durney-Crowley, 2000, pp. 9–13)

The Impact of Private and Professional Organizations on Assessment

The Pew Charitable Trusts funded a commission in the late 1980s charged with the responsibility of determining how to "ensure that today's students will contribute to and thrive as practitioners in tomorrow's radically different and ever-changing health care environment" (Shugars, O'Neil, & Bader, 1991). The deliberations of the Pew Commission were published in a series of four reports. The underlying premise for all the reports is that health professional programs need to reform curricula to prepare graduates with skills that complement a changing health care delivery system if graduates are to continue to be relevant to the practice of nursing. The commission "outlined a set of 21 competencies—to serve as a guide for helping professional schools redirect and redesign their curricula" (Bellack & O'Neil, 2000, p. 15). The commission concluded that students needed to acquire broad competences that included "critical thinking and clinical judgment skills, effective organizational and teamwork skills, service orientation, cost awareness, accountability for clinical outcomes and quality of care, continuous improvement of health care, population-based approaches to care, an ethic of social responsibility, and commitment to continual learning and development" (Bellack & O'Neil,

p. 16). These recommendations were consistent with changing society and health care trends.

The Pew Reports, beginning with the first one issued in 1991, mobilized nursing leaders who, along with professional nursing organizations, called for revolutionary changes in the ways nursing was practiced and students were educated. The American Association of Colleges of Nursing (AACN) and the National League for Nursing (NLN) were two highly visible organizations at the forefront of the curriculum reform movement. Nursing leaders from these and other nursing practice organizations began to identify and describe the competences that would advance the practice and education of nurses in maximizing nursing productivity outcomes.

In 1995, AACN constituted a task force to examine the right mix of knowledge and skills future nurses needed to possess in a rapidly changing health care environment demanding full accountability for nursing practice outcomes. The AACN task force defined the essential knowledge, values, and professional behaviors' expected of baccalaureate and graduate students at the completion of their programs. The results of these efforts were published in 1998 as *The Essentials of Baccalaureate Education for Professional Nursing Practice* and in 1996 as *The Essentials of Master's Education for Advanced Practice Nursing*. Articulated within these documents are core competences emphasizing critical thinking; communication; information management; and ability to use knowledge to improve health, prevent disease, and decrease health risks. Additionally, nurses must possess ethical reasoning skills, an understanding of human diversity and health as a global issue, knowledge of health care systems, and an understanding of how health care policy is shaped at the micro and macro decision-making levels within the social and political strata (AACN, 1998, 1999).

The National League for Nursing (NLN) promoted curriculum reform that would prepare graduates with skills to practice in community-based health care settings. It is projected that the majority of nursing positions and nursing practice will occur within a community-based context within the next decade. The set of competences that nurses will need to practice in a broader-based context is requiring a different mix of knowledge and skills and expanded learning experiences in which to develop these skills/competences. In response to the NLN call for curriculum reform, nursing faculty are experimenting with innovative curriculum designs and teaching practices that will prepare graduates to practice across a continuum of care from acute care settings to homes, schools, work, churches, and long-term care settings. Reflected in curriculum reform is the use of technology as a means to facilitate distributed educational commitments and as a teaching tool for enhancing student learning.

The National Council of State Boards of Nursing (NCSBN) in the 1990s revised the testing blueprint and structure for nurse licensure. This redesign was to complement increasing emphasis on critical thinking and clinical reasoning in the application of nursing knowledge and skill.

The Role of Accreditation

Professional accreditation has become a major external stimulus for encouraging the incorporation of relevant student learning outcomes in undergraduate and graduate curricula. "In nursing education, assessment of program outcomes has been incorporated in accreditation standards developed by the National League for Nursing Accreditation Commission and by the recently established Commission on Collegiate Nursing Education" (Thompson & Bartels, 1999, p. 170). In 1991, the NLN, which began accrediting nursing programs in 1938, required all nursing programs to define student learning outcomes. According to the NLN, "outcomes are performance indicators [that] demonstrate to what extent the purposes of the mission and goals of the program have been achieved" (National League for Nursing, n.d., p. 3). The membership of the NLN believes that this action is consistent with program improvement and public accountability for the graduates of nursing educational programs (NLN, p. 4). The National League for Nursing Accreditation Commission (NLNAC) went one step further in distinguishing core outcomes that must be a part of every program's evaluation. The design of the NLNAC to incorporate outcomes assessment into every school's evaluation set off a national movement to an outcomes orientation. Nursing faculty from across the country began struggling to define the NLNAC-required outcomes of critical thinking, communication, therapeutic nursing interventions, graduation rates, and patterns of employment that needed to be assessed as part of the accreditation process (Council of Baccalaureate and Higher Degree Programs, National League for Nursing, 1991).

The need to incorporate outcomes into program evaluation activities was, for many, a formidable task, requiring a transformation in philosophical thinking. For years, nursing faculty had focused on a system of internal accountability that emphasized a linear approach to curriculum development, implementation, and evaluation. Goals and objectives were established using internal deliberation and were employed as measures of success at the end of courses and completion of the program. It was assumed that a well-defined and monitored process yielded the desired educational product.

The move from a system of internal accountability to one of external accountability resulted from the public's concern about the product and cost of higher education. In response to this concern, nursing faculty needed to change their focus from process to outcomes in nursing education (Lindeman, 2000). Initially, nursing educators, given their original orientation, considered the terms *outcomes* and *competences* to be replacements for *program* and *course objectives*. The required changes were viewed as cosmetic rather than substantive. Eventually, with the benefit of national discussions, nursing faculty came to realize that a change in philosophical thinking was needed to address the public's concerns. Outcomes and competences needed to be crafted through dialogue with representatives from constituent interest groups.

Nursing faculty across the country looked for models that would assist in determining how to identify and define learning outcomes. They also explored tools to measure and strategies to summarize these outcomes data in ways that would be meaningful to their constituent interest groups, including their accreditation agency. For many nursing faculty, the assessment of student learning outcomes became an additional activity to incorporate into well-established program evaluation plans. This perception initiated skepticism and a lack of enthusiasm for increased workload. However, like faculty at the University of Memphis, faculty nationally have become increasingly grounded in and energized by these challenges (Luttrell, Lenburg, Scherubel, Jacob, & Koch, 1999).

The NLNAC's outcomes criteria posed an overwhelming struggle to faculty groups as they looked for existing models from other disciplines. One popular approach adopted by some faculty groups was to develop assessment plans based on the concept of a report card. In this approach, faculty principally "focus on the technical task of designing psychometrically sound instruments [for] producing a report card" (Keith, 1991, p. 14). A report card addresses accreditation expectations and provides information to make decisions for program continuation, deletion, or modification. The report card concept also has broad utility as a communication tool to many external constituents or stakeholders. Program outcome report cards can provide various publics with quantifiable information on how well programs are meeting their goals and mission.

Other faculty groups chose to approach assessment "as a conversation" (Keith, 1991, p. 14). This approach is more conceptual in nature. Assessment as a conversation appears to have been common in the discussions that culminated in a new accreditation body in the late 1990s. The Commission on Collegiate Nursing Education (CCNE) was created in 1997 as an autonomous accrediting agency of the American Association of Colleges of Nursing (AACN) to "ensure the quality and integrity of baccalaureate and graduate education programs [in] preparing effective nurses" (Commission on Collegiate Nursing Education, 1998). The CCNE is the second accrediting body for nursing education programs. The goals of this commission clearly focus on fostering continuous program quality improvement within the framework of program effectiveness and efficiency. The accreditation criteria generated for this process encourage a conversation among faculty as they assess existing mission and goals for relevance to the discipline and practice of nursing.

This conversational approach to accreditation and program review may prove to be most valuable in fueling the curriculum revolution undertaken in nursing education programs during the last decade. The focus on student learning is shaping the current "conversation" taking place in schools of nursing. The conversations focus on the skills and knowledge (competences) nurses must have to be prepared to meet the challenges of a new century. A refocused lens on productive learning is driving the search for effective classroom and practice pedagogies to facilitate student attainment of competences. The debates surrounding the place of technology in education are no longer focused singularly on distributed education needs but on the use of technology to create innovative teaching and learning techniques that complement diverse learning styles.

These conversations are consistent with the philosophy of continuous quality improvement now in place in nursing education. Nursing faculty have moved to generate models that will provide them with information necessary for maintaining highly effective, relevant undergraduate and graduate nursing programs. Continuous quality improvement is consistent with the approach of the CCNE. This conversational approach appears to be appealing to nursing educators across the country. In this lens, the cyclic "repackaging or relabeling [of] the same content, expectations, and traditional methods no longer will suffice" (Lenburg, 1991, p. 32).

Moving to a Competence-Based Education Model in Nursing

The educational lens has been refocused on competence-based education models, which is very different from the behaviorist approach that dominated the design of nursing curricula for the last half-century. Changes in educational models and curriculum design have been equivalent to a paradigm shift in nursing. Within this shift, faculty, as well as nursing leaders in general, are grappling with what constitutes necessary knowledge and skills for the education of future nurses as well as current practitioners. Developing competences that are clearly explicated within the context of best practice is the curriculum goal (Eichelberger & Hewlett, 1999; Luttrell et al., 1999). Nurse educators

are, like their colleagues in institutions of higher education, redefining learning and teaching to emphasize student abilities to demonstrate essential
competences.

Outcomes Assessment in Competence-Based Nursing Education

The focus on outcomes assessment has influenced the education of nurses in a
number of other ways. Faculty research and practice in education have actively
refocused on finding the keys to student success in nursing programs. Predic-
tion of success continues to be an elusive concept. Nevertheless, faculty remain
committed to constructing a predictive model to be used in the admission and
retention of students who demonstrate the greatest potential to meet program
outcomes. Outcomes assessment also challenges nursing faculty and administrators to seek optimal ways of using fixed or decreasing financial, material,
and human resources to support student learning and creativity in teaching
methodologies (Lenburg, 1991). Nursing faculty are carefully reexamining
their curricula to ensure that they are fostering the development of skills and
knowledge that will meet the demands of a dynamic but often unpredictable
health care system. This delicate balance between what students need to know
and what they need to be able to do is being made more complex by the
national higher education movement to clarify general education for our
future citizenry. As nursing faculty incorporate different skills or expand existing expectations, they need to identify or develop measures of student assessment for these different skills. Competence-based curriculum models appear to
be gaining popularity among nursing faculty who are seeking ways to become
more outcome- or student-learning focused.

Search for Competence-Based Models

As the emphasis on student learning and program accountability gained popularity in higher education, the call for increasing levels of accountability in
health care became louder. Both national and state nursing organizations took
an active role in defining and building competence-based models grounded in
professional practice standards that would be relevant to changes in the health
care system and address the different levels of educational preparation of
nurses. The Midwest Alliance in Nursing (MAIN) was among the early organizations to undertake the challenge of identifying competences based on differences between associate and bachelor degree education programs (Eichelberger & Hewlett, 1999). Other nursing organizations joined the efforts begun
by MAIN. The list includes the American Association of Colleges of Nursing,
the American Organization of Nurse Executives, the National Organization of

Associate Degree Nursing, and the Nursing Organization Liaison Committee, which represented 26 state nursing associations (Eichelberger & Hewlett, 1999).

Competence-based models continue to evolve within nursing education programs across the country. Inherent in the work of developing competence-based curriculum models are the identification and explication of critical competences that graduates must acquire as they begin their practice or expand their current arena of practice. Although the task seems rather transparent to others, it is not for nursing faculty. The issues that cloud the way forward include (a) the diversity that exists among different educational paths currently available within the profession, (b) the desire or need to differentiate nursing practice reflective of the differences that exist within different educational paths, and (c) the imperfection that results from continuing to envision the future of the health care system based on outdated predictive models.

Different groups of nurses across the country have taken steps to articulate competence models based on the knowledge and skills they believe graduates need as they begin or expand their nursing practice. Although the nursing discipline has yet to adopt one common model to serve the discipline, individual group efforts do exist. One such effort grew out of a collaboration between representatives from nursing education and nursing practice. In 1995, representatives from the Indiana Deans and Directors Council and the Indiana Organization of Nurse Executives worked together to create a competence-based model for the practice of nursing in Indiana. This model identified the concepts critical to the practice of nursing and the level at which these competences were to be met by graduates of associate, bachelor, and master's degree programs. This work was an attempt to differentiate nursing practice for Indiana nurses and their employers. It also was intended to forge a common understanding to help bridge the gap between nursing practice and nursing education regarding what practice expects from new graduates and what nursing education is able to accomplish. An excerpt of this work is presented in Table 5.1.

The Mississippi Schools of Nursing Council of Deans and Directors in 1997 approved a model that also included competences expected of graduates at the completion of a nursing program (Eichelberger & Hewlett, 1999). This model, like the models developed in Indiana, South Dakota, North Dakota, Colorado, New Mexico, and Nebraska, was conceived as useful to both nursing education and nursing practice in the continuing development of curriculum, job descriptions and performance evaluations reflective of differentiated practice, and a prescription for the practice of nursing (Eichelberger & Hewlett). It is important to note that the national licensure examination has yet

Table 5.1 Excerpts from Expected Competences of Associate, Baccalaureate, and Advanced Prepared Nurse Providers at Two Years Post Graduation

Competency	Associate	Baccalaureate	Advanced (MSN, etc.)
Planning of nursing care	Plans care in collaboration with other members of the health care team that is need driven for a specific population related to an episode of care: a. individualizes care pathways for specified individuals or groups in specific settings; b. sets therapeutic care goals in collaboration with client, families and other members of the health care team; c. incorporates client's lifestyle, cultural beliefs, health behaviors and support systems in setting care goals;	Plans and manages care collaboratively with individuals, families, communities and other members of the health care team in order to achieve therapeutic outcomes: a. prioritizes established therapeutic goals; b. identifies therapeutic interventions consistent with established goals (teaching/coaching, functional, somatic and emotional interventions); c. uses state-of-the art knowledge and technology in planning care;	Uses advanced knowledge and skills to function independently and interdependently as a member of the health care team to a. integrate unique client needs into the development and implementation of best practice interventions to prevent unintended consequences and enhance intended care outcomes; b. incorporate measures in the plan of care that assess care outcomes;

d. uses state-of-the-art knowledge and technology in planning care for a specified group of clients for specific episodes of care; and

e. makes appropriate judgments about discharge needs.

d. articulates nursing judgments and nursing therapeutics (verbally and in writing) and communicates rationale for care decisions to other members of the health care team, individuals, families, and communities;

e. makes appropriate judgments about discharge needs and support services as individuals move across the health care continuum; and

f. develops programs to deal with common problems of vulnerable populations as appropriate primary prevention.

c. designs cost-effective outcomes measures based on best practice consistent with resource allocations of the health care setting and the diversity of the client care population being served; and

d. refers clients and family members, as appropriate, to other providers and facilitates the movement of these clients across the health care continuum to maximize care outcomes.

Note. From "Expected Competences of Associate, Baccalaureate, and Advanced Prepared Nurse Providers." Copyright 1998 by the Indiana Deans & Directors and the Indiana Organization of Nurse Executives. Adapted with permission.

to distinguish different levels of educational preparation. The licensure examination is seen as a great impediment to differentiation of practice expectations.

Fundamental to these individual state efforts is a common agreement on what skills nurses need to bring to the practice of nursing. The basis for this common agreement was established by the early work of the Midwest Alliance in Nursing (MAIN) that identified the essential work of nursing as the "provision of direct care, communication, and management" (Eichelberger & Hewlett, 1999, p. 205). Although the discipline of nursing has yet to unite under a single definition of nursing practice or a single competence model that reflects current and future performance expectations for those practicing nursing, nurse educators have moved rapidly to identify student learning outcomes and methods of assessing these outcomes and are beginning to create models of best practice for student learning and nursing practice.

Defining Core Competences for Undergraduate Nursing Education

Nursing faculty have been engaged actively in defining program outcomes and competences for undergraduate and graduate programs. Without the advantage of a nationally accepted set of competences, this work is being accomplished program by program and school by school across the country. Faculty have sought input from representatives of various interest groups in identifying appropriate competences for their programs. Representatives include employers of new graduates, consumers of the services that graduates render, leaders who have an interest in the education and profession of nursing, faculty colleagues, recent alumni (as defined by faculty) who know the degree to which the program prepared them to secure a position and perform at or above expected performance standards for positions secured, and representatives from other programs who have an interest in program direction. The outcome of this dialogue has led to the identification of knowledge and skills graduates need to possess at program completion for each school.

Although nursing faculty nationally have had little difficulty in accepting the movement to an outcomes orientation or to increasing emphasis on student learning, faculty have debated how to embrace this movement. National forums sponsored by the NLN and the AACN have supported the exchange of ideas and experiences of faculty as they have experimented with the identification and assessment of student learning outcomes. These exchanges have led to a rich conversation and expression of opinions as to what nursing students need to be prepared to do when they graduate from their educational programs. Conversations are being shaped by geographical differences in the

American health care system, by philosophical differences among private colleges with a strong liberal arts mission, and differences in faculty beliefs and values about the education and practice of nursing.

Lindeman (2000) identified five outcomes that undergraduate students need to demonstrate if they are to be relevant for current and future nursing practice. These outcomes include development of reasoning skills, ability to deal with change in an environment that breeds ambiguity, commitment to the role of lifelong learner, effectiveness as a practitioner, and value as a contributing member of a collaborative health care team (pp. 10–11). Bowen, Lyons, and Young's (2000) research suggests that nurses also need "effective, accurate communication skills; legislative/policy awareness; leadership/ influence skills; crisis management skills; and effective organizational and prioritizing skills" (pp. 32–33). Enriching this list of competences is the thinking of Quinless and Elliot (2000) who recommend that undergraduate curricula emphasize "urban health care systems," the use of behavioral analysis skills to reform the health care system, the use of economics to balance both the cost and benefits of care sought and given, the underlying ethical considerations in the practice of nursing and medicine, and the ability to use literature to inform and diversify practice (pp. 88–89). This rather long list of skills and knowledge can be seen in many undergraduate program outcomes. Common among most undergraduate and graduate programs is the inclusion of critical thinking skills, communication skills, and the use of cultural concepts.

Critical Thinking as an Outcome

Critical thinking has been one of the most difficult outcomes for nursing faculty to define and assess. As a complex abstract concept, there is no consensus for a single definition that adequately reflects the domain of critical thinking for nursing practice. A national survey conducted in 1996 (O'Sullivan, Blevins-Stephens, Smith, & Vaughan-Wrobel, 1997) clearly delineated the range of behaviors that define a critical thinker. Many faculty relied on the components of the "nursing process" (a variation of the scientific problem-solving process) as the parameters for the definition and assessment of critical thinking. The critics of this approach argue that the "nursing process" models linear thinking that is the antithesis of a reflective thinking approach needed to foster conceptualizing, analyzing, synthesizing, and evaluating in moving to problem resolution. Despite the continuing debate, nursing faculty have defined critical thinking and are using a number of different measures in determining critical thinking skills of their graduates.

According to Banta (1993), faculty must make some assumptions about critical thinking. These assumptions appear consistent with the action the

NLN took in explicating critical thinking as one core outcome of nursing programs. First, faculty must assume that critical thinking can be operationally defined. Second, faculty must assume that critical thinking can be taught and, more importantly, is a skill that can continue to be refined. The teaching of critical thinking has been viewed consistently as the most difficult assumption to embrace as faculty are resistant to changing current teaching practices (O'Sullivan et al., 1997). Third, faculty must assume that reliable and valid measures exist or can be created to measure critical thinking as defined for practicing nurses. Fourth, they must assume that measurement results can be used in meaningful ways that can improve the way faculty teach and students learn to be critical thinkers at some acceptable level (Banta, 1993).

Nursing faculty have tended to adopt popular definitions of critical thinking. A 1999 review of the literature by May and coauthors found that critical thinking "has been defined as a process by Brookfield in 1987; as composite knowledge, attitudes and application skills by Watson and Glaser in 1980; and as cognitive skills and an intellectual disposition by Facione in 1991 and 1992" (May, Edell, Butell, Doughty, & Langford, 1999, p. 100). Definitions by Watson and Glaser and Facione have gained favor with nursing faculty as each definition has spawned a measurement tool that can be used readily in assessing the student's ability or disposition toward critical thought.

Faculty at Indiana University School of Nursing undertook the task of clarifying the concept of critical thinking as they moved to identify program outcomes. The attributes of critical thinking they thought important for the practice of nursing were intellectual curiosity, rational inquiry, problem framing, information validation, and evaluation of judgments (Dexter et al., 1997). These attributes were woven into competence statements that serve as anchors for assessing student abilities at the end of the program. In addition to the end-of-program competences, faculty developed complementary competence statements for each year of the three-year nursing major. The competences for each year built developmentally on the prior year's performance expectations. End-of-year competences serve as interval benchmarks for assessing student progression toward accomplishment of end-of-program competences and related outcomes.

Communication as an Outcome

Another core competence faculty believe graduates of nursing programs must demonstrate is effective communication. Communication generally is defined to include both verbal and written abilities. The challenges faculty face in defining this competence occur in the interpretation and measurement of "effective" and in the identification of the parameters of communication. The use of technological tools that support verbal and written exchanges of information must also be considered in defining communication abilities. There is general agreement that "effective" communication skills enhance the exchange of information that will affect patient care outcomes positively. The use of communication skills that will facilitate collaboration and networking within a team concept is another attribute supported among nursing faculty. The use of technology in the generation, translation, transformation, transference, and storage of information must be included within a definition of communication for practicing nurses. These attributes of communication have most consistently provided focus for the development of outcomes and competences expected of undergraduate and graduate nursing students.

Cultural Understanding as an Outcome

Nursing educators agree that nursing students must be competent in relating to diverse groups of people. Consistent with the increasing diversity in the world's population, nurses must understand not only the effects of different beliefs and values on individual, family, and community health behaviors but also how these behaviors influence health care outcomes. Nursing students must have a working knowledge of what constitutes diversity among people and how differences affect the health of individuals and groups, how these individuals or groups define health, and how they deal with acute and chronic health problems. Within this working knowledge base, students must learn to respect individual and group differences and work with these differences in determining appropriate health care outcomes and mechanisms that will work best in attaining positive health outcomes. This range of knowledge and skill is difficult to capture within the context of *cultural sensitivity, cultural awareness,* or even *cultural understanding,* which are the most common terms used in outcomes statements.

Assessment of Student Learning

Nursing faculty have not found it difficult to accept the growing public mandate for program accountability. Evaluation of student learning has been critical to every accredited nursing program since the inception of professional accreditation. The greatest challenge faculty have faced is how to develop valid assessment plans that will determine both individual student competences and group competences for learners at the completion of their educational programs.

Competence statements were valuable tools as faculty moved to implement curriculum revisions and assessment plans that focused on student learning from a performance perspective. Faculty continue to refine courses, learning experiences, teaching methods, and testing that facilitate student achievement of course, year, and end-of-program competences. Learning and assessment of learning clearly take center stage in a competence-based curriculum. Program assessment that includes assessing what students have learned should be guided by a carefully thought-through plan. The assessment plan starts first with defining outcomes and competences that are relevant both to the practice of nursing and to the values of the faculty. Outcomes and competences must be written in measurable terms. Faculty must decide when assessment should be carried out, who should be responsible for carrying out the assessment functions, and how to feed assessment information back into the curriculum for continuous quality improvement. The need to identify or construct valid measurement tools is critical to the success of data collection and interpretation. Finally, faculty must decide how to use assessment information.

Nursing Program Assessment Models

Nursing education has provided a number of models for assessment. One early leader in assessment was Alverno College. Outcomes at Alverno have been stated as "what the learner is able to do with what he or she knows as a result of a set of learning expectations" (Thompson & Bartels, 1999, p. 173). As indicated in their assessment plan, faculty assessed student performance across the program and at the completion of the program, looking for intended and unintended outcomes (Thompson & Bartels). Faculty analyzed a number of existing standardized instruments to assist with assessment in this model but found existing tools insufficient measures of their program outcomes. Given this review, they adapted an existing evaluation tool to meet their needs. Based on the Alverno faculty's experiences, Thompson and Bartels encourage others who are developing an assessment program to "enlist faculty support," "gain student support," "determine assessment methods and procedures," and "use assessment results" (pp. 175–177) if they are to be successful.

Indiana University School of Nursing moved to an outcome-oriented curriculum in 1998. The nursing faculty began the curriculum revision process in 1994 with a critical look at what characteristics/attributes students should possess at the completion of the baccalaureate nursing program. Once these attributes were identified, they were incorporated into program outcome statements. Accompanying end-of-program competence statements were also constructed. Competence statements became the operational definitions of the attributes used in measurement. Additional competence statements were developed to reflect the level of growth students should be achieving at the end of each of the three years of the nursing major.

Indiana University School of Nursing (IUSON) faculty valued an outcomes approach to curriculum separate from the requirements of accreditation. Initially, faculty incorporated the NLNAC's required outcomes of critical thinking, communication, therapeutic nursing intervention, graduation rates, employment rates, and pass rates on the national licensure examination. Faculty then proceeded to develop outcomes related to cultural competence; knowledgeable coordination of community resources; political awareness; competence as a health care provider; competence within recognized legal and ethical parameters of practice; professional role modeling for others; and responsible management of human, fiscal, and material resources (Halstead, Rains, Boland, & May, 1996).

Formative and Summative Components in Program Assessment

Assessment was viewed as having both formative and summative components in the outcome competence model designed by faculty. Determining at what point in the curriculum student learning was to be assessed proved contentious. Historically, faculty have assessed student learning in every course throughout the curriculum. There was concern that additional assessment would be time-consuming for students and faculty and require additional resources. However, faculty realized that there needed to be some data that would indicate how well students (singularly and as an aggregate) were meeting end-of-year competences beyond what they could determine by individual course assessment information. Three assessment times emerged from faculty discussions. Students would be assessed as they entered the nursing major; they would be assessed at the end of each of the first two years of the major; and they would be assessed again at the completion of the major. Figure 5.1 is a visual representation of the assessment model being implemented.

Faculty and administrators were mindful of the costs involved in implementing this assessment model and explored ways to incorporate existing assessment measures. As a number of assessment methods and tools already existed, the challenge became to enfold them in a revised assessment plan. Other considerations focused on (a) how to "group" individual course assessment together for end-of-year assessment, (b) what additional assessment measures needed to be developed to provide a comprehensive picture of students' performance, and (c) how to use this information to facilitate student success and quality assurance of the program.

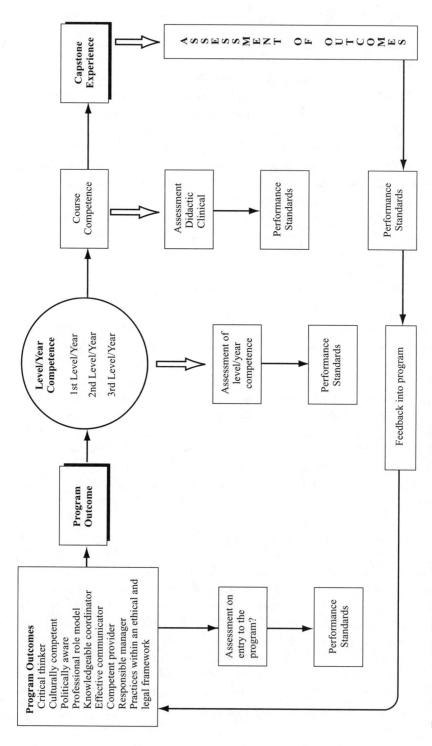

FIGURE 5.1 Baccalaureate in Nursing Program Assessment Model

As noted in the assessment model, the first point of student assessment is upon entry into the nursing major. All nursing programs traditionally assess students' potential for success in the program in some fashion consistent with the population served by the major. At IUSON, the faculty assess potential success using cumulative grade point average and the grade point average for prerequisite courses taken for the nursing degree prior to acceptance to the nursing major. Other tools have also been piloted but have not proven to offer faculty more reliable information. Many of these tools are being used by other nursing faculty and, given their student population, provide valuable feedback. These assessment tools are standardized critical thinking measures, including the California Critical Thinking Skills Test; the California Critical Thinking Dispositions Inventory; the Watson-Glaser Critical Thinking Appraisal; and the Nursing Entrance Test (NET), which broadly assesses critical thinking, reading, math, and learning styles (Educational Resources Incorporated, 1999). Additionally, an interview process is sometimes used to assess critical thinking, communication abilities, and an interest in and understanding of the discipline of nursing among potential applicants. Generally, graduate nursing programs require students to produce a writing sample to assess critical thinking and communication abilities. These writing samples are used primarily to assess the fit between student goals and program goals.

At IUSON, an "enhancement for success" program has been developed based on a profile built from information collected on how students performed in courses, specifically science courses; college entrance assessments; and high school record prior to entry into the nursing major. This program invites students who match the at-risk profile to study with mentors who help them develop tools for success that include critical thinking skills, reading skills, writing skills, test taking skills, and time management skills. In tracking students who have participated in this enhancement program, most were successful in completing the major.

The second assessment point occurs at the completion of the first year of the nursing major for IU students. Recognizing that student learning is assessed both in the classroom and laboratory/practice areas, it was important to identify a means of aggregating individual course assessment data from the eight courses that comprise this year's program requirements. The mechanisms identified for this level of assessment must also have applicability to the next year of the nursing major. Again, a number of standardized tests are available from nursing organizations and private publishing companies that can be used to assess student knowledge in a wide variety of content areas. However, curriculum/courses have to be constructed around these tools if they are to be valid indicators of student knowledge. Thus, this was not the curriculum design approach used at IUSON.

Given the curriculum design, the recommendation was to have a common core of assessment items on each laboratory/clinical practice course evaluation. This approach is consistent with the intent of the program and level competences that were written to focus on the application of knowledge and skills in the clinical practice setting. Clinical practice evaluations were designed to show both the growth in students' abilities to meet these competences for each year in the program and the increasing expectations for the students to perform. In the classroom, faculty use year-level competences as a guide in determining the structure of course content, the identification of skills to be developed or refined, and the construction of the evaluation of learning, including tests. Instead of requiring another assessment occasion at the completion of each year of the nursing major, faculty are experimenting with assessing students' didactic performance at the end of each semester by using the grades earned in nursing course work that semester. Using the class mean for grades, any student falling below the class mean for one or more courses within the semester just completed proceeds to the next semester with a written prescription for improving academic success. The written prescription makes it mandatory for students to attend peer mentoring sessions, consultation with course instructors, study sessions, test review sessions, and academic skill development sessions.

End-of-program assessment is incorporated in the capstone course, which is the last course in the nursing major required of students. The capstone is designed as an intensive clinical practice course. Students work with an experienced registered nurse in one of many health care agencies under contract with the school. This experience is designed to provide students with an opportunity to synthesize knowledge and skills learned throughout the program. Assessment is built on the same "core" clinical practice assessment items used throughout the program. Students also are expected to produce a scholarly project as part of a research utilization course that complements the capstone experience. The project requires application of knowledge students have accrued throughout the program. Students are required to demonstrate critical thinking and communication skills in addition to their understanding of the practice of nursing.

Comprehensive summative clinical assessments traditionally have been part of student performance evaluations. A number of innovative approaches published in nursing literature are worth mentioning here as examples of best practices. Faculty at the School of Nursing at Miami-Dade Community College designed a "Clinical Performance Manual" based on earlier work of del Bueno and Lenburg, recognized leaders in competence-based education (Woolley, Bryan, & Davis, 1998). The performance manual required faculty to assess students on abilities to demonstrate identified professional behaviors, appropriate performance of randomly selected clinical practice skills, ability to write a plan of care appropriate to selected patients' responsiveness to a simulated critical patient care situation, and acceptable level of completion on various course assignments (Woolley, et al.). This approach was consistent with program expectations and found to be a reliable and valid summative process for assessing student learning.

A less traditional approach to evaluation is through the use of narrative stories. This approach is consistent with the philosophy that "nursing is an integrative science that studies the relationships between the mind, body, and human worlds" (Benner, 1999, p. 315). Benner suggests that nurses must develop a "clinical grasp" that includes "clinical inquiry skills, problem identification, and clinical judgment" (p. 317). These characteristics can be assessed as students share their experiences with patients and families. Through these exchanges, faculty have opportunities to assess students' openness for learning and their ability to understand the context and content of the situation. Faculty and students together can validate information being collected for problem framing and identify which thoughts and actions are helpful in seeking problem resolution. Although this process of assessment is qualitative and relies on a dialectic exchange among students and faculty, it provides faculty with rich data for use in assessing student learning. The challenge in this approach is finding a mechanism to integrate assessment data for use in making decisions about program effectiveness.

As these formative assessment mechanisms become fully integrated into program assessment, there is a need to look at summative mechanisms that assess students' performance at the end of the program. Faculty at the Indiana University School of Nursing are exploring the utility of the portfolio as a summative assessment tool. Portfolios have gained popularity over the last few years among nursing faculty as a data collection method that facilitates judgments about student performance across and at the end of a program from a holistic perspective (Wenzel, Briggs, & Puryear, 1998; Karlowicz, 2000). Although guidelines for the development of a portfolio differ, it is important to identify which items are to go into a portfolio to represent adequately students' ability to meet course and program outcomes. The portfolio mechanism, like narrative stories, presents a challenge for translating individual assessment data into a meaningful aggregate for program decision making.

Challenges Within Assessment

Nursing faculty are continuing to face a number of challenges that affect assessment at the student and program levels. Many nursing programs admit "new majority" students who come with differing levels of academic preparation and experience. Many students are the first generation of their families to enter college and hold values different from one another and different from a rapidly graying faculty. There is often a disconnect between professional practice expectations and student-held personal learning expectations.

The need for access to nursing education has led nursing faculty to embrace technology. Beginning with telecommunication operations, nursing faculty are among the high-end users of the Internet to deliver credit and non-credit courses. Faculty continue to explore ways of using technology to enhance student learning. The use of simulated and virtual computer models will become increasingly more important in the student learning process as hospital settings place more restrictions on previously available learning opportunities. As the role of technology expands within the educational process, the challenges for assessment will multiply. Faculty will need to focus both on the assessment of technologically enhanced student learning as well as the effects of this technology on the learning process.

A number of creative initiatives are under way in nursing education. However, there are limited avenues for sharing. The traditional knowledge dissemination arenas (publications and presentations) are less amenable to "real-time" sharing of these best practice models, and this has fostered duplication of efforts and an atmosphere of trial and error.

The Future of Assessment in Nursing

Every indication is that assessment will continue to play a valuable role in the education process. Nursing as a practice discipline must be accountable to its many communities of interest/stakeholders. The emphasis on accountability will only increase within a rapidly changing dynamic health care industry. Nursing's future in this environment is uncertain, and the practice of nursing must continue to evolve in ways that are not yet clear to those educating the future nurse population. It is crucial, therefore, that nurse educators focus on skills and knowledge that will be adaptable and serviceable within a context of known and unknown change. Assessment is a key ingredient in ensuring that graduates will have the skills and knowledge necessary to meet today's and tomorrow's practice expectations effectively.

References

American Association of Colleges of Nursing (AACN). (1996). *The essentials of master's education for advanced practice nursing.* Washington, D.C.: Author.

American Association of Colleges of Nursing (AACN). (1998). *The essentials of baccalaureate education for professional nursing practice.* Washington, DC: Author.

American Association of Colleges of Nursing (AACN). (1999). A vision of baccalaureate and graduate nursing education: The next decade. *Journal of Professional Nursing, 15* (1), 59–65.

Baly, M. (Ed.). (1991). *As Nightingale said . . .* London: Soutari Press.

Banta, T. W. (1993). Toward a plan for using national assessment to ensure continuous improvement of higher education. *Journal of General Education, 42* (1), 33–58.

Bellack, J., & O'Neil, E. (2000). Recreating nursing practice for a new century: Recommendations and implications of the Pew Health Professions Commission's Final Report. *Nursing and Health Care Perspectives, 21* (1), 14–21.

Benner, P. (1999). Claiming the wisdom & worth of clinical practice. *Nursing and Health Care Perspectives, 20* (6), 312–319.

Bowen, M., Lyons, K. J., & Young, B. E. (2000). Nursing and health care reform: Implications for curriculum development. *Journal of Nursing Education, 39* (1), 27–33.

Commission on Collegiate Nursing Education. (1998). *CCNE Bylaws of the Commission on Collegiate Nursing Education* (CCNE: 925). Washington, DC: Author.

Council of Baccalaureate and Higher Degree Programs, National League for Nursing. (1991). *Criteria and guidelines for the evaluation of baccalaureate nursing programs.* (NLN Publication No. 15-2474). New York: Author.

Dexter, P., Applegate, M., Backer, J., Claytor, K., Keffer, J., Norton, B., & Ross, B. (1997). A proposed framework for teaching and evaluating critical thinking in nursing. *Journal of Professional Nursing, 13*(3), 160–167.

Educational Resources Incorporated. (1999). Mission, KS: Author.

Eichelberger, L. W., & Hewlett, P. O. (1999). Competency model 101—The process of developing core competencies. *Nursing and Health Care Perspectives, 20* (4), 204–208.

Halstead, J. A., Rains, J., Boland, D. L., & May, F. E. (1996). Reconceptualizing baccalaureate nursing education: Outcomes and competencies for practice in the 21st century. *Journal of Nursing Education, 35*(9), 413–416.

Heller, B. R., Oros, M. T., & Durney-Crowley, J. (2000). 10 trends to watch. *Nursing and Health Care Perspectives, 21* (1), 9–13.

Hill, M. (1999). Outcomes measurement requires nursing to shift to outcome-based practice. *Nursing Adminstration, 14*(1), 1–16.

Karlowicz, K. A. (2000). The value of student portfolios to evaluate undergraduate nursing programs. *Nurse Educator, 25* (2), 82–87.

Keith, N. Z. (1991). Assessing educational goals: The national movement to outcome education. In M. Garbin (Ed.), *Assessing educational outcomes.* New York: National League for Nursing Press.

Lenburg, C. B. (1991). Assessing the goals of nursing education: Issues and approaches to evaluation outcomes. In M. Garbin (Ed.), *Assessing educational outcomes.* New York: National League for Nursing Press.

Lindeman, C. A. (2000). The future of nursing education. *Journal of Nursing Education, 39* (1), 5–12.

Luttrell, M. F., Lenburg, C. B., Scherubel, J. C., Jacob, S. R., & Koch, R. W. (1999). Competency outcomes for learning and performance assessment. *Nursing and Health Care Perspectives, 20* (3), 134–141.

May, B. A., Edell, V., Butell, S., Doughty, J., & Langford, C. (1999). Critical thinking and clinical competence: A study of their relationship in BSN seniors. *Journal of Nursing Education, 38* (3), 100–110.

National League for Nursing. (n.d.). *NLN accreditation: Public accountability shared values.* NLN Accreditation National League for Nursing. New York: Author.

O'Sullivan, P. S., Blevins-Stephens, W. L., Smith, F. M., & Vaughan-Wrobel, B. (1997). Addressing the National League for Nursing critical-thinking outcome. *Nurse Educator, 22* (1), 23–29.

Quinless, F. W., & Elliott, N. L. (2000). The future in health care delivery: Lessons from history, demographics, and economics. *Nursing and Health Care Perspectives, 21* (2), 84–89.

Shugars, D. A., O'Neil, E. H., & Bader, J. D. (Eds.). (1991). *Healthy America: Practitioners for 2005, an agenda for action for U.S. health professional schools.* Durham, NC: Pew Health Professions Commission.

Thompson, C., & Bartels, J. (1999). Outcomes assessment: Implications for nursing education. *Journal of Professional Nursing, 15* (3), 170–178.

Wenzel, L. S., Briggs, K. L., & Puryear, B. L. (1998). Portfolio: Authentic assessment in the age of the curriculum revolution. *Journal of Nursing Education, 37* (5), 208–212.

Woolley, G. R., Bryan, M. S., & Davis, J. W. (1998). A comprehensive approach to clinical evaluation. *Journal of Nursing Education, 37* (8), 361–366.

6

ACCOUNTABILITY FOR PROFESSIONAL PRACTICE

Assessment in Social Work Education

Frank R. Baskind, Barbara W. Shank, and Elaine K. Ferraro

It has been more than 15 years since accrediting agencies, regional and professional, began requiring assessment activity. All academic programs are being asked to assess student learning in individual courses and the total program. Social work faculty face the same challenges with respect to student outcomes assessment as faculty in other professional disciplines. Many social work faculty are anxious about developing and implementing student assessment activities even though in their own graduate education all have studied evaluating service delivery and their own practice. They seem to have difficulty making the transition from practice evaluation to assessment of student outcomes. When mandated to develop a student outcomes assessment plan, either by their institution as part of regional accreditation and/or by their own professional accrediting association, faculty cite concerns about academic freedom, teaching to the test, time constraints, professional autonomy, challenges to required scholarship, and cost as reasons they have not developed and implemented student assessment plans. Although there may be some merit to each of these concerns, social work education has embraced student outcomes assessment as a recognized national standard for program evaluation.

This chapter focuses on assessment in social work education. It begins with a brief look at the foundations for assessment in the profession and includes a discussion about current assessment practices, a presentation of findings from two studies that evaluated these assessment practices, and three case studies. It concludes with remarks from Commission on Accreditation members about ongoing issues and lessons learned.

Social Work Education

Social work education is offered at the baccalaureate, master's, and doctoral levels in accredited colleges and universities. Baccalaureate programs prepare students for generalist social work practice, and master's programs prepare students for advanced social work practice in an area of concentration. Both the baccalaureate and master's levels provide a professional foundation curriculum that includes a common body of knowledge, values, and skills for the profession that is transferable among settings, population groups, and problem areas. Baccalaureate programs must include a liberal arts perspective and the professional foundation content to prepare students for direct services with client systems of various sizes and types. Master's programs must include the professional foundation content and concentration content for advanced practice. Professional social work education at the master's level requires the equivalent of two years of full-time academic work. Admission to a master's program in social work does not require the completion of a baccalaureate degree in social work (Council on Social Work Education [CSWE], 1994).

The purpose of professional social work education at the baccalaureate and master's levels is to enable students to integrate knowledge, values, and skills of the profession into competent practice. According to the Council on Social Work Education (CSWE) Curriculum Policy Statements, "The achievement of this purpose requires clarity about learning objectives and expected student outcomes, flexibility in programming and teaching to accommodate a diverse student population, and commitment of sufficient time and resources to the educational process" (CSWE, 1994, pp. 98, 136).

Professional accreditation in social work has for decades recognized the importance of doing assessment at the classroom, program, and agency levels. The three entities within the Council on Social Work Education that have provided leadership for addressing student outcomes assessment are the Board of Directors, the Commission on Education Policy (COEP), and the Commission on Accreditation (COA). The Commission on Accreditation of the Council on Social Work Education is recognized by the Commission on Higher Education Accreditation (CHEA) for accreditation of baccalaureate and master's degree programs in social work education in the United States. Doctoral programs are not accredited by CSWE. The COA is made up of 25 Commission members appointed by the president of CSWE, each serving a three-year term. It is staffed by educational specialists and a director in CSWE's Division of Standards and Accreditation (DOSA). The COA has sole authority to determine whether a program meets all accreditation standards. The COA can take various actions from granting candidacy, initial or reaffirmation status, conditional accredited status, to withdrawal of accredited status. Programs placed on conditional accredited status or withdrawn from accredited status are determined to be out of compliance with one or more accreditation standards. A standard often cited as an area of concern or out of compliance is Evaluative Standard 1, Program Rationale and Assessment.

Student Outcomes Assessment in Social Work Education: Historical Development

In 1919, the Association of Training Schools for Professional Social Work was formed, with 17 charter members, to establish professional standards for social work education. In 1932, the association adopted accrediting procedures and a curriculum policy intended to guide the development of graduate programs in social work. This curriculum policy outlined four basic subject areas, and it was not until 1944 that the four areas were expanded to eight (public welfare, social casework, social group work, community organization, medical information, social research, psychiatry, and social welfare administration). In 1933, the organization changed its name to the American Association of Schools of Social Work. Berengarten (1986) notes that, in the early years, social work education did not focus efforts on "a systematic examination of the outcomes of educational experiences for students."

In 1952, the Council on Social Work Education (CSWE) was recognized by the National Commission on Accreditation and the United States Office of Education as the duly-represented accrediting body for graduate social work education. As part of the accreditation process, CSWE developed a Curriculum Policy Statement that required the curriculum to be constructed in such a way as to permit an integrated course of study with a balance of subject matter and progression in learning for all students (CSWE, 1952). This two-and-a-half-page curriculum policy mandated curriculum areas of social services, human growth and behavior, social work practice, and field courses. It did not address educational objectives or evaluation of student outcomes.

Ten years later, the CSWE's 1962 *Official Statement of Curriculum Policy for the Master's Degree Program in Graduate Schools of Social Work* used

Boehm's *Social Work Curriculum Study* (1959) to fashion its statement of purposes for social work education. This Curriculum Policy Statement required the curriculum to be developed as a unified whole, including the major components of social welfare policy and services, human behavior in the social environment, and methods of social work practice. These components described the broad areas to be covered in class and field instruction. Also included in this curriculum policy statement were mandates related to program evaluation and student assessment. In the Introduction, it stated, "Each school is also expected to establish procedures for self-study and continuing evaluation of the effectiveness of its educational program." Under Learning Experiences, it stated "Curriculum objectives define what the student is expected to learn. Learning experiences, such as those provided through classroom courses, field instruction, laboratory exercises, tutorial conferences, and research projects offer the student the means to achieve the goals of social work education." The Conclusion notes that "Continuing appraisal of the effectiveness of educational process and programs within schools of social work and of practice within the profession as a whole will contribute to further progress in the development of curriculum policy and to the constant improvement of social work education" (CSWE, 1962, pp. 1,7,8). This curriculum policy statement serves as the primary introduction to the expectation for development of program goals, educational objectives, and the establishment of procedures for evaluation of the educational program. The 1969 *Curriculum Policy For The Master's Degree Program in Graduate Schools of Social Work* (CSWE, 1969) reiterated these expectations.

In 1974, the *Standards for the Accreditation of Baccalaureate Degree Programs in Social Work* (CSWE, 1974) were effected. These standards made explicit reference to objectives and educational outcomes. The document stated:

- The expected educational outcomes of the program shall be explicated and be in harmony with the objectives and ethical values of the profession of social work.

- Since the statement of objectives forms a basis for evaluation of the program, it is necessary that there be a detailed explication of how the design of the program enables the implementation of the objectives.

- The various components of a program should not be considered separate entities but rather should be viewed as parts of an interrelated whole that contributes to the expected student outcomes.

- Objectives of the program and of the parent institution shall be compatible and mutually supportive.

- While program objectives shall address the specific human needs of the region, they need not be limited to these. Program objectives should relate to issues in social work practice and service delivery and should take into account manpower needs.

In reviewing the 1974 standards, it appears that the baccalaureate standards were patterned after the *Standards for the Accreditation of Masters' Degree Programs in Social Work,* as the language on objectives and education outcomes is comparable.

Between July 1975 and July 1977, an undergraduate social work curriculum development project was conducted (Baer & Federico, 1978). It relied on consultation with leading social work educators and special workshops with educators, practitioners, and agency representatives. Existing research and curriculum studies were reviewed. From these efforts, 10 general competences necessary for the baccalaureate professional social worker were identified for validation in practice. These competences shaped the expected competences articulated in the 1982 curriculum policy statement and have evolved to become the basis for the baccalaureate and master's competence expectations today. These have been integrated with the evaluation standards for accreditation to form the nucleus for assessment in social work education. In addition, the 1982 *Curriculum Policy for the Master's Degree and Baccalaureate Degree Programs In Social Work Education* (CSWE, 1982) articulated the structure of social work education as follows: "The goal of social work education at every level is for students to integrate the values, knowledges, and skills of the profession into competent practice. The achievement of this goal demands institutional clarity about what students should learn . . ." (CSWE, 1982, p. 3). Corresponding accreditation standards required that programs assess outcomes of the total educational program and that data be submitted related to the percentage of students completing the program, class and field performance records, and graduate employment performance data. As part of the assessment process, programs were required to provide data such as the results of licensure examinations, attitudinal studies of graduates, and alumni achievements in professional associations (Berengarten, 1986).

Current Assessment Practices

In 1992, separate Curriculum Policy Statements for baccalaureate and master's social work degree programs were developed. Also, for the first time, the curriculum policy statements articulated 12 educational outcomes for baccalaureate graduates and 14 educational outcomes for master's graduates. For example, graduates of baccalaureate social work programs are expected to apply critical thinking skills within the context of professional work practice; practice within the values and ethics of the social work professional and with an understanding of and respect for the positive value of diversity; and use communication skills differentially with a variety of client populations, colleagues, and members of the community. The statements for master's graduates are similar (CSWE, 1994, pp. 99, 137–138).

The Commission on Accreditation Evaluative Standards for baccalaureate and master's social work programs were derived from and are consistent with the Curriculum Policy Statement. The Evaluative Standards for undergraduate and graduate programs address the following eight areas: Program Rationale and Assessment; Organization, Governance, and Resources; Nondiscrimination and Human Diversity; Faculty; Student Development; Curriculum; Alternative Programs; and Experimental Programs. The Evaluative Standard 1, Program Rationale and Assessment, and corresponding Interpretive Guidelines, set the stage for the assessment activities in social work education today. Evaluative Standard 1, Program Rationale and Assessment, for baccalaureate programs states:

> The educational program must provide a statement of rationale, including a program mission statement and program goals, consistent with social work's purposes, values, and ethics. The mission and goals are to include quality educational preparation for entry into beginning social work practice with individuals, families, groups, organizations, and communities. The program's goals must reflect the intent of the Curriculum Policy Statement.
>
> Once the mission and goals have been stated, the program must present its objectives, derived from its statement of mission and goals. The program's objectives must reflect the intent of the Curriculum Policy Statement B5.7 to 5.7.12 (for baccalaureate programs) and M5.7 to 5.7.14, M6.19, and M6.22 (for master's programs).
>
> The program must specify the outcomes measures and measurement procedures that are to be used systematically in evaluating the program, and that will enable it to determine its success in achieving its desired objectives.
>
> The program must show evidence that it engages in ongoing, systematic self-study based on evaluation of its total program, and show evidence that the results of evaluation affect program planning and curriculum design.

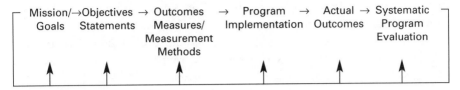

The Social Work Education Program

FIGURE 6.1   Key Ideas In Evaluation

The relationships among the key ideas inherent in this standard is illustrated in Figure 6.1.

The program defines its mission. Subsequently, specific program goals are laid out. Statements of objectives derived from the mission and goals are specified. The measures to be used to substantiate the degree of achievement of each objective, along with measurement methods (instruments, respondents, data gathering procedures, statistical procedures, etc.), are stated. The program then is implemented, or operates, until a predetermined point in time (e.g., during a course, at the end of a course, at the end of a year's work, at the end of all course work, at different stages of field practicum, at stated intervals after graduation) at which actual outcomes are evaluated. Findings are used to assess the extent to which objectives are achieved. The findings are fed back into curriculum or other program revision and possibly into revision of goals and objectives. In assessing attainment of objectives, a variety of sources of information (e.g., students, faculty, employers of graduates, field instructors, clients, consumers, student work products, and other reports or materials) may be used (CSWE, 1994, pp. 79–82, 117–119).

Internal Assessment

Two activities are contributing to revisions in the current policy statement and standards. These are the assessment of the 1992 Curriculum Policy Statement conducted by Michael Sheridan of Virginia Commonwealth University and the Commission on Accreditation Quality Assurance Research Project staffed by Ann Johnson, a DOSA educational specialist, and led by Mary Ann Suppes of Mount Mary College and George Metrey of Rhode Island College, both COA commissioners.

The purposes of Michael Sheridan's Assessment of the 1992 Curriculum Policy Statement (CPS) for the Commission on Educational Policy (Sheridan, 1998) were to identify the strengths and limitations of the current curriculum policy statement and to use this information to inform revisions that will be drafted in the next two years. Commission on Accreditation members, Division of Standards and Accreditation educational specialists, educators attending Baccalaureate Program Directors and National Association of Deans and Directors meetings in fall 1996, program faculty who used the 1992 statement and accreditation standards, and site team members who visited these programs were sampled via telephone interviews, surveys, and focus groups. The Sheridan study identified the following major themes regarding assessment:

1. The majority of social work programs found the emphasis on educational competences useful because it provided structure and guidance for curricular issues and/or assisted them in evaluating their programs.

2. A substantial majority of programs found the list of educational competences appropriate and inclusive and did not want to expand this list.

3. The majority of site team visitors stated that the 1992 CPS was useful . . . because it provided more flexibility and encouraged creativity and/or specificity of expectations, objectives, and outcomes.

4. Useful features mentioned by several members of the National Association of Deans and Directors of Schools of Social Work focus groups included promotion of ongoing assessment of program efforts.

5. Baccalaureate Program Directors group participants noted difficulties with the outcomes measures.

6. The CSWE Educational Specialists noted problems with terminology, especially relating to measurement; the material on educational competences; and vague or inconsistent language and references to measurement.

7. Commission on Accreditation (COA) members found the list of educational competences a useful feature, yet they noted that these were also the most difficult to interpret and apply.

8. CSWE Educational Specialists and COA members experienced more "problems" with the educational competences used for assessment than the other participants in the study.

In 1998, the Quality Assurance Research Project of COA was established to assure the quality of social work education by analyzing the accreditation process and its impact on programs. The COA assigned the project to its

Research Committee. Members of the committee forwarded findings in response to one element of CSWE's strategic plan, which was to analyze the current accreditation process as a resource or as an obstacle to program development and make recommendations for change.

The initial project included all programs that were in candidacy, received initial accreditation, or were reaffirmed between July 1, 1995, and June 30, 1998, plus a random sample of 59 other programs (N = 317 or 56% of all accredited programs). The response rate was 60.2% (n = 191). The COA decided to continue the project on an annual basis. Between July 1, 1998, and June 1, 2000, 22 programs received candidacy; 19 programs received initial accreditation; and 71 programs were considered for reaffirmation. The descriptive data for the additional programs were compared to the original groups of programs and found to be essentially identical in terms of program levels, decision categories, auspices, and number of faculty. For purposes of this study, descriptive data were analyzed as one data set.

Programs were asked to rate their agreement with a series of statements about the program's experience with each component of the accreditation process. On a scale of 1 (strongly disagree) to 4 (strongly agree), most programs found the accreditation experience to be positive (82.3%, N = 209) and believed that programs were improved as a result of the accreditation process (94.9%, N = 241). Both baccalaureate and master's programs ranked articulation of objectives and measurement of outcomes as the top two areas in which the accreditation process was most helpful to program development. The evaluative standard that addresses Program Rationale and Assessment was ranked second in the categories "most helpful" and "strengths to program development" (Metrey, Pebbles-Wilkins, Flynn, Mohan, & Johnson, 2000, pp. 1–7).

Although programs expressed favorable reactions to Evaluative Standard 1, a COA research committee report revealed that 96% (N = 70) of all programs that were reviewed for reaffirmation for the period February 1998 through October 1999 were required to submit an interim report for this standard (Metrey & Johnson, 1999). The interim report requires follow-up or submission of additional materials on specific program activities. The sections cited most frequently were the ones that addressed "outcome procedures and measures" and "outcome integration and ongoing evaluation."

When presenting this information to the members of the COA for their consideration, it was clear to the members that development of a faculty development training program addressing Evaluative Standard 1, Program Rationale and Assessment, could reduce the number of accreditation concerns related to assessment of student outcomes and reduce the number of required interim reports in this area. In 1999, faculty development training programs were initiated to assist faculty in understanding how to develop a mission statement, program goals and objectives, and a student outcomes assessment plan. As most faculty attending are preparing for an accreditation review, the COA Research Committee will attempt to determine if those program faculty who participated in EVS1 training are experiencing fewer problems in addressing this standard during their accreditation review.

Case Study—Columbia College

The social work major/program is one of four majors (Behavioral Science, Child & Family Studies, Psychology, and Social Work) in the Columbia College Department of Human Relations. The program was initially accredited in 1979 and has remained in continuous compliance with the CSWE Accreditation Standards. The most recent reaffirmation of accreditation occurred in June 1993 at which time the program was granted full accreditation with no concerns cited by the Commission on Accreditation. The next scheduled reaffirmation review is June 2001.

Until 1996, the program operated with two full-time faculty and adjuncts as needed. Currently the program has approximately 75 majors, three full-time faculty, and adjuncts as needed. Two important elements have characterized the program since inception: faculty stability and institutional support. Both of these elements are critical factors in developing and maintaining good assessment practices.

Faculty Stability

Faculty permanency is a key element in good assessment practices. This program has been blessed with faculty constancy that has encouraged the development of a collaborative understanding and commitment to program objectives and assessment. The program has had two program directors. The original director remained in the director's position from 1977 until 1998 when she moved to the department chair's position. The field coordinator who had been in that position since 1986 moved into the director's position. A new faculty member was hired as field coordinator. The continuity has allowed faculty to engage in informal assessment on an almost daily basis as well as formal assessment requiring long-range planning and implementation.

Institutional Support

The college is committed to specialized accreditation for programs that have such accreditation. Thus, outside accreditation is welcomed as evidence of academic excellence. The college supports the program with budget resources that allow (a) faculty to attend professional meetings to stay current with the nuances of accreditation, (b) periodic outside consultation, and (c) faculty to serve as site visitors and most recently on the Commission on Accreditation. With this support, accreditation becomes part of faculty development activities. Thus all faculty are knowledgeable concerning accreditation standards and processes.

The college is also committed to assessment. As a result of the last regional accreditation (1990), the college engaged in a campus-wide assessment initiative. All academic units were required to develop assessment plans, implement the plans, and report yearly the results.

Social Work Program Assessment Plan Pre-1993

The social work program since inception has been carefully monitored and modified as evidence for needed change emerged. The most recent changes occurred in 1991 in preparation for the reaffirmation review in 1993. The program was reaffirmed with no interim report and no concerns cited. Changes made prior to the 1993 review and the accompanying rationale follow:

1. The term *educational outcomes* was changed to *program objectives* to reflect the Accreditation Evaluative Standards and the Curriculum Policy Statement. Twelve program objectives were defined using the Curriculum Policy Statement.

2. Faculty (two at the time) reviewed the curriculum to determine the congruence with the new program objectives.

3. Assessment data from the following sources were used to make curriculum changes: score reports from the Area Concentration Achievement Test (ACAT); alumnae surveys; senior exit surveys; field evaluation instruments completed by the field instructor, the student, and field coordinator; and student performance in required courses.

Several consistent themes emerged: (a) students were not performing at the level expected in research; (b) students were having difficulty integrating policy and practice at the junior year; (c) a need for earlier screening of student compatibility with the profession existed ; and (d) the Human Behavior in the Social Environment (HBSE) course was unmanageable.

Faculty collaborated to make changes without requiring additional course work. In a liberal arts college, professional programs must balance professional requirements with liberal arts requirements while also providing students with electives. A three-semester-hour research course was changed to 3 two-semester-hour courses; the policy course was moved from the junior to the senior year and coordinated to run concurrently with the state general assembly; a two-semester-hour course in ethical problem solving was added as a prerequisite for the major; and a second HBSE course was added. The required hours for the major increased by just five because an introduction to social work course was eliminated and the content redistributed to other required courses.

Results: Student scores on the ACAT policy and research areas improved. Prior to the changes, these two areas produced the lowest scores consistently. For the past three years, these have been the highest score areas. More students decide that social work is not a career compatible with their value framework. Some improvement has been noted in student outcome performance in the HBSE curriculum area; however, students are not consistently performing at the program's established benchmarks. Assessment data are currently used to explore alternate pedagogical methods to assist students in mastering the volume of content required in this area.

Social Work Program Assessment Plan 1993 to Current

As a consequence of recommendations in 1991 from its regional accrediting association, the college engaged in a campus-wide assessment initiative. The college invited consultants to work with faculty to help them understand the principles of assessment and to engage faculty in a dialogue about multiple methods of assessment. The social work faculty already had fairly extensive assessment procedures in place and used this time to refine further the linkages of assessment methods with program objectives. The current plan serves as a campus model:

Procedures

1. The program director is responsible for collecting the assessment data and submitting the data to the department chair at the end of each academic year for the annual department assessment report.

All assessment reports follow a common format:

Program Objective	Method of Measurement and Benchmark of Achievement	Outcome/ Results	Recommendations/ Needed Action
Analyze and evaluate social policies. . . .	ACAT 50% of seniors will score above the national mean in the area of social welfare policy.	76% of the students scored above the national mean in the area of social welfare policy.	Criterion satisfied.

2. The social work faculty review the assessment report in the fall of each academic year and discuss needed action items.

3. The social work advisory committee reviews the report in the fall of each academic year and makes recommendations to the faculty for action.

4. Any required curriculum changes are presented to the department for approval and to the College faculty as a whole. Most recommendations do not require curriculum changes and are more pedagogical in nature.

The Plan

1. Assessment must be related to program objectives. This is critical. Each course objective is linked to a program objective. Each course objective is linked to a method of measurement. Courses are regularly evaluated, and faculty collaborate with each other to assure that all program objectives are assessed multiple times over the student's academic career. The assessment plan format for each course follows:

Program Objective	Course Objective	Method of Measurement	Results/ Outcome	Needed Action
Apply critical thinking skills within the context of professional social work practice.	Use statistical analysis to inform practice decisions.	Lab Exercises 80% of the students will earn a 3.0 or better on lab exercises.	64% of students scored a 3.0 or better on the lab exercises.	Comment from course evaluations for more lab time = will work to incorporate five additional lab days next semester.

2. Multiple methods must be used to assess each program objective, and benchmarks are clearly identified. Internal methods of assessment include course assignments, the Senior Exit Evaluation, and course evaluations. The senior exit evaluation is part of the field evaluation; this assures student completion and consistency in administration. External methods of assessment include the ACAT, the first and second semester field placement evaluations, the alumnae survey, and the American Association of State Social Work Boards–Licensed Baccalaureate Social Worker exam. Focus groups are also conducted annually with field instructors.

3. The ACAT is administered during the exam period in the senior policy class. This does two things: (a) impresses upon students the importance of their performance and (b) provides a consistent testing period for comparison of results. The senior policy course is completed during the last semester of the senior year.

Conclusions By institutionalizing this approach, assessment has become a way of thinking for the faculty. It is no longer an add-on—something done every eight years for accreditation. Faculty believe it has made them better teachers, more thoughtful about their assignments as they are reminded of the purpose for making them. The data collected make the program stronger; there is a rationale for change. If program objectives truly reflect what students should be able to do to be effective social workers and faculty hold themselves accountable based on assessment, then the profession and clients are the beneficiaries.

Case Study—Virginia Commonwealth University

At Virginia Commonwealth University, the faculty attended to the assessment of program objectives as they prepared for the self-study for reaffirmation of accreditation during the period of August 1992 to September 1994. At that time, the school was in transition. In 1990, its former dean moved to a position in central administration and a senior member of the faculty was appointed interim dean and provided leadership until January 1992, when the current dean arrived. At the graduate level, there were two concentrations, clinical social work and administration, each having four areas of specialization (mental health, health, children and families, and criminal justice). The master's degree program also had two off-campus sites in Virginia; one was 100 miles and the other 200 miles away. Curriculum comparability was lacking, and there was unevenness in course objectives and student outcomes in each of the specializations.

A two-day faculty retreat was held in August 1992. The revised Curriculum Policy Statement, which was approved by the CSWE Board of Directors in June 1992, was introduced at the retreat. The new curriculum policy opened the way to consideration of how to shape the curriculum for contemporary practice and attend to its sharpened expectations for program objectives and assessment. Focus groups with social work practitioners, field practicum instructors, and agency administrators were conducted across the Commonwealth of Virginia. The findings indicated the need to identify themes or organizing principles that cut across the concentrations and to eliminate the specializations within each concentration. The findings also helped to shape program and course objectives. These in turn became the framework for student outcomes. In an attempt to have course content become congruent with the demands of the field, these expectations became the lens through which the field education tool was developed.

Faculty first resisted being directed by an outside body on the topic of how to construct their content areas and course syllabi, and some members continued to "do it my way." Adjunct faculty members had the most difficulty identifying with an integrated curriculum and tended to teach for the student outcomes that they deemed necessary for practice. Strategies were developed in the self-study process to include each and every member of the faculty in the ownership of the curriculum. These included creating content teaching groups; assigning a senior member of the faculty to direct the self-study; appointing a member of the faculty to direct the MSW program with particular responsibilities for curriculum development; and biweekly meetings in which mission statement, program goals, course objectives, and student outcomes were discussed, consensus achieved, and votes taken. This contributed to the two-year period of self-study highlighted by a focus on curriculum development and consensus in decision making. Student outcomes were identified as the means by which program objectives would be achieved and measured. The MSW faculty noted in their self-study (Virginia Commonwealth University School of Social Work, 1994, p. 259) that evaluation of outcomes of the MSW program is an ongoing process using data from multiple sources. These data sources and the types of outcomes assessment include the following:

Students: Summative evaluations of course outcome objectives and teaching effectiveness are completed by students at the end of each semester for each course; exit group interviews use a focus group method with a sample of full-time on- and off-campus students and advanced standing students; and an evaluation of the field

	agency, field instructor, and field liaison is completed at the end of each field placement.
Faculty:	Course grades constitute a summative evaluation of course assignments designed to meet course learning objectives, and field evaluations are completed by the agency-based field instructor and field liaison each semester.
Graduates:	A follow-up study describes the employment of graduates and summarizes graduates' assessments of major MSW program outcomes.
Practitioners:	A study using focus groups of practitioners is conducted in the three areas of the state where the MSW program has on- and off-campus sites.

The undergraduate social work education program process was different. This program has had a faculty member serving as program director and, because of the nature of its curriculum, always has had a single focus, the preparation of generalist practitioners. There was also a stable cadre of faculty assigned to this program. The BSW faculty began the self-study process by reviewing and revising program objectives. First, each faculty member designed his or her own list of student outcomes. These were discussed and revised until there was complete consensus in the group. In developing program objectives and student outcomes, an effort was made to assure that these reflected the reality of practice. Information was utilized from a national survey, from research, and from field instructors. The objectives for each course in the curriculum were designed to support and implement program objectives and student outcomes. The self-study (Virginia Commonwealth University School of Social Work, 1994, pp. 107–108) noted the following:

The BSW faculty began discussion of assessment by working with a university consultant and using an instrument developed by the Center for the Study of Higher and Post-Secondary Education at the University of Michigan. This instrument is designed to stimulate discussion about the interaction of liberal education objectives and professional education. Using the Michigan instrument, faculty identified writing and critical thinking as areas where there seemed to be important discrepancies between the ideal and actual performance of students. Four assignments were designed that would replicate the types of writing tasks required in professional social work practice. In Spring 1990, these writing tasks were embedded in the introductory course. The writing tasks were graded by the faculty member as part of the course requirement. Then they were evaluated by the assessment team using a holistic rating scale developed for use with Advanced Placement Examinations. The process was repeated when this cohort of students was enrolled in the final senior practice course. Results were quantified and reported at several professional conferences and in an article prepared for publication.

This assessment strategy was in the forefront of the university's assessment activities and became a model for other departments. The project had both internal and external benefits. Faculty became more aware of the qualities and behaviors associated with writing and thinking. Course objectives and assignments were revised and the BSW admissions policy was modified. In addition to the usual forms of evaluation common to an academic setting (exams, papers, and oral presentations), the BSW program utilizes videotaping, learning logs, process recordings, an alumni survey, and a senior focus group/exit interview. Since few BSW graduates choose to take the state licensure exam, these results are not utilized.

The site team arrived in the winter of 1995. Their report (CSWE, 1995) noted the following:

> Both the BSW and MSW programs use multiple methods to obtain outcome measures. These include standard tests, senior satisfaction surveys, meetings with field instructors and faculty liaisons, the general education assessment project, senior exit interviews, course evaluations, course grades, follow-up studies describing the employment of graduates, practitioner focus groups, graduates holding the Licensed Clinical Social Worker credential, and alumni surveys. The outcome measures confirm that the program objectives are being accomplished. (p. 3).

However, upon review of the self-study documents, the report of the site-visit team, and the response from the two programs, members of the Commission on Accreditation noted that the program "does not link each method and measure to specific educational objectives. The program is asked to demonstrate in specific terms which measures address which objectives" (COA letter, 1995, p. 2).

This request for additional information led to resentment on the part of the faculty members who became invested in the self-study process. Those not as invested were less concerned and saw this as "just another hurdle" in the accreditation process. The response in the interim report described the linkages between the objectives, outcomes, and curriculum implementation for the BSW and MSW programs and then described the outcome measures used by the programs and the relationships to each program's objectives. To illustrate the integration of assessment as learning, they traced one outcome from each program throughout the curriculum. The report was accepted by COA.

Today, the same faculty are preparing the self-study for reaffirmation of accreditation and the site visit in the year 2003. Both programs are using a variety of measures to evaluate the extent to which educational outcomes and ultimately program objectives are being achieved. For the next self-study, measures will be described (course evaluations, field practicum evaluations, exit interview focus groups, alumni survey, input from practitioners), examples provided on the use of results, and each measure linked to outcomes and objectives. There is an expectation that the assessment process will continue to improve the curriculum of the two programs in regard to shaping objectives and related content that contribute to student outcomes.

Case Study—College of St. Catherine/ University of St. Thomas

In 1992, preparing for reaffirmation of the undergraduate and graduate social work programs, faculty in the School of Social Work at the College of St. Catherine and the University of St. Thomas developed a multiple measure plan to assess student outcomes. Prior to 1992, faculty had components of an assessment plan in place, but the newly released Curriculum Policy Statement and the new Evaluative Standards of the Council on Social Work Education (CSWE) greatly expanded program requirements for assessment of program objectives. Programs were now mandated to specify a statement of rationale, program mission and goals, program objectives, outcome measures, and measurement procedures and to demonstrate that the results of evaluation would be used to determine success in achieving program objectives and to affect program planning and curriculum design (CSWE, 1992, pp. 80–81).

Faculty were determined to develop an assessment plan that included goals and measurable objectives. They wanted the objectives to include what faculty expected students would learn in terms of knowledge, skills, and values by the end of the program. They also were interested in obtaining an average score for each objective as a means of determining how well their objectives were being met. Faculty met to discuss elements they deemed important for a successful assessment plan and to review existing instruments or measures for possible application to the program. Faculty determined that the assessment plan must employ multiple quantitative and qualitative measures, use direct measures of student learning, include external assessment of student learning, and produce data that could be used to improve student learning and program operation. The faculty decided that each year data collected from assessment would be used as part of the annual curriculum review and planning for the next year.

As a first step, faculty carefully reviewed the stated educational missions of the College of St. Catherine and the University of St. Thomas, the Curriculum Policy Statement and the Evaluative Standards of the Council on Social Work Education, and their own stated beliefs and philosophy about professional social work practice. The College of St. Catherine and the University of St. Thomas both are liberal arts institutions at the undergraduate level and committed to the integration of liberal arts at the graduate level. They believe that liberal arts and development of career competence are compatible and complementary. Keeping in mind the guides mentioned, faculty developed an overall mission statement for the school and individual mission statements for the undergraduate and graduate programs that clearly reflect social work's purposes, values, and ethics through emphasis on the enhancement of well-being and social functioning, service to meet basic human needs, promotion of social justice, and advancement of human rights. From the mission statements, faculty derived six overall goals for the baccalaureate program, including preparation of students for beginning generalist professional practice and preparation for graduate education in social work. Four goals were developed for the graduate program with a focus on development of analytical skills and substantive knowledge essential for clinical social work practice, for assessing the effectiveness of current social work methods, and for developing more effective practice procedures. The goals of each program reflect the overall educational missions of the institutions as students prepared as beginning generalist professional practitioners and clinical social work practitioners are committed to social and economic justice, to be responsible citizens, to have an understanding and appreciation of diversity, to be competent and morally responsible, and to be committed to self-understanding and lifelong learning.

From the program goals, faculty developed 18 program objectives for the baccalaureate program and 20 for the graduate program. These objectives reflect the requirements of the CSWE Curriculum Policy Statement that specified what all graduates will be able to do and the unique focus of each program. Flowcharts and tables were developed that clearly showed the linkage and consistency between program goals and objectives; assessment methods were determined; and an implementation plan was articulated. The programs adapted the schema presented in the CSWE Evaluative Standard to illustrate the implementation of the assessment plan. The schema for both programs are comparable. (See Figure 6.2)

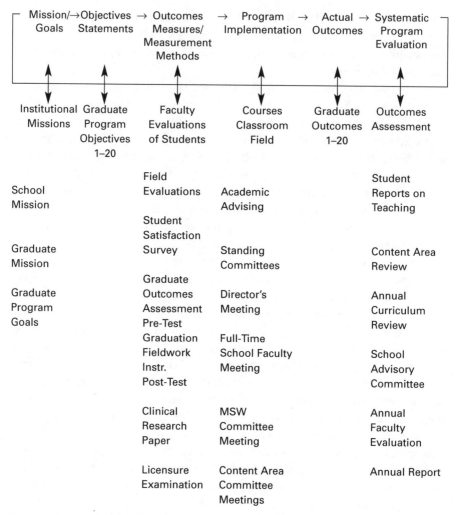

FIGURE 6.2   Evaluation Schema

The baccalaureate and master's program assessment plans include ongoing pre-graduation and post-graduation measures. In the pre-graduation program evaluation process, the baccalaureate and graduate programs each use four means to evaluate educational outcomes as achieved by students and supported by the program. The evaluation process is supported by findings from (a) faculty evaluations of students and student evaluations of the instructor and the course, (b) the field practicum, (c) a student outcomes assessment study, and (d) a student satisfaction survey. In the graduate program, the clinical research paper is used instead of the student satisfaction survey. The post-graduation assessment process uses primarily three means of evaluation: (a) the outcomes assessment study, (b) the state licensure examination, and (c) alumni survey (baccalaureate only).

Academic Course Evaluations

Program objectives are operationalized in course objectives, including knowledge and skill objectives. Faculty use both quantitative and qualitative methods for evaluating students' achievement of course objectives, including research papers, oral presentations (individual and group), class participation, role plays, video and audio taping, papers, quizzes, and examinations. At the end of each term, students evaluate the course and instructor using a college/university-wide assessment tool. The collated quantitative data and qualitative comments serve as valuable information for faculty review and development. In addition, faculty supplement formal end-of-term evaluations by a variety of periodic and ongoing feedback measures suggested by Angelo and Cross (1993) in *Classroom Assessment Techniques.*

Field Practicum

Field evaluations, including ongoing input from field instructors and student self-assessment, measure student performance in their field placement. The learning contract requires identification and specification of measurable learning goals and serves as the primary criterion of progress and achievement. Questions on the field evaluation were developed to measure specific program objectives.

Outcomes Assessment Study

A student outcomes assessment study derived from the goals of the program (linked to school and institutional missions) is administered to students, field instructors, and alumni. Prior to beginning the program, students complete a student profile, which in addition to demographic data requires them to rate themselves on multiple competences created to measure each program objective. Students retake the outcomes study before graduation and then again 18 to 24 months post-graduation. As part of the assessment process at the end of the final field placement, fieldwork instructors rate the students using the same instrument, providing a critical validation procedure. Students rate the competences on a scale of 1 (totally unprepared) to 5 (very well prepared). The ratings are averaged for objectives with multiple competences, with the goal to achieve an average rating of 3.5 for each objective. A score of 3.5 or higher on both student post-test ratings and field instructor ratings is required for an objective to be considered met for the year. Scores below 3.5 are referred to the appropriate content area committees for review and discussion. Scores above 4.0 are considered areas of strength.

Student Satisfaction Survey

Students are asked to rate their satisfaction with each of the nine content areas of the social work curriculum on a five-point scale, ranging from 1, low satisfaction, to 5, high satisfaction. The goal is to reach a minimum satisfaction rating of 3.5 in each content area. In addition, students are asked two qualitative questions: What would you change about any content area? and What do you view as strengths of the program?

Clinical Research Paper (Graduate Level Only)

All graduate students must complete a clinical research paper prior to graduation. The clinical research paper assesses the students' comprehension of the research process, including research ethics, methodology, and dissemination, as well as their ability to contribute to the knowledge of the social work profession.

Alumni Survey (Baccalaureate Level Only)

Alumni are surveyed 12 months after graduation regarding the nature of their employment, job title, salary, full- or part-time status, interest in graduate education, and success in passing the licensure examination.

Licensure Examination

Licensure test scores of students serve as a measure of student competence. The Association of State Boards of Social Work provides composite student passing rates annually for both baccalaureate and master's graduates with comparison to national pass rates.

Data gathered from each of the measures is used to evaluate whether stated program objectives are achieved, to tell how well the total program supports the specified educational outcomes, to identify and respond to changing educational and professional conditions, and to strengthen and improve the baccalaureate and graduate programs. Faculty meet regularly to discuss curriculum revision based on the results of all components of the assessment process.

The outcome of the last reaffirmation review is one indicator of the success of the assessment program. In 1995, both the baccalaureate and graduate programs were granted full accreditation with no concerns cited by the Commission on Accreditation. The next reaffirmation review is scheduled for

March 2004. Another indicator of success relates to current campus-wide assessment initiatives. Both the College of St. Catherine and the University of St. Thomas are accredited by the North Central Association of Colleges and Schools. All academic units were required to submit an assessment plan and then annually report on assessment activities conducted during that academic year. The School of Social Work submitted its plans in 1998, and both plans were approved. Strengths noted by the Assessment Coordinating Committee included the effective description of the links between school and institutional mission through program objectives; inclusion of easy-to-follow, intuitive grids and flowcharts; the longitudinal and developmental approach to assessment that assists students in understanding their own patterns of change throughout their educational experience; and the integration of the results of licensure examinations, introducing an objective measure along with the subjective outcomes assessment study.

Over the past 15 years, faculty have learned a great deal about assessment, student learning, and programs through the assessment process. First, they have learned that implementation of an assessment plan is challenging and requires attention. It is not a periodic event but an ongoing, integrated process. It is not something that can be assigned to one member of the faculty to "take care of" but is a collective responsibility. Faculty have learned the importance of designing measurable objectives and collecting data that can be used to inform and guide curriculum change. Secondly, they have learned that assessment must be student-centered, focused on what students completing the program have learned and can do. Finally, faculty have learned that, by systematically assessing student learning, they have useful data for program and curriculum design.

Lessons Learned and Ongoing Issues: Commissioner Observations

One of the major difficulties for faculty is the confusion that exists with terminology. Commission on Accreditation commissioners[1] define student competences as what students should be able to do when they graduate and use the CPS statements of expected educational outcomes as program objectives. Many faculty do not make this connection and thus do not use program objectives as the framework for assessment. This often results in multiple lists of "student outcomes" that have little or no relationship to program objectives and/or assessment methods. The biggest problem that COA commissioners and several Division of Standards and Accreditation staff see is the lack of congruence between the field practicum evaluation instrument and the program objectives/

competences. One commissioner observed that programs struggle because they do not devote the necessary time and effort to learn what is being asked. For example, most programs use a variety of measurement methods but they often do not tie the method to a specific objective/competence. The key to a good assessment plan is for faculty to be clear about the competences or learning objectives that are to be measured and to use these to guide curriculum development.

At the baccalaureate level and for the first year of master's education, defining student competence is heavily influenced by the accreditation requirements and the current Curriculum Policy Statement. Most programs use the CPSs of educational outcomes as student competences, either exactly as they are stated or with slight modifications. Some faculty would not have learned how to evaluate the program as extensively if it were not for the accreditation requirements.

The process of accreditation is helpful and also causes resentment. It is helpful because it provides periodic opportunities for thoughtful self-study. Commissioners note that programs on their campuses that have external accrediting bodies are among the strongest and generally have the easier time meeting the assessment requirements of the regional accrediting associations.

The process causes tension for many and resentment for some. Some perceive it to be an intrusion or perceive it as judgmental with underlying possibilities for sanction or public disapproval. The value of the process appears to depend partly on whether the program dean or director is able to provide leadership to use the experience as an opportunity for growth and strengthening the profession. For the process to work, there has to be a degree of tension, much like taking an examination.

The strategies for fostering good practice with respect to assessment include the following:

- Begin with a planning session with faculty using Evaluative Standard 1, Program Rationale and Assessment, as the orienting guide.

- Keep the assessment plan manageable and vest the primary responsibilities with one person for coordination.

- Work with faculty to develop skill in writing course objectives consonant with stated program objectives/competences.

- Support innovative teaching strategies and the use of assessment methods that challenge the creative thinking of faculty.

- Send faculty to workshops and conferences other than those in social work education, such as those sponsored by the American Association for Higher Education and the International Society for Exploring Teaching Alternatives.

Today, the profession is revising its curriculum policy statement and accreditation standards. The *Bylaws* of the Council on Social Work Education (1993) require the members of the Commission on Educational Policy to "prepare at periodic intervals not to exceed seven years, a statement of social work curriculum policy to encourage excellence in educational programs and to be used by the Commission on Accreditation in formulating and revising accreditation standards" (p. 3). Representatives from the Commission on Accreditation and the Commission on Educational Policy are working together in the revision process. The new document will be called *Education Policy and Accreditation Standards* (EPAS), and it is intended to revise and integrate the two documents. In accordance with CHEA accreditation standards, there will be a stronger focus on the outcomes-based approach, a program's development, and its continuous improvement. To highlight this focus, a revised evaluative standard, program assessment and continuous improvement, will be introduced. The standard will state:

> The program has an assessment plan and procedures for evaluating the achievement of each program objective. The plan specifies the measurement procedures and method(s) used to evaluate achievement of each program objective. The program reports an analysis of its assessment data for each program objective and links this analysis to program goals. The program shows evidence that the analysis of its assessment data is used continuously to improve the program. (CSWE, 2000, pp. 16–17)

During the 2000–2001 academic year, the revised policy statement and evaluative standards will be sent to deans, directors, program faculty, and members of constituency groups for comment. The CSWE Board of Directors will vote on approving the EPAS at its meeting in June 2001.

Good assessment requires time and commitment. The best strategy is for assessment to become a natural part of the teaching process and to move away from being an "add-on" or an activity undertaken solely for accreditation.

Note

1. The authors want to recognize the comments provided by Marilyn S. Flynn (University of Southern California), Charles Zastrow (University of Wisconsin–Whitewater), Terry L. Singer (University of Louisville), and Ann M. Johnson (Council on Social Work Education). These were incorporated into the lessons learned.

References

Angelo, T., & Cross, P. (1993). *Classroom assessment techniques: A handbook for college teachers.* San Francisco, CA: Jossey-Bass.

Baer, B. L., & Federico, R. (1978). *Educating the baccalaureate social worker: Report of the undergraduate social work curriculum development project.* Cambridge, MA: Ballinger Publishing Company.

Berengarten, S. (1986). *The nature and objectives of accreditation and social work education.* Austin: University of Texas School of Social Work.

Boehm, W. W. (1959). *Social work curriculum study (1957–1959).* New York: Council on Social Work Education.

Council on Social Work Education. (1952). *Curriculum policy.* New York: Author.

Council on Social Work Education. (1962). *Official statement of curriculum policy for the master's degree program in graduate professional schools of social work.* New York: Author.

Council on Social Work Education. (1969). *Curriculum policy for the master's degree program in graduate schools of social work.* New York: Author.

Council on Social Work Education. (1974). *Standards for the accreditation of baccalaureate degree programs in social work.* New York: Author.

Council on Social Work Education. (1982). *Curriculum policy for the master's degree and baccalaureate degree programs in social work.* New York: Author.

Council on Social Work Education. (1992). *Curriculum policy statement for baccalaureate degree and master's degree programs in social work education.* Alexandria, VA: Author.

Council on Social Work Education. (1993). *Bylaws.* Alexandria, VA: Author.

Council on Social Work Education. (1994). *Handbook of accreditation standards and procedures.* Alexandria, VA: Author.

Council on Social Work Education. (1995). *Site-visit report.* Alexandria, VA: Author.

Council on Social Work Education. (2000). *Working draft of the educational policy and accreditation standards.* Alexandria, VA: Author.

Metrey, G., & Johnson, A. (1999). *Interim report project, Commission on Accreditation research committee.* Alexandria, VA: Council on Social Work Education.

Metrey, G., Pebbles-Wilkins, W., Flynn, M., Mohan, B., & Johnson, A. (2000). *Commission on Accreditation research committee quality assurance project report.* Alexandria, VA: Council on Social Work Education.

Sheridan, M. J. (1998). *Assessment of the 1992 Curriculum Policy Statement.* Alexandria, VA: Council on Social Work Education.

Virginia Commonwealth University School of Social Work. (1994). *Self-study for reaffirmation.* Richmond, VA: Author.

7

ASSESSMENT OF STUDENT COMPETENCE IN BUSINESS

Neil A. Palomba and Catherine A. Palomba

Assessment of student learning is a subject of keen interest in business schools across the nation. Much of that interest reflects the influence of the business accreditor, AASCB—The International Association for Management Education (formerly the American Assembly of Collegiate Schools of Business). In this chapter, we describe AACSB's expectations concerning assessment and we highlight the experiences of several business schools that are doing outstanding assessment work.

AACSB's Expectations

In April 1991, AACSB adopted new criteria for accreditation and by 1993 the association was reviewing business schools using standards that are "mission-linked" and centered on continuous quality improvement (Martinez, 1995). Cognizant of the profound changes forcing businesses to become more mission oriented and quality conscious, AACSB sought to encourage business schools to emulate these characteristics. AACSB now requires business schools to develop their own mission statements against which their progress can be measured. In what has been described as a "near-miraculous transformation in its approach" (Dill, 1998, p. 20), AACSB broadened its focus to include outcomes measures, as well as traditional input measures. Although AACSB continues to examine criteria such as faculty credentials, library resources, and teaching loads, it now places emphasis on outcomes measures that monitor achievement of program objectives (AACSB, 2000).

According to AACSB's "Curriculum Content and Evaluation Standard" (AACSB, 2000), business schools must systematically review their degree programs in order to assess their effectiveness. Campuses are expected to revise their programs to "reflect new objectives and to incorporate improvements based on contemporary theory and practice" (p. 20). As a basis for judgment on this standard, business schools must demonstrate that they have processes in place for planning, monitoring, and revising their curriculums. The implication of this standard is that, in order to establish eligibility for initial and continuing accreditation, business schools must develop credible processes for assessment of learning, carry out effective assessment activities, and use assessment information to improve their programs. Although the standards do not explicitly use the phrase "assessment of student learning," AACSB clearly expects its members to examine the quality of their educational offerings and to "anticipate rising expectations, even within a given mission" (p. 1). Assessment of student learning is viewed as an important factor in strengthening the curriculum. AACSB does not require any specific processes or activities but has asked campuses to review the placement of their graduates and to analyze information from alumni and employer stakeholders.

AACSB is helping business schools meet the new standards by providing them with comprehensive information about assessment. For several years, the topic of assessment has been featured in presentations and workshops at AACSB's annual *Continuous Improvement Symposium*. Since spring 1998, AACSB has conducted an annual *Outcome Assessment Seminar* under the leadership of Jay M. Kridel, director of professional development. This conference features addresses by nationally known assessment experts and sessions by business school faculty and administrators who candidly describe assessment efforts on their own campuses. Both conferences provide tremendous opportunities for faculty to exchange information and learn more about assessment. Many of the examples reported in this chapter are drawn from the assessment projects described by faculty at conference sessions.

Taking advantage of resources from AACSB and elsewhere, faculty and administrators in many business colleges and departments have developed and implemented thoughtful approaches to assessment; but the process has not been without challenges. Similar to faculty in other disciplines, business faculty have struggled with identifying goals and objectives for learning; planning and organizing their assessment efforts; involving colleagues, students, and other stakeholders; selecting and implementing assessment activities; and using assessment results for improvement. Some of their experiences with assessment are described here.

Identifying Goals and Objectives for Learning

Perhaps because of AACSB's strong emphasis on the link between assessment and the curriculum, a number of business schools have spent considerable effort developing statements of expected competences for students. AACSB (2000) has provided guidance about the learning goals and objectives that member schools must address. Although specific courses are not required, member schools are to provide students with an understanding of "perspectives that form the context for business," including ethical and global issues; the influence of political, social, legal, environmental, and technological issues; and the impact of demographic diversity on organizations (p. 17). Students must master the foundation knowledge for business, including accounting, behavioral science, economics, mathematics, and statistics. In addition, AACSB has identified written and oral communication skills as important competences for students to possess. AACSB expects that general education courses will comprise at least 50% of a student's four-year program. In keeping with the concept of unique missions, member schools consider AACSB's guidance as they develop a set of competences that are campus-specific. Because AACSB has not been entirely prescriptive about required learning outcomes, a great deal of variety exists in the outcomes statements of business colleges. Most have statements for each major, as well as for the business core. The core is made up of courses such as introductory accounting, business law, and economics that all business students are required to complete regardless of their major.

In the College of Business Administration at Winthrop University, all graduates are expected to be competent in the areas of communication, teamwork/diversity, adaptability, problem solving, and accountability/ethics. Students are expected to master three or four specific competences within each of these areas. For example, with respect to communication, graduates should be able to organize information, draw and support conclusions, and access and communicate information using modern technologies. With respect to adaptability, graduates should be able to respond to changing markets and needs of stakeholders and understand how the concepts and theories of quality and continuous improvement are incorporated into business practice (Weikle, Spears, Bradbard, & Maner, 1999). In the Pamplin College of Business at Virginia Polytechnic Institute and State University (Virginia Tech), all departments have developed their own sets of learning goals that include competences specific to the major. However, the expectation that students will develop communication skills, citizenship/service skills, and appreciation of international and multicultural perspectives is common across departments (R. Sorensen & N. Spencer, personal communication, June 2000).

In 1996–97, faculty in the W. Paul Stillman School of Business at Seton Hall University adopted a new core curriculum that was based on the development of five broad competences, including change management, communications, critical thinking, teamwork, and technology. After the new program was approved, teams of faculty worked on operationalizing the learning objectives associated with each of these competences. The teams made recommendations about which courses should stress the development of the competences and eventually developed a document mapping courses to competences and objectives. The entire faculty approved the work of the teams before it was implemented (Boroff, Martin, & Mayo, 1999).

Working from the course level to the program level, faculty in the College of Business Administration at Northern Arizona University (NAU) found that "learning outcomes can be developed in a piecemeal fashion" (Tallman, E. Jacobs, & N. Jacobs, 1999, p. 2). Early in the process, assessment leaders recognized that the content of the core curriculum "belongs to the faculty as a whole rather than an area" (p. 6). Faculty began their efforts at writing learning outcomes by developing a new format for master syllabi. Under the new format, syllabi must contain student outcomes written in the active voice. The intent of stressing outcomes is to identify curricular strengths and weaknesses and to communicate to stakeholders what is being accomplished in the courses. Faculty teaching core courses drafted the new syllabi and submitted them to the curriculum committee for review. The learning outcomes assigned to core courses were reviewed for validity and assessibility at small group faculty retreats and later presented to the full faculty. After the outcomes for each core course were complete, faculty synthesized them into a set of learning outcomes for the core. The final list was comprised of seven expectations for student learning, including the abilities to understand the benefits of a free market economy, communicate and defend ideas, identify opportunities and solve business problems, and use organizational and leadership skills to solve problems. In contrast to Seton Hall, NAU's business faculty found it easier to develop course outcomes before developing outcomes for the entire core. The process helped faculty understand the core as an integrated unit rather than a collection of courses. As part of ongoing procedures, area coordinators review course syllabi each semester to ensure conformity with the master syllabi.

In a process similar to that at Northern Arizona University, College of Business faculty at Ball State University (BSU) began their assessment efforts with a thorough look at the curriculum, first looking at the business core and later at each major. The faculty teaching each course developed specific learning objectives for the course using worksheets created by the university's Office of Academic Assessment. Then, using the statements developed by faculty, the college's Undergraduate Curriculum and Assessment Committee identified seven overall learning objectives for the core. These include skills, such as formulating a business problem and implementing a business decision, that are common to all graduates of the college. Next, all courses in the core were reviewed to determine if the seven learning objectives were appropriately addressed, reinforced, and sequenced in the courses. A curriculum review was also conducted in the MBA program. After common learning objectives were developed for all MBA graduates, faculty were asked to complete checklists indicating which learning objectives were covered in their courses. The Graduate Curriculum and Assessment Committee used these lists to review the overall coherence of the MBA program (Hill, 1996).

Faculty in the School of Business at Southern Illinois University Edwardsville employed grids to examine their curriculum. Using a matrix that listed learning objectives as column titles and course names as row titles, faculty indicated whether the particular objective was (a) a prime (major curricular) objective, (b) an important objective (one that received significant emphasis), or (c) a basic objective or recurring theme. The grid enabled faculty to see how well the learning objectives they had established for their students were being addressed (Eder & Hirsch, 1999b).

Planning and Organizing Assessment

Leadership for assessment can come from many directions. In some cases, new committees or task forces are created for this purpose. However, at BSU's College of Business, the existing undergraduate and graduate curriculum committees assumed leadership for the process and changed their names to "curriculum and assessment" committees in order to reflect their new assignments. In addition to providing general guidance about assessment, the committees review department level assessment plans and reports that are submitted according to an established timetable. Administrative assistance is provided by the college's undergraduate and graduate program coordinators.

The curriculum and assessment committees asked faculty to develop appropriate plans for assessing the core and major programs. To aid the process, faculty were given a list of "desirable characteristics" for assessment programs. As the list indicated, successful assessment programs (a) identify assessment procedures to address all learning goals; (b) use efficient procedures such as sampling student work and drawing on university-wide data where appropriate; (c) include multiple measures; (d) describe the people, committees, and processes involved; and (e) contain plans for using assessment information (N. Palomba & C. Palomba, 1999).

At Virginia Tech, state-level requirements for developing plans and reporting assessment results have had an impact on the organization of assessment. Responding to a request from the Virginia legislature, Virginia Tech first developed a set of university-wide expectations for learning. Then, every five years, each department participates in a two-year process of goal setting, plan implementation, and report publishing. At the Pamplin College of Business, some department heads appoint a faculty committee to develop and implement their entire assessment plan. In other cases, the department head writes the assessment plan with consultation from faculty. Other than the state-mandated department plans and reports, the college has also participated in a six-year continuous improvement project, originally in partnership with Westinghouse Corporation. Analysis of input from several sources including recruiters, parents of students, and benchmark institutions has led to several program modifications (R. Sorensen & N. Spencer, personal communication, June, 2000).

In addition to state requirements, institutional requirements can have a substantial impact on the development of assessment processes and activities. At Ohio University, all departments are required to submit annual reports about their assessment activities that are reviewed by the university-wide Assessment Review Committee (Williford, 1997). At Southern Illinois University Edwardsville, all seniors are required to participate in Departmental Senior Assignments (SRAs). The SRAs provide baccalaureate graduates the opportunity to demonstrate how well they have met both major and general education expectations. Completion of an approved SRA is required for graduation. The university's Committee on Assessment (COA), made up of students, faculty, staff, and administrators, supervises all phases of the campus-wide assessment process. The COA's main task has been to help departments match their SRAs to the educational objectives they have chosen for their students. In response to this requirement, the School of Business is using its capstone business course to evaluate writing samples and research reports submitted by students (Eder, 1996).

Involving Stakeholders

Mindful of the great importance of widespread involvement in assessment, several business colleges have designed assessment programs that draw heavily on faculty participation. The need to provide appropriate materials and resources for both faculty and students has also been recognized by many business colleges.

All faculty from the School of Business at Southern Illinois University Edwardsville are required to participate in writing-through-the-curriculum workshops that are offered in partnership with English and speech faculty. Faculty are trained to rate papers that are required in both the capstone course, Written Communication and Analytical Thinking, and the cornerstone course, Foundations of Business (Eder & Hirsch, 1999a). At Virginia Tech, faculty are widely involved in workshops that address issues to improve student learning. Topics have included using group projects in the classroom, integrating writing across the curriculum, and expansion of technology in the classroom. Within the Pamplin College of Business, a real effort has been made to orient faculty to the purposes of assessment and how it fits into the culture of the field. Accounting faculty, for example, benefited from discussing the differences between the precise nature of their discipline and the more probabilistic nature of assessment (R. Sorensen & N. Spencer, personal communication, June 2000).

All new faculty at King's College, including those in the McGowan School of Business, attend workshops when they arrive on campus. The workshops, led by faculty teams, introduce new colleagues to the King's College Course Embedded Assessment Model, which incorporates assessment into the courses of each program. All faculty receive the *Handbook on Assessment,* as well as materials that are specific to their own department. Accounting faculty, for example, receive the *Course Embedded Assessment Program Handbook* that describes, through competency growth plans, how the Department of Accounting achieves each liberal learning skill that is common to King's College graduates (Williams & Parsons, 1999).

At BSU's College of Business, the assessment process was based on the principles that faculty involvement would be widespread and that assessment would draw primarily on locally developed strategies. Development of local methods allowed faculty to closely align assessment techniques with the curriculum and to maximize faculty involvement. All faculty assumed specific assessment roles, including serving on committees, participating in the development of plans, contributing to data collection and analysis, and/or making recommendations based on assessment findings. In order to ensure faculty success, several workshops were conducted, helpful materials were generated and shared with faculty, and faculty meetings and retreats were held to monitor progress and discuss results. One MBA faculty member developed a particularly effective handout that delineated the roles of various stakeholders in assessment, including the Graduate Curriculum and Assessment Committee, students, faculty, and external stakeholders. As described in the handout, faculty are expected to provide checklists of course coverage vis-à-vis MBA program objectives, course syllabi, assessment plans for their own courses, and assessment reports. This statement and the overall assessment plan for the

MBA program were submitted to the entire faculty for approval before they were put into effect. The statement had the great benefit of making expectations for involvement clear to all stakeholders (Palomba & Banta, 1999).

The leadership of BSU's College of Business recognized, however, that assigning responsibility and providing training are only part of what is needed to make assessment successful; the issue of faculty rewards is very important. Assessment leaders made clear to faculty that assessment is a separate process from faculty evaluation and that assessment findings would never be used in a punitive manner. With that reassurance, the evaluation form that faculty use for their annual reports, and that is considered during salary deliberations, was modified to reflect contributions to the assessment effort. Faculty are now encouraged to include their assessment activities in the Instruction/Teaching section of their reports. This opportunity provides clear evidence that assessment is valued in the college.

Students also need support as they participate in assessment. Informational materials that explain the purposes of assessment and clarify expectations for student participation in assessment activities can be very helpful. Several business colleges have developed written materials for their students. BSU's faculty developed a brochure entitled *Academic Assessment and the Business Student*. This brochure is given to students in the business communications course, which is the first required course in the business core. The brochure addresses several questions, including the following: What is academic assessment? Who participates? When and where does assessment take place? Both university-wide and college-level activities are described. The brochure lets students know that they are considered active learners in the college and that they share responsibility for their learning with faculty and administration. As such, they are an integral part of the assessment process.

At Duquesne University's Graduate College of Business, graduate students receive a statement entitled *Commitment to Student Outcomes*. Students are informed that successful completion of their course of study will lead to development of a number of outcomes. In addition to skills such as problem solving and communication, one outcome is "a portfolio of demonstrated competence in applying the skills and disciplines acquired throughout the program" (Presutti Jr., 1999, p. 7).

Faculty in the W. Paul Stillman School of Business at Seton Hall University have developed an indexed manual for their students that describes the entire assessment process. It includes a description of all expected assessment activities, definitions of key terms related to the program's expected competences, and general guidelines about assessment. Students are told that assessment is a process that will help mark their growth with respect to their educational studies, in addition to allowing the school to monitor the quality of its undergraduate program. The general guidelines include a number of expectations about student performance. For example, students are expected to contribute to team assignments, strive for professionalism in assessment presentations, and maintain high standards of integrity with respect to their projects. The school offers workshops for students prior to their participation in assessment panels (Boroff et al., 1999). In the College of Business and Public Administration at the University of Louisville, personnel in both the Advising Center and the co-op office communicate with students about expected outcomes (Srinivasan & Wright, 1999).

Alumni of business colleges, employers of graduates, and practitioners in the field are important groups of stakeholders. Faculty and administrators in the College of Business and Administration at the University of Colorado at Boulder have developed one survey for alumni who graduated three to five years previously and another for employers and recruiters. Names and addresses for the latter survey are obtained from the University Career Service and the college's Placement Office (Palmer, 1999). The College of Management at North Carolina State University has developed a questionnaire for employers who hire their graduates. Employers are asked about the characteristics they typically look for when screening resumes to select candidates for interviews. *Related work experience,* such as internships and co-ops, tops the list. The survey also asks employers about the characteristics they look for when interviewing candidates. *Communication skills* tops this list, followed by *motivation* (G. Hankins, personal communication, June 2000).

Ohio University's program for Human Resource Management (HRM) benefits greatly from the involvement of an advisory board of practitioners. Recently, this group constructed a mission statement that defined reasons for the HRM major to exist, discussed changes in the field that should be reflected in the curriculum, and helped faculty develop a set of expected competences for their graduates. The latter include the abilities to manage change and function as change agents. The advisory board helps faculty design realistic and practical projects to assist students in mastering the competences. The use of face-to-face meetings and assigned tasks helps ensure that practitioners remain committed to the assessment effort (Thacker, 1999). Practitioners have been very important in helping BSU's entrepreneurship faculty assess their program. In particular, employers serve on juried panels where they evaluate business plans written and presented by seniors during the last semester of their programs. Projects are graded on a pass-fail basis, and a student must pass in order to graduate from the program (Kuratko, 1996).

King's College business faculty seek feedback from employers about the internship experiences of their students. Employers evaluate the students' strengths and weaknesses both in subject matter knowledge and the liberal learning skills covered in the competency growth plans. The school has created a Business School Advisory Council for each major. Typically, council members attend annual meetings held on two consecutive days and use some of their time on campus to conduct a thorough review of the major. Council members visit classes, serve as guest lecturers, and attend department meetings (Williams & Parsons, 1999).

Implementing Assessment Activities

Although faculty differ in how they proceed with assessment, once learning goals and objectives have been identified, they typically feel ready to select their assessment strategies. After completing a curriculum review, BSU's business faculty committed themselves to a variety of assessment procedures. Assessment of the core includes a pre-post test that is given to students midway through the program after they have completed the pre-business courses in accounting, statistics, economics, and computer usage that are required for admission to the college. It also includes cases, problem sets, oral reports, and group work in the capstone core course and an alumni survey of recent graduates. The latter survey is conducted by the university's Office of Academic Assessment. The survey is distributed to all alumni two years after they have graduated from the university. Because the office disaggregates results by college and department, business faculty receive findings for their own graduates that they can compare with university averages. The survey asks students to rate their preparation in various areas and to indicate how important these areas are in their work. In addition to the evaluation techniques already described, some core courses, including business law and marketing, are assessed using information generated from already existing and newly developed classroom activities.

In order to assess undergraduate majors, faculty in each program identified assessment methods for their students, including portfolios, pre-post tests, internship evaluations, and focus groups of students and employers, as well as surveys of current students and alumni. In most majors, faculty collect some assessment information in their capstone course. Assessment activities in the MBA program now include surveys of graduating students, a review of taped cases from the capstone course, an objective test administered to students at entry and exit from the program, and course-based assessment in all courses. The MBA faculty are reviewing these techniques to see which are most useful and to create a time line for future assessment activities (N. Palomba and C. Palomba, 1999).

In Winthrop's College of Business Administration, assessment activities include surveys for graduating seniors, alumni, and employers, as well as portfolios, a capstone test, and capstone cases (Weikle et al., 1999). Faculty in Virginia Tech's Pamplin College of Business use a variety of measures, including exit interviews of a sample of seniors, placement data, portfolios and projects in capstone courses, focus groups of students, surveys of alumni, surveys of Advisory Council members, and employer surveys and telephone interviews. Although there is sentiment that standardized tests measure learning more directly than the methods that are currently used, faculty have not adopted standardized tests (R. Sorensen & N. Spencer, personal communication, June 2000). A number of campuses do use the Major Field Test in Business available through the Educational Testing Service. In the early 1990s, AACSB participated in the development of a standardized exam, but that effort was abandoned. More recently, AACSB has worked with Educational Benchmarking, Inc., to help them pilot benchmarking tools including student and faculty surveys. In 1998, 142 and 71 schools, respectively, participated in these surveys (Detrick, 1999).

In those business colleges in which faculty in each major develop their own assessment plans, the difference in approaches between departments can be quite striking. At Central Missouri State University's Harmon College of Business Administration, entry-level assessment in management is conducted during an orientation course open only to management majors. In this class, students learn about the college's assessment-as-learning paradigm, participate in pre-assessment exercises that measure outcomes, and obtain feedback about their current ability levels. Entry-level assessments include in-basket exercises, a case analysis that includes oral and visual presentations, and a writing exercise that results in a printed document. Exit assessment for this program occurs in a course that also is exclusive to management majors. This capstone course includes a number of assessment activities such as case analyses, in-basket exercises, and videotaped presentations that are evaluated for both major outcomes and general outcomes. The latter are based on the general outcomes adopted by the university, including interacting, communicating, thinking, valuing, and learning. The Department of Management has operationalized these university-wide general outcomes so that they reflect the language and specifics of their own curriculum. In contrast to the management department's use of entry and exit courses for assessment, the Department of Economics and Finance has developed a number of classroom-based activities that occur throughout the program. In the public finance course, students are given statements of the competences they must master in order to receive a grade of *A* or *B*. To make expectations clear, three levels of proficiency are described for each competence, with higher levels of proficiency requiring the use of application or judgment. Each student then compiles a portfolio that is jointly reviewed by the teacher and student in order to determine the grade. Although specific assessment activities vary by department, the entire college is committed to active learning and the use of feedback to enhance student achievement (Andrews & Neal, 1999).

A key feature of the assessment program in the School of Business at Southern Illinois University Edwardsville is the use of the capstone course. In this course, students submit written papers that are graded by multiple readers. The intent is not only to assess individual performance but also to examine cohort performance and the curriculum itself. Students were originally asked to submit three papers that were written prior to the course. The course was offered on a pass-fail basis, and students were allowed to redo their existing papers. When faculty found that students were not taking advantage of the option to revise their work and were not motivated to take the "pass/fail" course seriously, the course was revised to include a letter grade. In addition, students are now required to complete a new paper in the course. A grading chart has been developed using primary trait analysis. Using a six-point scale, papers are graded on factors such as organization, evidence, references/citations, and overall impression. Originally, only curriculum committee members and administrators read the papers. Now, in order to distribute the workload and involve more faculty in the assessment process, all tenured faculty participate in reading the papers (Eder & Hirsch, 1999a).

Assessment centers and panels represent unique approaches to evaluating the learning of students. An assessment center involves the use of exercises, simulations, leaderless discussion groups, and paper-and-pencil measures to evaluate participants' knowledge and skills. Trained assessors conduct the evaluations. Their results are compiled and provided to participants along with developmental feedback. Both Valparaiso University (VU) and Arizona State University–West (ASU–West) have created such centers. Faculty at VU's College of Business Administration believe that learning outcomes cannot be measured effectively by student surveys or course grades and that a center allows them to examine skills directly. They developed a set of activities including oral presentations, in-basket exercises, and role-playing. In one scenario, students assume the role of plant managers who are meeting with the company president to discuss budget cuts. Students meet as a group to come up with a plan for allocating the cuts. Both videos and practice cases are used by VU business faculty when they train assessors how to evaluate students and how to provide students with constructive and supportive feedback. Faculty are planning to use the center to evaluate students at three points in time: at the beginning of the sophomore year, in the middle of the junior year, and at the end of the senior year. ASU–West's School of Management conducts day-long assessment centers at which 15 to 20 students are evaluated. They use upper division seminar students, faculty, and government and private industry managers as assessors. Assessment activities include in-basket exercises, group discussions, cases, interviews, and paper-and-pencil measures. Some of the challenges involved in using the center include motivating students to do their best, providing appropriate feedback to students, and using the information for program improvement (Christ et al., 1999).

Seton Hall's assessment program in business is comprised of four phases, including pre-assessment, the sophomore assessment panel, the senior assessment panel, and the final assessment. Every student participates in the pre-assessment, the final assessment, and one of the two panels. In the pre-assessment, students complete a vocabulary test in which they are asked to define key terms associated with competences developed in the program. They complete an English skills test that measures their ability to communicate in written form and take the Watson-Glaser Critical Thinking Appraisal. All of these tests are completed in orientation. Half of the sophomore class is required to participate in the sophomore panel. For the panel, students work in teams to complete questions and exercises. On the assessment day, the teams must use technology to present prepared answers to case questions. The cases are complex and multidisciplinary and require students to engage in critical thinking to resolve the issues presented. During the assessment, students are required to submit individual work, including a sample of writing and answers to several questions about topical material drawn from the curriculum. Students prepare both self- and team evaluations and are assessed by a business practitioner. Seniors who do not participate in the sophomore panel are required to participate in the senior panel. This panel parallels the sophomore panel with a mix of team presentations and individual work. It includes a post-assessment critique by the assessor. Assessors include alumni, business partners, or graduate students in business who are trained and may be paid. (Students pay a fee for participating in the panels.) Faculty are encouraged to observe the panel assessments and are required to attend at least one assessment panel every two years. The final assessment includes a vocabulary test of key terms, a writing sample, and a battery of nationally normed standardized tests (Boroff, et al., 1999).

Reporting, Sharing, and Using Results

Business faculty take various approaches to reporting and distributing assessment results. In order to provide comparability across required assessment reports, the curriculum and assessment committees in BSU's College of Business developed a report outline that was distributed to college faculty. The outline asks faculty to describe their assessment methodology including the who, how, when, and where of assessment activities; the relationship between assessment techniques and learning goals; and assessment results. The outline asks faculty to include recommendations for action based on their assessment findings, as well as plans for future assessment activities. Based on critiques of both plans and reports, the committee provides faculty with specific feedback about areas for improvement in the assessment process. However, the committee does not make recommendations for improvements in academic programs. This remains the responsibility of faculty teaching in the program.

Each department in the McGowan School of Business at King's College submits an annual review of their assessment program. The reports must include a description of assessment activities and an explanation of how assessment results will be shared with faculty (Williams & Parsons, 1999). At Virginia Tech's Pamplin College of Business, a number of accountability checks help ensure that department-level reports actually are used. The reports are public, shared with all faculty in the department, and are included in the department head's annual review with the dean. The dean refers to these reports when he meets annually with each department. Further, the report itself asks the department to indicate what will be done with the information, and subsequent reports ask what was done with information collected in previous assessments. Based on their experiences, Richard Sorensen and Norrine Bailey Spencer, Dean and Associate Dean for Undergraduate Programs of the college, recommend that faculty involved in assessment go public with their results "even if it shows some large deficits or needs for radical change." As they indicate, "one has to know the starting point" in order to improve student learning. They advise that it is important to demonstrate how assessment information was used. This is critical in motivating people to spend time on assessment (Personal communication, June 2000).

Reviewing Assessment

A final element in successful assessment is to review the process and make necessary changes. Similar to other business colleges, BSU's College of Business has benefited greatly from introspection about the assessment process. Several faculty meetings and retreats are held each year to discuss assessment procedures and findings. In addition, the opening faculty meeting each fall includes a review of assessment prepared by the college's undergraduate and graduate program coordinators. The review includes both a summary of what was accomplished in the previous year and assessment plans for the coming year. For example, in the fall 1997 report, the undergraduate program coordinator Janice Replogle thanked the faculty for "a tremendous amount of work." She noted how during the first round of assessment "most plans were quite ambitious and that this ambition caused there to be a diffusion of focus. . . ." (Replogle, 1997, p. 1). As a result, some plans were modified to accomplish more modest objectives.

Implementing Changes

Assessment has led to many changes at Virginia Tech's Pamplin College of Business including creation of more writing and teamwork assignments, development of a center for leadership studies in management, reorganization of course content and sequencing in management, creation of an advising position in marketing, and reorganization of principles teaching in accounting (R. Sorensen & N. Spencer, personal communication, June 2000).

BSU's College of Business has modified its curriculum based on assessment findings. It has introduced a required communications course for all majors and has redesigned its production course to include more total quality management concepts. As a result of discussions among faculty, there is more coherence across multiple-section courses, and prerequisite courses are doing a better job of preparing students for later courses. In the MBA program, two-credit courses offered in pairs have replaced discrete three-credit courses that were offered previously.

Assessment has created a cultural change within BSU's College of Business. Faculty view the curriculum as a coherent whole rather than a collection of discrete courses. They now take responsibility for the entire curriculum rather than just for the individual courses they teach. The college has found that, while assessment measures and techniques are necessary to provide evidence for discussion, the discussion itself is just as important as any assessment findings. Northern Arizona University reports similar kinds of changes. Assessment has helped faculty "break down functional blinders" (Tallman et al., 1999, p. 2) and think about the core in a more integrated way. As a result of their efforts at curriculum review and assessment, "An environment of change was created" (p. 28).

Fostering Success

Several colleges of business are able to draw on university-wide support as they carry out their assessment programs. Winthrop University, Ohio University, and BSU all provide colleges and departments with extracts of institutional surveys (Palomba & Banta, 1999). BSU's College of Business receives other kinds of support from the Office of Academic Assessment, including consulting, informational materials, and summer grants for faculty involved in assessment projects. Although small in dollar amount, the grants are helpful in getting faculty to work together on specific projects that provide momentum for assessment. For example, one summer project was used to design the MBA program's assessment plan, and another was used to create the college's assessment brochure for undergraduate students. A third project involved the development of a matrix that aligned learning goals with suggested assessment techniques.

Another success factor in BSU's College of Business was the willingness of the dean and committee leaders to be flexible in implementing the process. They recognized from the beginning that it takes a long time to do assessment well and that faculty could expect considerable trial and error in the process. Although the college started with a written assessment plan, faculty deviated from that plan when it became necessary. The current assessment plan that includes alternating assessment of the core and the major is quite different from the original conception of a cyclical assessment process with two departments assessed per year. College faculty quickly realized that it was more important to make progress each year than to stick to a rigid plan. NAU's College of Business Administration faculty also benefited from flexibility in their process. For example, in defining learning objectives, they originally felt they could proceed from mission to core and then to course-level objectives. Instead, they found that developing core outcomes was too large an initial task for faculty who felt more comfortable dealing with course learning outcomes (Tallman et al., 1999).

The strong impetus for assessment coming from AACSB is a prominent factor in the success that many business colleges have experienced with assessment. Because BSU's business faculty take significant pride in having the college accredited, they were willing to expend a great deal of effort in designing and implementing an assessment program that would satisfy AACSB's requirements. Because AACSB is flexible about the specifics of assessment, faculty had many occasions to be involved in creating the program. Throughout the process, faculty were given several opportunities to become familiar with assessment purposes and methods and to voice their opinions and reservations about assessment. Faculty who initially asked "Why are we doing assessment?" gradually became comfortable with the idea that its overriding goal is to improve educational programs, not to fill out reports or demonstrate accountability.

The Dean and the Associate Dean for Undergraduate Programs of Virginia Tech's Pamplin College of Business believe that AACSB "has served as a model for doing assessment and using it; just by requesting college mission statements, goals and target audiences, and data to evaluate progress," AACSB has helped colleges of business develop habits of "taking measures, implementing change, and revising goals" (R. Sorensen & N. Spencer, personal communication, June 2000). William Dill (1998) credits AACSB with "real efforts to help schools anticipate and engage emerging issues for business and society" (p. 20). For their part, AACSB leaders remain committed to fostering campus assessment programs. They too are introspective about their role in accreditation and assessment. With so much change during the previous few years, AACSB staff recognize how important it is to make sure teams are well prepared for their campus visits. They continue to help team members get ready to carry out this important responsibility (Martinez, 2000).

The examples cited in this chapter indicate that faculty, administrators, and staff in many business colleges have been thoughtful, imaginative, and committed to developing successful assessment programs. Numerous business schools have become more explicit in describing their missions, have committed themselves to measuring their progress against their missions, have carefully examined whether their goals and objectives for learning are being achieved, and have sought input from their stakeholders. Clearly they recognize the potential of assessment to improve learning. It appears that AACSB is making progress toward achieving its goal of helping business schools enhance their educational quality and improve the learning of their students.

References

AACSB—The International Association for Management Education. (2000). *Achieving quality and continuous improvement through self-evaluation and peer review: Standards for accreditation.* St. Louis, MO: Author.

Andrews, K., & Neal, J. C. (1999, February). *The basics of outcomes and assessment.* Paper presented at the AACSB Outcome Assessment Seminar, Clearwater Beach, FL.

Boroff, K., Martin, D. T., & Mayo, A. (1999, February). *Competencies development in the undergraduate business curriculum.* Paper presented at the AACSB Outcome Assessment Seminar, Clearwater Beach, FL.

Christ, M. Y., Mainstone, L. E., McCuddy, M. K., Pirie, W. L., Waldman, D. A., & Silberman, J. (1999, February). *Assessment centers in business schools:*

Lessons learned from Valparaiso University and Arizona State University–West. Paper presented at the AACSB Outcome Assessment Seminar, Clearwater Beach, FL.

Detrick, G. (1999, February). *Utilizing comparative data analysis to support assessment and continuous improvement: Examples from the front lines.* Paper presented at the AACSB Outcome Assessment Seminar, Clearwater Beach, FL.

Dill, W. R. (1998, July/August). Specialized accreditation: An idea whose time has come? Or gone? *Change: The Magazine of Higher Learning, 30* (4), 18–25.

Eder, D. J. (1996). Assessing student achievement in the major: The departmentally owned senior assignment as an assessment mechanism. In T. W. Banta, J. P. Lund, K. E. Black, & F. W. Oblinger (Eds.), *Assessment in practice: Putting principles to work on college campuses.* San Francisco, CA: Jossey-Bass.

Eder, D. J., & Hirsch Jr., M. L. (1999a, February). *Assessment planning and implementation strategies.* Paper presented at the AACSB Outcome Assessment Seminar, Clearwater Beach, FL.

Eder, D. J., & Hirsch Jr., M. L. (1999b, February). *Setting assessment program and outcome objectives.* Paper presented at the AACSB Outcome Assessment Seminar, Clearwater Beach, FL.

Hill, I. B. (1996). Assessing student achievement in the major: Setting the context for assessment. In T. W. Banta, J. P. Lund, K. E. Black, & F. W. Oblinger (Eds.), *Assessment in practice: Putting principles to work on college campuses.* San Francisco, CA: Jossey-Bass.

Kuratko, D. F. (1996). Assessing student achievement in the major: New venture creation—the ultimate business course assessment. In T. W. Banta, J. P. Lund, K. E. Black, & F. W. Oblinger (Eds.), *Assessment in practice: Putting principles to work on college campuses.* San Francisco: Jossey-Bass.

Martinez, K. (1995, June). *Assessment, quality, and accreditation in schools of business.* Paper presented at the AAHE Conference on Assessment and Quality, Boston, MA.

Martinez, K. (2000, June). *The role of assessment in professional accreditation.* Paper presented at the AAHE Assessment Conference, Charlotte, NC.

Palmer, M. (1999, February). *Designs for data collection.* Paper presented at the AACSB Outcome Assessment Seminar, Clearwater Beach, FL.

Palomba, C. A., & Banta, T. W. (1999). *Assessment essentials: Planning, implementing, and improving assessment in higher education.* San Francisco: Jossey-Bass.

Palomba, N. A., & Palomba, C. A. (1999, May–June). AACSB accreditation and assessment in Ball State University's College of Business. *Assessment Update, 11* (3), 4–5, 15.

Presutti Jr., W. D. (1999, February). *Outcomes assessment: One school's experience in planning for and monitoring outcomes.* Paper presented at the AACSB Outcome Assessment Seminar, Clearwater Beach, FL.

Replogle, J. C. (1997). *Review of assessment progress.* Muncie, IN: Ball State University College of Business.

Srinivasan, S., & Wright, A. L. (1999, February). *Stakeholder involvement: Examples from the University of Louisville.* Paper presented at the AACSB Outcome Assessment Seminar, Clearwater Beach, FL.

Tallman, G. D., Jacobs, E. L., & Jacobs, N. W. (1999, February). *Developing course learning outcomes.* Paper presented at the AACSB Outcome Assessment Seminar, Clearwater Beach, FL.

Thacker, R. A. (1999, February). *Improving assessment effectiveness through stakeholder involvement: An example and specific actions.* Paper presented at the AACSB Outcome Assessment Seminar, Clearwater Beach, FL.

Weikle, R. D., Spears, M. C., Bradbard, D. A., & Maner, C. D. (1999, February). *Assessment planning from general design to a method of student learning outcomes.* Paper presented at the AACSB Outcome Assessment Seminar, Clearwater Beach, FL.

Williams, B. H., & Parsons, A. L. (1999, February). *Stakeholders involvement in assessment: Processes, applications, and continuous improvement.* Paper presented at the AACSB Outcome Assessment Seminar, Clearwater Beach, FL.

Williford, A. M. (1997). Ohio University's multidimensional institutional impact and assessment plan. In P. J. Gray & T. W. Banta (Eds.), *The campus-level impact of assessment: Progress, problems, and possibilities* (New Directions for Institutional Research, No. 100). San Francisco: Jossey-Bass.

8

ASSESSMENT OF STUDENT COMPETENCE IN COMPUTER SCIENCE

Gordon E. Stokes

Competence assessment, to be of real value, consists of three parts: (a) the determination of the competences to be assessed, (b) the utilization of an effective evaluation instrument based upon the selected competences to be assessed, and (c) a feedback mechanism in which the process of competence acquisition can be improved. Computer science presents an interesting study in the use and effectiveness of an assessment process in the development of the discipline.

Computer science is a young discipline whose history is well known. Professional societies existed in the computer area before an academic discipline was developed. These societies have influenced the determination of the concepts and competences that make up the discipline and continue to influence the definition of the computer science field. The field is very dynamic, with the scope of the discipline constantly expanding. In fact, new disciplines such as information systems, software engineering, and large segments of computer engineering have been developed out of the concepts of the computer science field. Many of the techniques and tools of assessment, from individual student assessment to institutional assessment, have been influenced and enabled by the application of technology coming from computer disciplines.

This chapter includes discussions of the influence of professional societies on defining the discipline, early efforts at assessment in the computer science area, the justification for the development and implementation of accreditation in the area to assist in evaluating valid programs, and some of the effects of the accreditation effort. The changes that are currently taking place in program and institutional assessment and some innovative methods of assessing student performance in particular computer science competences are presented. Because the history of the computer science discipline is so brief, the chapter takes a historical approach to the development of the discipline and of assessment in the discipline.

The Birth of a Discipline

In the late 1940s, after several years of experimentation and theorizing about the ability to carry out numeric computations electronically, working computers emerged from laboratory settings into functional activities solving interesting numeric problems. In the early 1950s, the production of computing machines as a business activity emerged and interest in the computing phenomenon began to increase.

Very early in the life of the computer as a viable device to solve real problems, a group of pioneers in the discipline formed a professional society to assist them in the exchange of ideas and to provide a forum for discussion. The society was called the Association for Computing Machinery (ACM). In the late 1950s, a vigorous debate went on among many practitioners about the characteristics, computing machines, and skills needed by the people who worked with the machines. This debate was carried out in the pages of the professional journal published by ACM.

Several phenomena contributed to the debate. Computers were being recognized as symbol manipulators or information processors as well as numeric computational devices. The theory driving the development of the field of computing came from mathematics (discrete mathematics), physics (devices and storage medium), linguistics (languages), psychology (symbol manipulation), and philosophy (formal logic). Practitioners came from the same collection of disciplines. Needs emerged for formal data structures to organize the data, organized approaches to algorithm development to solve problems being worked on by the computer, and software systems to control and exercise the computer to meet users' needs. By 1965, educational efforts for training computer professionals in the growing collection of needed competences were begun at the graduate and undergraduate level at 20 to 30 universities.

In 1968, the ACM published the first set of curriculum guidelines for training bachelor of science degree level students in a discipline that was called *computer science* (ACM Curriculum Committee on Computer Science, 1968). The foundation concepts of the discipline were established, and a set of competences was described. The first academic departments formed were closely associated with mathematics or physics departments, and the majority of early faculties came from these departments.

The body of material in computer science as defined by the ACM committee consisted of data structures, computer organization and architecture, systems programming, compiler construction, computational theory, programming languages, database systems, computer graphics, systems simulation, and artificial intelligence. The mathematics that supported the theory of computation was discrete structures.

Early Experiences and Issues

A body of knowledge was now defined, and assessment of students to check on their skills within that body of knowledge could begin. There was considerable experience in the assessment of learning in mathematics, but how do you assess a student's ability in nonmathematical areas? Is skill in programming demonstrated by the mastery of the syntax and the semantics of a programming language? Could having a student find programming errors in an already developed program check their programming skills? Could multiple choice questions be designed that would accurately measure programming skills?

The assessment of programming skill is not a simple task. A skilled programmer is expected to take a problem described in a conversational language; convert that description to a problem definition; derive a logically correct algorithm that will solve the problem; convert the algorithm to a programming language using proper syntax and semantics; submit the program to a computer system; and, using the error analysis output from the computer's attempt to execute the program, find and correct the syntactical and logical errors in the program. The programmer will repeat the execute and correct cycle until the program runs without errors.

Could students' programming skills be assessed without having their programs run on computers? The most demanding part of the programming exercise is the development of the algorithm to solve the problem and the modification of the algorithm to be logically correct. The adequate assessment of that portion of programming knowledge requires students to use computers. Computer science is a laboratory science in which computers are the central laboratory component. In fact, computers are the objects of study in computer science as well as a tool to help students learn computer skills. Any kind of accurate assessment of students' computer science skills has to include use of the computer as part of the teaching and part of the assessment.

The rapid increase of the use of computers in research laboratories of industry and government and their extensive use in the financial components of these enterprises from the mid-1960s to the mid-1970s created an insatiable demand for employees who could organize and utilize computer systems. Programs to teach computing-oriented skills sprang up all over the nation. Many of these programs had no computers, but they advertised that they could train students without them. In the early 1970s, the ACM organized many information campaigns warning prospective students of the ineffectiveness of computer training without computers. The ACM accreditation committee even investigated some type of accreditation standard for these training programs, but the task was beyond the means of the organization.

During the 1970s, the computer science departments of the major academic institutions resisted any attempts to impose an accreditation standard on the discipline at the university level. It was felt that the discipline was changing too fast to be constrained by a set of standards. There was also fear that the publication of a set of minimum requirements would encourage many administrators to accept the minimum standards as an acceptable level for their institutions. Computer science would then be shackled with an academic atmosphere in which many of the departments would be unable to move beyond the minimum requirements. Academic excellence in the discipline would be discouraged by academic administrators because of the cost of the laboratory-oriented discipline.

Accreditation Arrives

In the late 1970s and early 1980s, there was a decline in overall student enrollment at many institutions but computer science remained a very popular major that attracted many students to an institution. There was a big demand for computer science faculty. Some colleges and universities located in large population areas, unable to attract computer science faculty and having an excess of other departmental faculty, sent several of their faculty from a variety of departments to summer short courses in computer science topics and formed computer science departments with these faculty members. The ACM and the Institute of Electrical and Electronic Engineers (IEEE) Computer Society felt that they could no longer ignore this perversion of the discipline and this fraud upon students of the computer science programs at these institutions. The ACM and the IEEE Computer Society formed the Computing Sciences Accreditation Board (CSAB) with the intention first to establish accreditation standards for computer science and then to follow with the accreditation of other computer-related disciplines. The first Accrediting Commission of CSAB was the Computer Science Accreditation Commission (CSAC) formed during 1986 and 1987.

The accreditation criteria for assessment of computer science programs were developed by a joint committee appointed from the two sponsoring societies. In the late 1970s and early 1980s, both societies had produced curriculum documents relative to the developing field of computer science (ACM Curriculum Committee on Computer Science, 1979; IEEE Computer Society Educational Activities Board/Model Program Committee, 1983). These documents were used as the accreditation standards were drawn up. The desire of the committee working on the assessment standards was to leave the institution considerable flexibility but to maintain the integrity of the discipline and its academic content.

At the institutional level, the committee was concerned with faculty qualifications, the minimum number of faculty available, and the necessity for adequate computer laboratory facilities for students and faculty. They also were concerned about classroom space and equipment. They required an investigation of administrative and financial support for the computer science program by the college and university administration. The committee was also concerned with the interaction between computer science and other computer-related programs at the institution. These issues deal with the environment and the stability of the academic program in the setting of a particular institution.

In concerns directly related to students and the validity of program offerings, the committee specified broad levels of concept coverage in core courses and advanced courses. The concepts specified were drawn from the curriculum recommendation documents of the sponsoring societies. Concept requirements came from the supporting areas of science and mathematics as well as from the computer science discipline. Accreditation requirements also checked on the process used to validate a student's completion of the program specified by the computer science program of an institution.

The accreditation standards were approved by the sponsoring societies, and the formal accreditation process was first implemented in 1987. That process requires program faculty to conduct a self-study evaluating the program against the accreditation requirements. The first year, about one-third of the programs that applied for accreditation dropped out of the process early because in the self-study it became obvious that they had additional work to do.

For many years, the main assessment done by any academic computer science programs had been to ask, "Do our students find employment?"; for almost everyone, the answer was yes. If students were employable, faculty were satisfied with their programs. Accreditation caused departments to take a new look at themselves and to consider a larger set of questions.

As the new millennium begins, the Accreditation Board for Engineering and Technology (ABET) and the Computing Sciences Accreditation Board

(CSAB) have joined and introduced a new set of criteria for accreditation stressing the intent of accreditation requirements and leaving it to the institution to demonstrate that they meet the intent of the requirements. It is hoped that some of the rigidity of quantifying will be removed from the accreditation process and that accreditation groups will be able to examine the effectiveness of programs.

Accreditation has defined the minimum requirements for a computer science discipline and has passed that identity on to employers and to prospective students. This is a benefit to students and to society. Corporations that monitor the quality of computer science academic programs have observed a significant improvement in the quality of facilities and curriculum offerings of computer science programs across the nation. These improved programs have been a large contributor to the readiness of students who are better prepared to meet the challenge of producing the increasingly complex software required by the insatiable needs of the growing information society.

The Assessment of Student Competence

As computer science departments move to meet the intent of the accrediting agency criteria, they have been required to develop a description of competences they expect the graduates of their programs to acquire. After an extensive review of curriculum recommendations from professional societies, a review of accreditation requirements, a review of inputs from an industrial advisory group, and consideration of the mission statement of the University, Brigham Young University (BYU) Computer Science Department faculty derived a set of goals for computer science graduates. The department curriculum committee then developed enabling objectives that can be assessed to see if a goal is met. The goals and objectives for the BYU program are similar to those of the many other departments that were examined as these goals and objectives were established. The set of goals and objectives approved by the department faculty follow.

BYU Goals
The Bachelor of Science program of the BYU Computer Science Department will produce students who are

1. Qualified and capable of functioning as professional computer scientists in the workplace.

Enabling Objectives
A graduating student will

a. Have sufficient knowledge of discrete and continuous mathematics to support the concepts covered in the CS curriculum.
b. Be able to use an object-oriented approach to program design.
c. Be able to utilize internal data structures such as lists, trees, graphs, and so on.
d. Be familiar with external data structures and data processing environments such as indexes, hash tables, access methods, transaction processing, concurrency control, and the physical implementation of a distributed data management facility.
e. Have a good theoretical foundation in the basis of computing so that a student can perform needed analysis and read and understand the available research literature.
f. Have knowledge of existing algorithms for implementing computable operations and have the ability to analyze algorithms to determine their efficiency and effectiveness.
g. Have knowledge of computer hardware organization and computer architecture that will enable the student to make knowledgeable decisions in selecting hardware systems for enterprise tasks.
h. Understand programming languages, how they are specified, designed, and constructed. Be able use the algorithms that have been developed for implementation of a variety of programming language features.
i. Be familiar with operating systems, their construction and implementation, sufficient to be able to take advantage of the features of an operating system in the construction of software utilizing the operating system. The constructed software should be able to interact freely with the operating system in a distributed, heterogeneous environment.
j. Have a knowledge of the logical organization of data, data modeling, data normalization, data storage and retrieval, and the effects of the logical and physical organization of the data on the integrity of the data.
k. Have a knowledge of processes and procedures for the production of quality software. This should include specification, design, implementation, and testing of software as well as an understanding of the functioning of a team in the software production environment.

l. Have a knowledge of networking that includes the features and capabilities of lans, wans, internets, extranets, and intranets. The knowledge level should be sufficient to enable a student to select, implement, and utilize networking facilities in his/her programming environments.

m. Have a knowledge of the elements and structure of quality user interfaces. This will include information about human computer interaction, the creation and use of graphics environments, the use of animation, and the validation of the implementation of the interface.

n. Have a knowledge of the tools for working with information—lexical analyzers, parsers, code generators, program analyzers, and so on.

o. Have the ability to design, code, debug, test, and implement significant (> 10,000 lines of code) software systems.

2. Prepared for successful performance in graduate education programs in the computer science field.

Enabling Objective
In addition to meeting the objective for Goal I, a graduating student will have sufficient mathematical preparation and experience with the application of theory to perform well in graduate level studies.

3. Equipped with skills to enable lifelong learning in the computer science field.

Enabling Objectives
A graduating student will

a. Be able to master new concepts and technical skills without the assistance of an instructor or a teaching assistant.

b. Be able to solve problems not encountered before by utilizing his/her educational training, using the technical literature, and conferring with colleagues to assist in the development of the solution.

4. Literate and capable of communicating well in both the oral and written communication domains.

Enabling Objectives
A graduating student will be capable of writing well-structured and coherent technical reports and have the skills to organize and present information orally to both large and small groups.

5. Well grounded in ethical and moral values relating to their personal and professional lives.

   Enabling Objectives
   A graduating student will

   a. Have studied about personal and professional ethics.
   b. Have formulated and written out a personal code of ethics to assist in his/her life endeavors.

6. Broadly educated to enrich one's life experiences.

   Enabling Objective
   A graduating student will have studied at least two and one-half semesters in religion, history, the arts, and sciences in addition to his/her major classes.

Ohio State University Goals

At Ohio State University, faculty in the Computer Science and Engineering (CSE) Program within the Computer and Information Science (CIS) Department have developed a set of program and learning objectives that are available through the Web at http://www.cis.ohio-state/neelam/ugsc/programs/cseobjectives.html/. The latter site is maintained by Associate Professor Neelam Soundarajan who is chair of the department's undergraduate studies committee. The program and learning goals for CES majors are as follows:

1. To provide graduates with a thorough grounding in the key principles and practices of computing and in the basic engineering, mathematical, and scientific principles that underpin them.

   Students will

   a. Demonstrate proficiency in the areas of software design and development, algorithms, operating systems, programming languages, and architecture.
   b. Demonstrate proficiency in relevant aspects of mathematics, including discrete mathematics, as well as the appropriate concepts from physics and electrical circuits and devices.
   c. Successfully apply these principles and practices to a variety of problems.

2. To provide graduates with an understanding of additional engineering principles and the mathematical and scientific principles that underpin them.

Students will

a. Demonstrate an understanding of differential and integral calculus, differential equations, physics, and several areas of basic engineering sciences.
b. Have the ability to work with others and on multidisciplinary teams in both classroom and laboratory environments.

3. To provide graduates with an understanding of the overall human context in which engineering and computing activities take place.

Students will

a. Demonstrate an ability to communicate effectively.
b. Obtain familiarity with basic ideas and contemporary issues in the social sciences and humanities.
c. Obtain an understanding of social, professional, and ethical issues related to computing.

4. To prepare graduates for both immediate employment in the CSE profession and for admission to graduate programs in computing.

a. A large fraction of graduates will be immediately employed in high-technology companies that utilize their computing education.
b. Strong graduates from the program will be prepared to enter good graduate programs in CSE.

Many ways are available to develop evaluation instruments to check on the achievement by individual students of the objectives cited here. The traditional approaches of subjective and objective norm-referenced examinations are not well suited to check on a student's ability to design and implement software algorithms. Individual student assessment instruments using criterion-referenced evaluation, administered as a carefully designed mix of formative and summative exercises, hold more promise for meaningful assessment of student achievement.

Some Examples of Student Assessment

A description of the assessment program at Brigham Young University follows. This is followed by a brief sketch of the approach to assessing students employed in a large class at Michigan State University.

Brigham Young University

Given a set of objectives for a student's education, how do we measure the achievement of these objectives? As an example, let us look at Objective 15 under Goal I of "BYU Goals"—have the ability to design, code, debug, test, and implement significant (> 10,000 lines of code) software systems. How do we evaluate a student's mastery of this complex set of skills?

Faculty at Brigham Young University have struggled with this problem for several years and are convinced that, as students are introduced to the concepts and structures that assist in the development of working, reliable software, they must have extensive practice at actually producing such software to develop comprehension, retention, and transfer of those concepts. At BYU, classes that introduce and develop these concepts require many software development projects. In a project environment, it is difficult to assess an individual student's comprehension of the concepts involved because of the accessibility of teaching assistants, friends, and copies of projects from previous semesters. To validate a student's understanding of the concepts required to complete a project, faculty have designed objective exams given in a controlled testing environment. Assessment procedures in the introductory courses require a student to write short programs given a problem description or to produce program segments to perform specific operations. These evaluations require positive student identification and are monitored and timed. This environment can be created in the computer laboratories of the department and performed in real time, or the evaluations can be provided in a testing center with the solutions to the problems written out in the student's handwriting. The evaluations are designed so that students who have done their own work and have sought an understanding of the concepts being practiced have little difficulty in doing well on the evaluation. Students who have relied on a lot of outside help have a great deal of difficulty with these evaluations. Faculty have found that it takes a couple of evaluations before students begin to believe that the best way to prepare for the evaluation is to complete the projects assigned and to understand what they did to make the assigned projects successful. The evaluations are teacher—and teaching assistant (TA)—intensive for short periods of time in the correcting of the evaluations, but faculty have been able to handle courses with more than 600 students per semester using this style of evaluation.

In the course in which students finally do a large comprehensive project requiring design, programming, testing, debugging, and implementation of a complex set of requirements, the responsible faculty have used a slightly different approach to evaluation. After three semesters' experience, they have concluded that this approach is working well. The course requires students to employ a different programming language and a different programming environment than they have been using in previous courses. They have been using JAVA in an NT environment and are moved to C++ in a UNIX environment. If they have understood the concepts taught in the earlier courses, the transition to the new environment should be simple. When students begin the class, they are given three problem descriptions that are similar to problems they have solved in earlier courses. After four weeks in the course, students come to one of the department's programming laboratories and are given one of the three problems handed out earlier. They have three hours to design, program, test, and debug their program in the new environment of the current course. The most common reason for poor performance on this evaluation is the failure to prepare by working on the solutions to problems before the exam time. The next most common problem is that students have relied too heavily on assistance from teaching assistants (TAs) in previous courses and have not learned the concepts themselves. The course continues with the assignment of a problem that is complex and requires a substantive program to carry out the solution. Students are graded on the completed project; then, as a final check, they have an additional assessment. Students submit their completed projects to the course TAs, who then insert carefully selected errors (or bugs) into the objects and methods of the working programs. Students again come into the programming laboratory in a timed environment and are given their damaged projects to find the errors and correct them. If the programs are well designed, testing processes have been incorporated into the products, and students understand the entire design of the project, then the repair efforts are quite simple and students finish well within the time limits. Students are graded upon how many of the bugs they are able to find and correct. Faculty have found this evaluation process to be very effective in classes that have as many as 150 students per semester.

When the computer science department faculty try new approaches, such as those just described, the results are carefully monitored by the department's undergraduate curriculum committee. If the assessment approach seems to have merit, the undergraduate curriculum committee will make recommendations to the faculty and other faculty members will decide if the process is workable in their courses.

At BYU, faculty found many years ago that the most effective upper-division courses in preparing competent graduates were those that require large projects. Faculty have reached similar conclusions as they have been on accrediting teams visiting other institutions' programs. In the operating systems course at BYU, students build a multi-user operating system. In the compilers course, they implement a compiler for a specified language. In the computer architecture class, they design a computer architecture to meet certain specifications and create a simulator that will test the performance of that architecture. In the database class, they design, create, populate, and query a significant database system using good design principles such as normalization and mathematical analysis. Faculty are incorporating the form of the evaluation procedures of the programming class described in the previous paragraph into these project-oriented courses as rapidly as possible because they are assured that the evaluation process described is effective.

Michigan State University

At Michigan State University, the Computer Science and Engineering department had the task of designing a course to accommodate 1,800 students per semester. The faculty involved with the course rejected the traditional assessment and evaluation procedures that depend upon tests and quizzes that examine static recall (Urban-Lurain & Weinshank, 1999). They designed a course in which assessment

1. is entirely lab-based. The lab exercises build on concepts from the reading and homework,

2. replaces competitive grading with a collaborative learning model, and

3. replaces "points" with a series of mastery learning "Bridge Tasks."

A complete list of publications about this course and the approach faculty use for evaluation can be found at http://www.cse.msu.edu/~urban, "CSE 101 Papers and Presentations." A brief description of their evaluation process is given here.

Bridge tasks consist of a set of concepts and competences that are synthesized and applied to solve a set of real tasks. Bridge tasks are evaluated on a mastery/pass/fail basis, and the successful passing of a bridge task accumulates grade points toward the final score in the class. A student is allowed three attempts to pass a bridge task. The passing of the first bridge task locks in a grade of 1.0 for the course. The passing of four additional bridge tasks worth 0.5 each will bring the student's grade to 3.0, and then the student can choose a semester project that, successfully completed, can raise the grade to 3.5 or 4.0. The score for the project depends upon the complexity of the project the student chooses to complete.

The grade in the class is an indication of which concepts and competences a student has actually mastered. The first four bridge tasks have a specific set of competences and concepts. The fifth bridge task allows a student to specialize a bit to match his/her individual interests. There are three tracks of concepts and competences for the fifth task, and students can select one of the specified tracks to accumulate points toward their grade.

Part of the genius of the course is the way the bridge tasks are organized and generated. A bridge task is made up of a series of subtasks that evaluate the concepts and competences of interest. Each subtask has a set of instances that check the competence being evaluated, but each instance gives the student a different view of the problem. The collection of subtasks and instances are stored in a database. When a student requests a bridge task, the task is generated by choosing a specific instance under each subtask that makes up the bridge task. This allows every bridge task to be generated individually for each student. When a student attempts a second or third try at a bridge task, the problem they see will be different than the previous problems they have seen, but every generated task for a given bridge task level checks the same set of concepts and competences. An example of how instances of a subtask can vary follows.

One of the bridge tasks contains a subtask to test the concept of using Boolean operators to narrow searches in databases. Within that subtask, there are about 30 instances. Each instance requires a student to search the appropriate database to locate citations appropriate for a particular problem. Each search instance requires the student to use not only different search terms but also different combinations of Boolean operators. Thus, the concept is checked but the problem description varies. The selection of instances that check the various subtasks of a bridge task are generated as an HTML webpage that can be presented to the student as a problem assignment.

By utilizing the flexibility of the database of instances of subtasks, bridge tasks can be delivered in real time to a student's computer screen for administration in a supervised laboratory. Each student in the laboratory working on an evaluation has a custom webpage generated.

The Michigan State course design incorporates collaborative learning and a totally different approach to teaching and learning than is seen in the traditional university setting. The assessment and evaluation approach the faculty have devised is the key to making the whole system work.

Assessment of Department Performance

Both ABET in engineering accreditation and CSAB in computer science accreditation emphasized assessment in their year 2000 accrediting criteria. The assessment requirements of the CSAB accreditation process are given for an example. The accreditation requirements document can be accessed at http://www.csab.org.

Accreditation Criteria 2000

I. Objectives and Assessments

Intent: The program has documented, measurable objectives, including expected outcomes for graduates. The program regularly assesses its progress against its objectives and uses the results of the assessments to identify program improvements and to modify the program's objectives.

Standards:

I-1. The program must have documented, measurable objectives.

I-2. The program's objectives must include expected outcomes for graduating students.

I-3. Data relative to the objectives must be routinely collected and documented and used in program assessments.

I-4. The extent to which each program objective is being met must be periodically assessed.

I-5. The results of the program's periodic assessments must be used to help identify opportunities for program improvement.

I-6. The results of the program's assessments and the actions taken based on the results must be documented.

In their guidance for interpreting the criteria, CSAB indicates that faculty should seek input from students, faculty, and computing professionals in industry and government as they assess their programs. Faculty also are expected to examine information about the initial placement and subsequent professional development of students.

The CSAB requirements for program assessment have generated a flurry of activity in computer science departments across the nation. The first activity required to do responsible assessment is to develop the goals of the department's educational program.

The computer science discipline is a rapidly changing environment. It is important that students learn foundation principles that will carry them through a multitude of changes during their professional careers. Some of these principles have been presented in the curriculum documents of professional societies. Other principles come from the application of developing theories to the practice of the discipline. It is important to assess a student's comprehension of these foundation principles.

An additional source of guidance to academic departments about assessment of performance comes from the academic community's participation with practitioners of the discipline in the "real world." As computer science departments at the academic institutions form working relationships with various enterprises in their area, valuable feedback is provided to the academic institution about the performance of their graduates in the working world. Another important source of information is the performance of graduates of the undergraduate program in the various graduate programs that they enter for advanced educational degrees.

The true assessment of student competence must come from not only the student's performance in the undergraduate academic setting that checks an individual competence; but it must also come from the program graduates' extended experiences after leaving the undergraduate program.

Faculty in the Computer Science and Engineering (CSE) program at Ohio State University provide an excellent example of preparing for an ABET/CSAB accreditation self-study on the Web at http://www.cis.ohio-state.edu./ ~neelam/. Several of their assessment activities are described. For example, the faculty use surveys to query the program's graduating students, the program's alumni, and managers who are likely to hire their graduates. The surveys relate directly to program objectives of the department and ask for an evaluation of the importance of each objective and an evaluation of whether each objective was achieved. CSE graduates-to-be complete the survey on-line as a graduation requirement. The survey of CSE alumni is administered two and six years after graduation and gathers information about level of preparation and satisfaction with educational experiences. The managerial/supervisory questionnaire is sent to alumni of the College of Engineering who graduated 15 years prior to survey administration. The survey gathers opinions about the skills and abilities that are most important for future CSE graduates. An analysis of the replies to the department's 1998 and 1999 surveys are graphically presented on the website.

In addition to the surveys of graduates and employers, the department conducted a course content analysis. Faculty grouped their courses under five headings (Programming Languages, Computer Graphics, Software Spine, Software Engineering, and Theoretical Foundations) and carried out an extensive analysis of how each course in the group contributed to the department's desired learning objectives for their graduates. The faculty have matched each course in their program with ABET objectives as well as with CSE program objectives.

Minutes of the department's curriculum committee and faculty meetings are presented on the website. These minutes document the process of program and curriculum changes that occurred as the result of studying and evaluating the information from the department's assessment documents. The Ohio State process described on the referenced webpages is worthy of study and emulation. The process involves the creation and utilization of the program's objectives, the utilization of a set of existing accreditation requirements, and a thorough review of whether the department's program meets the desired outcomes.

In a meeting of the Computer Science Accreditation Committee at Arlington, Virginia, July 21–22, 2000, the methods of program assessment used by the computer science departments reviewed during the past year were summarized. The methods of assessment were

1. Student course evaluations

2. Exit interviews

3. Alumni surveys

4. Advisory committees

5. Employer surveys

6. Students' performance on exams and assignments

Focus was on the documentation, or lack thereof, of the goals of the departments and the results of the surveys and meetings. Departments need to keep minutes of the committee and faculty meetings in which goals and objectives are discussed and in which data are presented to help the faculty make decisions. It is not only important to collect data; it is also important to track how assessment data are used in improving the department's programs.

Lessons

How can a computer science department put in place a comprehensive assessment program to guide curriculum development and to build a quality program to produce a high level of student competence? Several components are needed:

1. A clear statement of the department's goals and objectives for learning should be developed. This effort should involve the faculty, and the goals and objectives adopted should be used in determining needed assessments.

2. Regular student assessment of the course material and faculty must be ongoing.

3. Some of the faculty must be involved in professional meetings in which curriculum reports are previewed and input from attendees is requested.

4. Some of the faculty should be involved in accreditation activities of the professional societies and should visit other computer science programs as program reviewers to enlarge their views of the educational effort.

5. Faculty should be well acquainted with professional society curriculum recommendations and with the discipline's accreditation requirements.

6. Departments should form industrial alliances that utilize practicing computer science professionals on department advisory councils to keep the department aware of the changing environments in the practicing world.

7. Student competence evaluation in the department's academic offerings should be closely examined and evaluations designed that truly test the acquisition of desired competences.

8. Regular feedback from graduates of the program should be sought to assist in determining the program's effectiveness in preparing graduates for employment or graduate education. The department might consider surveys of the graduates in the second and fourth years after their graduation.

9. A mechanism, such as a very active department curriculum committee, should be put in place to incorporate the feedback from the assessment documents into the department's curriculum upgrade and faculty replacement efforts.

References

ACM Curriculum Committee on Computer Science. (1968, March). Curriculum '68—Recommendations for academic programs in computer science. *Communications of ACM, 11* (3), 151–197.

ACM Curriculum Committee on Computer Science. (1979, March). Curriculum '78—Recommendations for the undergraduate program in computer science. *Communications of ACM, 22* (3), 147–166.

IEEE Computer Society Educational Activities Board/Model Program Committee. (1983). *The 1983 IEEE Computer Society Model Program in Computer Science and Engineering,* New York: IEEE Computer Society.

Urban-Lurain, M., & Weinshank, D. J. (1999, April). *Mastering computing technology: A new approach for non–computer science majors.* Paper presented at the Annual Meeting of the American Educational Research Association, Division C, Section 7, Montreal, Canada.

9

ASSESSING STUDENT COMPETENCE IN ENGINEERING

John A. Muffo

Engineers are problem solvers, can-do people who identify difficulties that need to be fixed, then fix them. The problems often have to do with a mechanical or industrial process in areas like transportation, construction, mining, or biotechnology. The range of issues with which engineers deal is broad. The important thing in the end is that there is a problem, usually physical in nature, that must be addressed for an organization or activity to move forward; and the engineer is the one who addresses it.

This central theme helps explain engineering assessment: Engineers are analytical thinkers who seek the best solution to a problem, usually by the most direct means. One would expect, therefore, that engineering assessment would be straightforward and direct, just like engineers themselves. This is the way that it has been until recently. Changes in the accreditation process have left engineers in a world somewhat alien to them, one placing increased emphasis on "soft" subjects such as communication and lifelong learning while seeming to take traditional knowledge in mathematics, the physical sciences, and engineering for granted. This has occurred in an environment shifting to an emphasis on outcomes over inputs, again one that is quite different from that of the past.

Accreditation and Assessment

The organization that accredits engineering programs is known as the Accreditation Board for Engineering and Technology, or ABET. It began in 1932 as the Engineer's Council for Professional Development (ECPD) and became ABET in 1980. It now accredits some 2,300 engineering, engineering technology, and engineering-related programs.

What is unusual about ABET among accrediting organizations is that it is a federation of 28 professional engineering and technical societies. Its Board of Directors sets policy and approves accreditation criteria. Engineering, like law, medicine, dentistry, nursing, and a few other fields, has licensure requirements that normally include graduation from an accredited institution of higher education, so ABET accreditation is critical for a school or college of engineering. Not all engineers seek licensure, and it depends a bit on the field of study whether or not licensure is necessary or even desirable; but not being accredited would be a real setback, since it would make licensure very difficult to achieve in many states. Alternatives to sitting for the licensure examination are technically possible but rarely used.

Licensure normally requires passing a written examination in addition to having an accredited degree, but the degree usually is required in order to sit for the examination in the first place. In addition, many graduate programs in engineering require that the bachelor's degree be from an accredited institution if the prospective student is to be admitted. Waivers are often granted for international students and the few who enter from nonengineering undergraduate programs. The latter have to make up engineering courses, however.

Another distinction that sets ABET apart from most other accrediting bodies is the strong role of industry representatives. A large percentage, though less than half, of those serving on visiting committees is drawn from industry rather than academe. The presence of professionals from the field on the visiting teams lends a more industrial and product-oriented perspective than one would find on more traditional teams.

In the past, ABET accreditation was well known for being input-oriented and focusing on details. The emphasis was on teaching and verifiable evidence of course quality as opposed to student learning. Colleges and universities worried about receiving citations for minor violations at an extremely fine level of measurement. Searching to find a student file with one missing credit hour of this or that was considered by some reviewers to be exemplary behavior. Slavishly obeying rigid rules was the norm. Few questions were asked about results or output other than student placement. As in most traditional accreditation, the assumption was that if all the inputs were of high quality and the rules were followed closely, then something of high quality would have to result. This led to an ever-increasing number of required courses in engineering programs and fewer technical and nontechnical electives, along with a general rigidity about the curriculum. It appeared that nothing could be considered for change and, especially, for elimination, because "ABET requires it."

In the late 1990s, ABET 2000 came along to stand the entire process on its head (Muffo & Kurstedt, 1997; Rogers, 1999; Shaeiwitz, 1999). *ABET 2000* is the term used to describe the new accreditation standards gradually implemented during that time, with 2000 being the last year in which a third of the engineering programs could still be accredited under the old criteria. The standards emphasize outcomes and nontechnical skills to a much greater extent than anything seen previously. They are much less rigid as well. "Considerable latitude in the choice and arrangement of subject matter in the curriculum is allowed. While the qualitative factors are more important than the quantitative assignment of credit hours to any particular area, the general principles outlined in the criteria will be checked closely by analyzing each particular curriculum. The coverage of basic information rather than the offering of specific courses is the important criterion" (II.D.1 of the 2000–2001 Policy Manual, p. 5, available at http://www.abet.org/accreditation/).

Criterion 3 — The Cornerstone of ABET's Assessment Initiative

The most outcomes-oriented component of ABET accreditation is known as *Criterion 3*, the one that specifies which outcomes are required in an accredited program. Unlike in the past, when the focus was on specific courses and course content that engineering faculty felt comfortable in discussing, Criterion 3 addresses knowledge and skills described in a general way. Worse yet from the engineer's point of view, many of the abilities described in Criterion 3 are considered "soft" and difficult to measure. Criterion 3 states that engineering graduates should possess:

A. An ability to apply knowledge of mathematics, science, and engineering

B. An ability to design and conduct experiments, as well as to analyze and interpret data

C. An ability to design a system, component, or process to meet desired needs

D. An ability to function on multidisciplinary teams

E. An ability to identify, formulate, and solve engineering problems

F. An understanding of professional and ethical responsibility

G. An ability to communicate effectively

H. The broad education necessary to understand the impact of engineering solutions in a global and societal context

I. A recognition of the need for and ability to engage in lifelong learning

J. A knowledge of contemporary issues

K. An ability to use the techniques, skills, and modern engineering tools necessary for engineering practice

The challenge presented to engineering faculty by such a list is that it does not state *how* such knowledge and abilities are supposed to occur, just that they are. In addition, there is ample room for interpretation, even in areas such as design, where the faculty feel very much at home. Besides the fact that such things as an appreciation for lifelong learning are difficult to measure, there has been a nagging concern that the loosely constructed standards somehow might be used against them.

Observations About ABET 2000

Many of the following observations are drawn from several years of working with the SUCCEED Coalition, a group of eight southeastern universities with engineering programs. The coalition, which was funded for nearly a decade by the National Science Foundation, consisted of Clemson University, Florida A&M University, the Georgia Institute of Technology (Georgia Tech), North Carolina A&T University, North Carolina State University, the University of Florida, The University of North Carolina at Charlotte, and the Virginia Polytechnic Institute and State University (Virginia Tech). One of the projects that was part of SUCCEED had to do specifically with assessment of engineering programs and was aimed at assisting member institutions to be successful with the ABET 2000 criteria. More information about the activities and products of the SUCCEED Coalition can be found at the website at http://www.succeed.vt.edu/.

One of the unusual aspects of ABET 2000 from an outsider's point of view is the apparent lack of support for the new criteria among many of the faculty affected by it. Discussions with faculty at a number of colleges and universities reveal little support for the new criteria or understanding of the concepts behind them. It is as if some outside agency, influenced by industry and government, had imposed this new approach rather than their own accreditation body.

Related to the apprehension concerning the ABET 2000 criteria themselves is a concern about reviewer training. Campus faculty worry that some reviewers trained under the old system will not be able to make the mental switch and will fall back on searching for small infractions. Those responsible for ABET implementation have similar concerns and may not permit some people trained under the old system to be reviewers for ABET 2000. Like all culture changes, this one presents its own set of challenges.

One other unique aspect of ABET accreditation is that each discipline has its own accreditation criteria *in addition to* the more general ABET criteria. So, not only does a department have to meet the usual ABET requirements, it also has to meet the requirements of its own professional society.

Assessment Practices in Engineering

How have engineers assessed their programs, whether for ABET or internal purposes, or both? The first step has been to challenge themselves to consider student learning rather than teaching alone, asking how students learn and apply basic science and engineering principle to provide engineering solutions to real problems. Faculty also have asked how students in their classes learn to understand and use engineering principles and which principles they learn and why. Faculty have described how they know that the students have learned what faculty say they should be learning. It was rough going at first, but once faculty began addressing the issues from a learning standpoint, a great deal began to happen. Often they liked the idea of setting goals and objectives and then matching measures of student learning to those, since such an approach is quite logical and engineers appreciate logical solutions. Most try to stay current in their fields also, so their courses already do many of the things encouraged by assessment but often not in such an organized and documented manner. The step-by-step, rational approach to assessment has been quite appealing to engineers when implemented in the right way.

The example here of the logical thinking of engineers comes from the Department of Electrical Engineering at Virginia Tech. Using the following suggested format put forward by Professor Kwa-Sur Tam, the faculty adopted the ABET a–k criteria to describe the major learning objectives of all courses, thereby linking course objectives directly to ABET accreditation requirements. The experiment proved to be so successful that this format is now required for all new course and independent study proposals. The faculty outside the department found the process to be so useful that it is now required by the entire college for all new and existing courses.

Course Objectives/Criteria Reference Chart

Course: _____ Prepared by: _____ Date: _____

Course Learning Objective	Overall Educational Objective (Enter level number defined below)										
1	A	B	C	D	E	F	G	H	I	J	K
What will be measured to demonstrate that this learning objective has been achieved?											
2	A	B	C	D	E	F	G	H	I	J	K
What will be measured to demonstrate that this learning objective has been achieved?											
3	A	B	C	D	E	F	G	H	I	J	K
What will be measured to demonstrate that this learning objective has been achieved?											
4	A	B	C	D	E	F	G	H	I	J	K
What will be measured to demonstrate that this learning objective has been achieved?											

Overall Educational Objectives

    A. To develop the ability to apply knowledge of mathematics, science, and engineering

    B. To develop the ability to design and conduct experiments, as well as to analyze and interpret data

    C. To develop the ability to design a system, component, or process to meet desired needs

    D. To develop the ability to function on multidisciplinary teams

    E. To develop the ability to identify, formulate, and solve engineering problems

    F. To provide an education on professional and ethical responsibility

    G. To develop the ability to communicate effectively

    H. To provide an education on the impact of engineering solutions in a global and societal context

    I. To develop the ability to engage in lifelong learning

    J. To provide an education on contemporary issues

    K. To develop the ability to use the techniques, skills, and modern engineering tools necessary for engineering practice

Level
   1. Major emphasis of the course
   2. Discussed in the course and covered in homework or quiz
   3. Mentioned in the course but not covered in homework or quiz
   4. Not mentioned in the course

One of the benefits of using this approach is that it enables a department or the college to identify gaps in the curriculum as well as providing an overview of what each course is attempting to accomplish.[1]

Once a list of goals and objectives has been identified, there are a number of ways to determine how well those are being met. In engineering, common sources have included student, alumni, and employer feedback. The Department of Industrial and Systems Engineering report at the Virginia Tech website (http://www.aap.vt.edu/reports.html) provides good examples of these. Here, faculty have been encouraged to do what is easiest in their specific environments. Sometimes departments have done exit interviews for years, so that sort of student feedback has already been gathered. If this is the case, one must ask whether faculty have gotten the kind of information that has been helpful for program improvement and whether changes have been made where appropriate. Other departments have done student surveys or focus groups. At Georgia Tech, the university assessment coordinator, a nonengineer from outside the department, conducts focus groups with seniors (Joseph Hoey, personal correspondence, August 2000). Most engineers are not trained in survey research and often are not comfortable developing surveys from scratch. Having someone provide them with existing instruments and critique their draft surveys has contributed substantially to survey improvement. Engineering faculty are the content experts and retain control of the survey text in these situations, but those assisting with formatting questions and providing similar technical expertise have provided a valuable service.

In thinking about generating all forms of feedback, including that from students, creativity is important. For example, the tradition of advisory committees is one that is helpful in engineering assessment. It is something that is common and trusted in the culture and that can be a good source of information on a variety of topics. One department at Virginia Tech has used an industrial advisory committee to aid in obtaining unbiased information from current students. The department has used one of its advisory committee meetings to bring together current students and the committee of alumni and other industry experts in the field. They give the members of the advisory committee a set of questions to ask students, then leave the room. The committee members chat with students for a time, then summarize the results for sharing with faculty after students have left. In this way students feel free to say what is on their minds, since faculty are not in the room to hear them, but faculty get the information from students via the advisory committee. The committee members are familiar with the discipline and consequently understand most of the issues involved, so there are few translation problems. They also acquire better insight into departmental matters as a result of the exercise.

Alumni feedback normally comes in the form of written survey responses, since graduates are dispersed around the globe and not very easy to reach, even by telephone. As with student surveys, alumni surveys require technical assistance if the instruments are to produce information useful for program improvement purposes. Where program improvement is the primary goal, limiting the survey population to relatively recent graduates has been the norm. Identifying mailing lists and related issues are important considerations, though some engineering departments and colleges have their own alumni newsletters and consequently may have a better address database than the institution as a whole. Alumni advisory committees have been another source of valuable feedback when members are approached in a systematic fashion.

Electronic surveys increasingly have been used in place of the paper-and-pencil variety. Web-based surveys of existing students have become commonplace. The day when alumni, especially those who have graduated recently, have easy access to such surveys is nearly upon us as well. A central unit, such as the dean's office, that supports such surveys for all departments has been a boon to assessment at the academic unit level. The hard work of developing a good survey instrument still must involve the department, however.

Employer feedback has been a tricky topic with engineers. Since they tend to be more externally oriented than academics in many other disciplines, engineers often want to know what employers think about their graduates and about the department/school/college generally. At the same time, however, they have favored an easy approach, that is, mailed surveys. Unfortunately, mailed surveys of employers often attract return rates of only 10–15%. Many engineering faculty do not like to hear that and conduct such surveys anyway, with predictable results.

Even some industry representatives have argued that such surveys are possible and encouraged faculty to try them on an experimental basis, again with the predicted outcome. As an example, the assessment work group in the SUCCEED Coalition, which included corporate representatives, was determined to create a model mail survey for universities to use for ABET accreditation purposes. Return rates were very low despite a sound instrument and the best advice of the corporate members.

Engineers have some alternatives in obtaining information from employers. One set of options has to do with using contacts that are close by. Advisory committees often are composed of those who hire graduates, though they may not be representative of all employers. Internship and cooperative education supervisors are evaluating students in their programs already. Although they employ students and not necessarily program graduates, they provide a lot of information to the faculty about strengths and weaknesses of students nearing the end of their programs. Another group providing employer data consists of those who come on campus to conduct interviews with graduating students; taking some of the interviewers to dinner has revealed a lot about perceived program strengths and weaknesses.

Going beyond existing networks, faculty in some engineering programs have telephoned 10 or more employers, asking about strengths and weaknesses. Even if some employ only one graduate of the program, soon common patterns emerge from the responses that suggest factors beyond individual differences among alumni. A side benefit has been that many industry people enjoy being contacted for their opinions and not just, as some have said, when the institution wants money, the placement of a student, or some other favor. Faculty at North Carolina State University and elsewhere have collected the names and telephone numbers of employer supervisors from alumni (Hoey & Gardner, 1999). Though the number of names collected has been small, it has been sufficient to permit calls that help to identify patterns of strengths and weaknesses. This approach also has eliminated the concern of some faculty that contacting employers without graduates' permission infringes the privacy of these former students. Obviously none of these techniques yield random samples; they just may be the best that can be done under the real-world circumstances in which assessment operates.

Employers send mixed messages about their feedback. Many say they want institutions to improve their programs so that graduates can handle the complexities of working in today's environment. Those hiring engineers make even stronger pronouncements about this than others. At the same time, one often hears that employers do not have time to talk to engineering educators about the alumni they have hired and for legal reasons will not talk about individuals in any case. This reluctance was encountered by the SUCCEED assessment group in talking with employers.

The use of surveys, while desirable, does not yield as much information about student learning as do direct measures such as course assignments and exams. Here, the first step has been to use existing tools. The senior design course in engineering has a long history and is widely accepted by faculty as a useful learning and assessment experience. If well conceived, such a course reveals much about what a student knows and is able to do. Often, design courses are based on real-life problems solicited from industry, with presentations of possible solutions provided back to industry. In other cases, students initiate the projects, for example, in aeronautical engineering designing an airplane that flies on the computer, followed by a model of it that flies in a wind tunnel. Sometimes the projects require group work, since industry has long told engineering educators that smooth group process is necessary for success in today's work environments. Sometimes multiple faculty are involved in evaluating the projects, and often industry representatives assist with evaluation as well. Many aspects of the educational experience have been included in the projects. These are extremely time-consuming but rewarding experiences for students. The very nature of the design project, as with those involving groups, has presented special assessment challenges, but the availability and thoroughness of the tool have made it well worth exploring.

While it is common for senior engineering design courses to be used to provide assessment data, at the same time these design courses address real industry problems, often with the assistance of design engineers in the field. Often the best student projects are entered into national competitions. As an example, the American Institute of Chemical Engineers (AICS) has an annual design competition. AICS presents a general design problem, and practicing design engineers specify and refine it. In recent years at Virginia Tech, engineers from the Radford Army Arsenal have worked with the faculty member teaching the course to present real problems and to judge, along with the faculty member, student solutions to them. The two best student projects are sent on to national competitions, and all students receive feedback in a number of areas of expertise, including communication and teamwork as well as engineering creativity, feasibility, and so on. Common student strengths and weaknesses are noted and reported to the faculty as a whole; this information is used in curricular planning. It is not uncommon for industry representatives, such as those at the Radford Arsenal, to be so impressed that job offers are made to graduating design students.

In recent years, much attention has been given to portfolios for engineering assessment, particularly with the advent of computer storage capabilities that make electronic portfolios more feasible. Rose-Hulman Institute of Technology has been among the leading proponents of portfolios in engineering (Rogers & Williams, 1999). The usual drawbacks apply here as elsewhere: Who keeps all of the projects? How can they be assembled in such a way as to be assessed easily? Who makes such judgments? By what criteria? Can sampling be used? The fact that there are challenges should not preclude the use of portfolios, but it does mean that such issues need to be addressed before the move to portfolios is implemented. The size of the academic unit and institution may have a major impact on the feasibility of such an approach. On the other hand, it has been possible to collect in a portfolio individual examples of class assignments that meet specific goals and objectives in an engineering program.

Regardless of the data-gathering techniques used, engineering students are similar to other students in the types of faculty behavior that yield maximum student learning. A study conducted by researchers at Penn State and involving six other universities yielded the following conclusion: "Findings show that the instructional practices of Instructor Interaction and Feedback, Collaborative Learning, and Clarity and Organization are significantly and positively associated with gains in students' self-reported gains in problem solving skills, group skills, and understanding of engineering as a occupation" (Cabrera, Colbeck, & Terenzini, in press).

In the past few years, engineering faculty and those with assessment expertise from outside engineering have been encouraged to work together more closely by research projects sponsored by the National Science Foundation (NSF) and other federal agencies that require assessment of results by an external evaluator. NSF instructional grants now require that assessment be built into the proposal, along with a budget and an identified assessment expert. Increasingly, engineering and other faculty seeking such grants ask for assistance from an outside expert in writing the assessment portion of the proposal; if the grant application is successful, they use part of the grant funds to support personnel and other expenses in the home unit of the assessment expert. Often the funds are used for student assistance to do the detail work on the assessment portion of the grant, with the assessment expert's time being used for the required matching funds. For a guide on structuring such projects, see Olds and Miller, 1997. A monograph by Rogers and Sando (1996) can be used for these projects or assessment of entire programs.

Special Features of Engineering

A few examples of special assessment approaches used by engineering faculty have been mentioned previously, but there are other ways in which engineering appears to be different from other disciplines and thereby provides special assessment opportunities and challenges.

The first of the special features is the Fundamentals of Engineering (FE) examination. Like a number of other fields, such as accounting and nursing at the undergraduate level and law and medicine at the graduate/professional level, engineering has an examination that is required for licensure and is administered externally, usually by the state. Department faculty often use high FE pass rates as a sign of program quality, but pass rates alone do not say much about the strengths and weaknesses of an instructional program. Thus, they are not particularly helpful in suggesting areas for program improvement. FE score reports by section can help faculty determine whether students are especially weak in statics or dynamics or some other portions of the examination. These reports can be and are used in program improvement.

Another feature of the FE examination is that, depending on the discipline, varying proportions of students sit for the exam. In fields such as civil engineering, where licensure is necessary for a variety of jobs, the rate may be high, but in electrical engineering or other areas, it may be low. Some departments and colleges require all students to take the FE examination, with predictable results in those cases where students are not interested and see no benefit in taking it. One must look at the percentage of students taking the exam and their academic profiles as compared to other students before accepting high (or low) FE pass rates as a sign of quality.

Another of the special features of engineering that can have applications in undergraduate assessment is the frequent use of competitions that test student knowledge and skills, as well as showcase talent to potential employers. Student groups, often following internal institutional competitions, compete with groups from other institutions to see who can design the best solar automobile to race cross-country or the best concrete canoe or the best human powered submarine. Egg drops from high places are popular, as are a number of other projects. Engineering faculty are understandably proud of doing well in such competitions. But one must be careful here, too, in accepting such results as signs of student learning excellence, since the teams often are highly selective and not representative of the average or typical student.

Cooperative education is another common practice in engineering academic units, though some nonengineers also participate in co-op and unpaid internship experiences. In co-op programs, students alternate going to college for an academic term and working for an academic term. Co-op programs have a long history in engineering and are intended to help students understand why they do certain things in the classroom while they are acquiring valuable work experience. Employers tend to prefer co-op students over those without such work experience, and faculty often say that they can distinguish the co-op students in their classes from those who do not have co-op experience because they differ in maturity. Traditionally, co-op programs require the hiring company to complete evaluation forms about student abilities. For assessment purposes, these can be revised to include more questions aimed at identifying program strengths and weaknesses.

Many disciplines, often as a result of employer and alumni feedback, have been working on improving student oral and written communication skills. In some cases, this has led to the formation of strong communications programs in engineering departments themselves. For example, at Indiana University–Purdue University Indianapolis, technical writing faculty from the English department have been hired to work with engineering faculty and students. Similarly, in the College of Engineering at Virginia Tech, technical writing faculty from the English department have been appointed to work with engineering faculty in particular and directly with the students to a lesser extent. Such specialization may not be as necessary outside engineering, but the disciplines within engineering differ substantially from each other in their writing requirements and traditions. Civil engineers, for example, need to write for state and federal government regulators, while engineering scientists need to keep records in such a way as to protect patent rights. The other disciplines differ similarly. As a consequence, the type of writing needed must be learned in engineering by engineering students. Many faculty do not feel comfortable correcting grammar, spelling, and so on, so having an English professor nearby who is familiar with engineering can assist both faculty and students. Assessment can and should help determine how well the process is working. After assessment results demonstrated the success of the initial writing program in the Engineering Science and Mechanics department at Virginia Tech, the program was expanded into the entire college, with financial support from industry.

The Culture of Engineering

One of the basic principles of assessment in any discipline is that the culture of the discipline influences the assessment and working with the academic unit generally. In the case of engineering, the issue of culture is perhaps even stronger than in other disciplines. The first curriculum at the U.S. Military Academy at West Point was an engineering one (Rudolph, 1962, pp. 228–229), and a high percentage of Reserve Officer Training Corps (R.O.T.C.) scholarships still goes to engineers. The freshman year in many programs is well known for academic rigor, with a heavy load of such courses as mathematics, chemistry, physics, and/or some introduction to engineering. These programs are known also for high dropout/transfer rates and a "survival of the fittest" mentality. Long hours of lab work and pressure to raise research money and publish are strong in colleges of engineering at large universities and exist to a lesser degree at smaller institutions.

Perhaps the most important part of the engineering culture from the assessment standpoint is the level of certainty that engineers have in their work. As a colleague who designs airplane landing gear once said, if his design fails even once in 1,000 times, people die. In assessment, on the other hand, if something works more than half of the time, that is probably a successful program. The levels of certainty at which most engineers operate is so far beyond those common to assessment that engineers find assessment hard to comprehend. They are trained in disciplines such as mathematics, chemistry, and physics and use the tools of these fields as study, applications, and research become more sophisticated. In these fields, there is generally one answer to a question, one best solution. That landing gear (or bridge) has to work every time or people die. The more probabilistic techniques used in assessment are foreign territory and suspect at first glance.

Since assessment depends a great deal on social science methodologies, there tends to be an inherent distrust of it. The field employs what many engineers would consider to be pseudoscience or soft methodologies to study student learning—not something in which most engineers are interested. Faculty in the branch of industrial engineering that focuses on such matters as human-machine interaction are most likely to develop an interest in assessment. Unfortunately, this creates an imbalance among engineering disciplines with respect to involvement in assessment.

Engineers and engineering faculty care deeply about whether or not something works to solve a problem. They may not implement the solution themselves, but they create the methods and products that will be used. This distinguishes engineering faculty from those in many other disciplines. In assessment, this creates opportunities for using such common curricular features as the capstone design experience for assessment purposes. Applied engineering design courses are common as capstone experiences and capture much of the student learning in a program. Such courses can serve as a useful assessment tool while at the same time being widely accepted by the faculty.

Reward systems affect the success of assessment throughout academe; those institutions that do not reward assessment or even good teaching cannot expect successful assessment processes. The reward system in engineering, especially at larger universities, is often connected to research funding and publications even more than in other fields. In addition, engineering faculty have opportunities for industrial consulting, patent applications, spin-off companies, and a range of industry-related activities that draw them away from campus even when the work is related to teaching and other campus-based activities.

Faculty in engineering today are producing students who command generous salaries and benefits and even signing bonuses at the bachelor's level, let alone at the graduate level. Those who receive daily telephone calls from recruiters wanting to hire their students have difficulty understanding why anyone wants to examine the quality of what they do. The very fact that their graduates are so attractive to industry in itself is sufficient evidence of high quality from their perspective. It is not easy to convince them that, even if they are successful at this point, improvements can still be made and assessment can assist in the process.

Not all of the features described here as part of the culture of engineering have negative repercussions for assessment; in fact, a number of them can be quite positive. First, engineers can be very straightforward, telling you exactly what they think at the outset. While such bluntness can seem harsh sometimes, you usually know where you stand with them. There are no games. Second, the direct, military approach can have its advantages when, as is the case now, disciplinary as well as regional accreditation requires assessment. The faculty understand requirements and will provide the effort needed to meet them, though in some cases with the least amount of effort possible.

Lessons Transferable to Other Disciplines

Up to this point, the chapter has focused primarily on engineering and related disciplines. One might ask how all of this applies to other fields of study. While engineers may appear to be a different breed, a number of lessons learned from examining engineering are transferable to other disciplines.

Probably the most overarching lesson is that of disciplinary culture, especially at larger universities. The culture of the discipline must drive the assessment process. What faculty trust in the way of data and approaches to problems has much to do with their field of study. Engineers tend to want data and a single correct answer to a problem while English professors seek writing samples and are more comfortable with ambiguity. One size does not fit all. Trying to impose numerical data requirements or writing samples on all departments will not end in success because all of the faculty will not trust the results.

Each discipline has tools in its curriculum for assessment; for example, engineering programs routinely employ capstone design courses in the curriculum, while music and theater programs have performances, art has exhibits, and mathematics requires proofs. Using the tools available makes the assessment process much easier and gives the results more credibility. Faculty determining how they should approach assessment first should identify the kinds of things that are going on already that might be adapted for assessment purposes. Often, good things have been going on for a long time but have not been called *assessment* or require only slight changes in order to be useful for assessment purposes. Similarly, assessment does not have to look the same within the same general field. For instance, some engineering units do exit interviews of seniors while others depend on surveys; some use portfolios while others rely entirely on senior projects.

A corollary lesson for nonengineers is that the perspectives of engineering and other fields can be helpful in looking at assessment in a different way. It is common, for example, to see flow diagrams in engineers' discussions of the assessment process, since this is how they describe physical processes that they study. There is a tendency among engineers to approach assessment from a systems point of view (see DiBiasio, 1999, for an example from the Civil Engineering Department at Worcester Polytechnic Institute). Not only is this helpful for them in communicating with each other about the issues involved but also it can provide new insights to nonengineers who have worked with assessment in other contexts.

Specialization can be a barrier to progress in all fields. Being experts themselves, many engineering faculty would prefer to leave assessment to other experts rather than having to be involved with it themselves. In other cases, faculty are more comfortable with solutions to assessment problems that are presented by members of the discipline than by those outside it.

Faculty reward systems, especially at large research-oriented universities, do not provide much incentive for faculty to be heavily involved in assessment. In a few instances, a line of research in education in the field might be developed and produce findings publishable in the appropriate journals, but this often is not considered high-status research by other faculty who make the initial promotion and tenure recommendations. Even getting education grants from agencies such as the National Science Foundation does not have the same status as more scientific research.

Where disciplinary assessment exists, many of the approaches are still in a transitional phase. Those that have been more successful have been implemented on a gradual basis with a lot of discussion within the field, while those getting less support have been implemented in a more radical or drastic fashion. Most people prefer gradual over radical change if change must occur.

Random sampling and other statistical procedures, while desirable, do not necessarily result in representative samples. A higher proportion of successful alumni, for instance, may respond to an alumni survey than do those who consider themselves less successful. Those companies hiring only a few employees are less likely to be reached by employer surveys than those with a lot of employees. Sometimes convenience samples of various kinds have to be used to gather data in the absence of anything else. All that one can do in some cases is to try to minimize bias as effectively as possible so that the measures being used apply to most students or alumni, not just the best and the brightest. For example, some faculty will state that most of their students go on to graduate school. This usually tends to be far from the truth but does represent fairly the thinking of those faculty who are teaching primarily the few who do go on to graduate or professional school. Sometimes in assessment one has to settle for the best data available, which would not necessarily be the best data if one were free to define the circumstances.

Finally, old ways die hard in assessment as elsewhere. It is difficult for successful people to give up approaches to teaching and learning that have helped make them successful while using methodologies alien to them to find out if there are other approaches that work better in enhancing student learning. A lot of empathy is needed to be successful in assessment.

Note

1. Special thanks to Professor C. E. Nunnally for sharing this format.

References

Cabrera A. F., Colbeck C. L., & Terenzini P.T. (2001). Developing performance indicators for assessing classroom teaching practices and student learning: The case for engineering. *Research in Higher Education,* 42 (2), 327–352.

DiBiasio, D. (1999). Outcomes assessment: An unstable process? *Chemical Engineering Education,* 33 (2), 116–120.

Hoey, J. J., & Gardner, D. C. (1999). Using surveys of alumni and their employers to improve an institution. In J. Pettit & L. H. Litten (Eds.), *A new era of alumni research: Improving institutional performance and better serving alumni.* (New Directions in Institutional Research, No. 101) San Francisco: Jossey Bass.

Muffo, J. A., & Kurstedt, P. (1997). Assessment in engineering begins a new era. *Assessment Update,* 9 (4), 4, 15.

Olds, B. M. & Miller. (1997). A measure of success. *ASEE Prism,* 7, 24–29.

Rogers, G. M. (1999). Outcomes assessment: Opportunity on the wings of danger. *Chemical Engineering Education,* 33 (2), 106–115.

Rogers, G. M., & Sando, J. K. (1996). *Stepping ahead: An assessment plan development guide.* Terre Haute, IN: Rose-Hulman Institute of Technology.

Rogers, G. M., & Williams, J. (1999). Building a better portfolio. *ASEE Prism,* 8 (5), 30–32.

Rudolph, F. (1962). *The American college and university: A history.* New York: Random House.

Shaeiwitz, J. (1999). Outcomes assessment: Its time has come. *Chemical Engineering Education,* 33 (2), 102–103.

IO

ASSESSING STUDENT COMPETENCE IN THE VISUAL ARTS

Kristi Nelson

As a profession, the visual arts require talent, skill, knowledge, inspiration, and creativity. Yet, artists and designers do not need a license to practice; and, as professionals, respect and success are based on one's work as an artist rather than on academic credentials. Education in the arts developed as educators sought to provide an environment that could maximize an individual's artistic learning potential. Following the European example (the Art Academy with practical applications), institutions of higher education throughout the United States now provide a broad range of opportunities for study in the visual arts.

To some extent, outcomes assessment, although not called by that name, has long been an integral part of the education process and, ultimately, student learning in the visual arts. While this is not the forum in which to debate the definition of the visual arts, suffice it to say that education in the visual arts is concerned with results. Innovation, creativity, and experimentation are urged in the production of works of art and design. The development of a portfolio (mandatory in nearly all visual arts disciplines), the ongoing use of the critique as a means for providing feedback to the student about his or her work, and the public exhibition of student work have all been and continue to be part and parcel of every art program in the country. Throughout higher education, outcomes assessment in the visual arts has always been continuous and remains one of the driving forces of the education of visual arts students.

Many of the techniques long practiced in the visual arts have now been adopted by other disciplines and stand as salient features in a formal assessment program or have become standard elements used to measure student learning outcomes. For many educators and administrators in the visual arts, the onset of "assessment" and "accountability" as formalized mechanisms or programs did not seem unusual, since many of the tools of assessment were already universally imbedded in every studio arts program in the country.

However, as literature began to appear on the subject of assessment, as conferences addressing the topic began to emerge, and as more and more states and regional accrediting bodies began to embrace the rhetoric of assessment and put pressure on institutions of higher learning to measure what students were actually learning during their enrollment, visual arts educators and administrators began to probe the topic more deeply. Their efforts were intended to understand how assessment with a more programmatic and more integrated approach could address both internal and external pressures coming from state legislators, the general public, employers, and regional accreditors. The issue to be confronted was how to take the concept of the personal and make it programmatic. Since the training and education of the artist and designer are centered on fostering self-assessment skills, how does one re-center an outcomes approach so that it is programmatically based?

Similarly, assessment concepts have been embedded in the visual arts accreditation standards since the inception of the National Association of Schools of Art and Design (NASAD). In this chapter, I take a look at how NASAD has assisted institutions in understanding the assessment movement and what it means for them in their own visual arts departments. I review some of the literature in the area that has been prepared by NASAD, particularly in light of the assessment movement, and analyze some institutional examples to see how faculty and administrators have implemented assessment plans in the visual arts. In my concluding remarks, I provide some thoughts on where art schools are today with regard to assessment.

National Association of Schools of Art and Design (NASAD)

The National Association of Schools of Art and Design was established in 1944. It is operated by member institutions; representatives of member institutions hold elected offices and serve as volunteers in the accreditation process. Since 1981, it has shared the same national office, executive director, associate director, and staff with the National Association of Schools of Music (established in 1924), the National Association of Schools of Theatre (established in 1965 but reorganized in its present autonomous form in 1980), and the National Association of Schools of Dance (founded in 1981). The four associations share a common philosophy about accreditation and its role, scope, and purpose, including the development of standards and guidelines that have been validated by professional consensus, extensive self-evaluation by the unit to be accredited, on-site review by peers to verify the self-study, final review of all documentation by an independent commission of peers and public members, and public designation of institutions and/or programs that have received accreditation. The arts accrediting associations have attempted to maintain a balance between tradition and change in their approaches to all aspects of the accreditation process. Analytical and conservative attitudes have been taken in the study of emerging trends to determine whether they are meaningful and relevant for the visual arts. The organizations have been leaders in such areas as competence-based accreditation standards, statistical services in support of accreditation, and outcomes assessment in on-site evaluation (Council of Arts Accrediting Associations, 1997).

Accreditation by its nature is an assessment and development approach. It focuses on accountability and improvement while promoting and protecting institutional and academic freedom. The concepts of "assessment," "accountability," "improvement," and "outcomes" have always been part of the accreditation process in the visual arts since the inception of NASAD. Assessment has always been understood broadly with regard to all aspects of accreditation and program development, not just the student learning outcomes connection with assessment.

Beginning in the late 1980s, however, NASAD began to monitor the issues surrounding the national movement of "accountability" in higher education through the annual meetings held for the membership each fall. Through a series of sessions, NASAD encouraged the membership to debate the pros and cons of outcomes assessment and how it might be applied to art and design programs. With the caveat that most educators favor the general concept of assessing the effectiveness of the educational process as a guiding principle, cautious deliberation was urged. In particular, NASAD suggested that to apply standardized assessment measurements across the board for the visual arts disciplines could be problematic. For example, while accurate and meaningful measurement of student achievement through standardized testing might be valid for some disciplines, it could be quite problematic for the visual arts. To overlay a canned assessment formula on visual arts curriculum and programs had the potential to be viewed as a bureaucratic process not relevant for the visual arts. From the outset, it was seen as crucial for the visual arts to monitor the situation in order to be able to design assessment techniques and processes in keeping with the nature of the visual arts and not to have something more suitable for other disciplines imposed on art programs. Furthermore, central to the philosophy of NASAD is the view that accreditation respects the uniqueness of each institution and that standards do not mean standardization. It is more important to see that functions are being served rather than that particular methods are being employed (Council of Arts Accrediting Associations, 1997).

Early Adopters

One of the sessions held during the annual meeting at Indianapolis in 1989 was entitled "Accountability: The Continuing Discussion on Assessments and Outcomes." NASAD representatives from the University of Tennessee and Rochester Institute of Technology examined various regional manifestations of the outcomes assessment movement and provided the opportunity for responses by the membership. The questions NASAD prepared for the membership to consider demonstrate the interest it took in educating attendees about the assessment movement. From the beginning, NASAD found it critical for its members to be knowledgeable about the movement and what it might mean for their institutions. To that end, the questions suggested for reflection and discussion included: "What is the scope and nature of the outcomes assessment movement? Is it here to stay or is it just another fad? What can we, as art and design program administrators, do to deal with the current pressures for assessment? To what extent can, or should, art and design outcomes be defined in measurable terms? How should we respond when there are conflicting demands for assessment, e.g., a university-wide program versus an accrediting agency's expectations? Are any relevant models available to assist us in developing assessment programs?"

The leaders of the discussion presented several assumptions as a way to introduce the session: gathering and documenting evidence has value; taking the initiative in assessment provides advantages; art professionals should determine the assessment process to be used; art professionals should resist any imposition of inappropriate assessment processes; and honest and candid assessment processes are best.

The case of Rochester Institute of Technology (RIT) is especially informative because the faculty have continued to refine their "assessment" activities for more than 10 years. In 1989, the assessment methodologies implemented at RIT focused on clarifying how the applied art graduate would be able to utilize a whole range of skills in his or her work. According to John Cox, one of the NASAD presenters, faculty initiated these efforts in order to address shortcomings they had noted with students' skill development. Faculty were curious as to whether a conglomerate of courses really provided the skills their graduates would need in their careers. Faculty identified objectives for individual course projects and for each course as a whole. The acquisition of a skill set for each course was identified, and a clear set of evaluative criteria for grading projects was devised. Students were assessed according to three categories. The first consisted of primary evidence or art growth on the basis of performance or work produced—art objects, courses, portfolios, and exhibitions. The second centered on inferential evidence or conceptual growth—critiques, faculty assessments, and student initiative; while the third was directed toward external evidence—competitions, grants, fellowships, outside evaluations, graduate school acceptances, alumni achievements, and benchmarking among peer programs and institutions. Professor Cox's viewpoint is that, from the start, the faculty never said, "let's do assessment"; rather, they focused on fine-tuning the curriculum and the whole instructional process. The end result was something that could be assessed. Since 1989, the system has evolved and become more refined. The faculty are constantly learning new angles and finding new challenges that had not been considered previously. The college has moved forward with implementing an assessment system across all the disciplines, and the art department will serve as the model based on its long involvement with the assessment of student learning (John W. Cox, 1995, 1993, personal communication, August 2000).

Thus, early adopters of assessment plans in the visual arts capitalized on time-honored evaluation techniques already in place throughout the field but organized them into more coherent plans that could be presented and explained to an external audience.

Publications

NASAD maintains an ongoing publications program, including the *NASAD Handbook,* that addresses accreditation standards and guidelines for educational programs in art and design. It is published in odd-numbered years; addenda may be published in even-numbered years. In the *Handbook,* NASAD has a strong standard about assessment under the category "Evaluation, Planning, and Projections." For example, the standard states that the art/design unit shall demonstrate that "the educational and artistic development of students is first among all evaluative considerations" and that "students completing programs have achieved the artistic and educational levels and competencies outlined in applicable NASAD standards" (NASAD, 1998, p. 66). NASAD expects institutions to have assessment procedures in place but does not impose specific procedural mandates on institutions. NASAD visitors focus more on student outcomes than on assessment processes. The *NASAD Self-Study Format* was last published in 1998 and in general is revised every five years. Higher Education Arts Data Service (HEADS) data summaries for art/design programs include composite statistics from annual reports of NASAD members relative to enrollments, financial information, and teaching-load practices and are published annually. *NASAD Executive Summaries of Future Issues* and *Briefing Papers* are presented periodically.

In addition to the regularly prepared materials just outlined, beginning in the 1990s, NASAD prepared a series of publications to assist member institutions and programs in understanding the context for assessment in the visual arts. One of the first of these was *Outcomes Assessment and Arts Programs in Higher Education,* a briefing paper prepared by the Council of Arts Accrediting Associations (CAAA, 1990).[1] The paper explored national outcomes issues from the perspective of arts programs in higher education with the intent to assist institutions and programs in reviewing outcomes assessment as both an internal and external force. It was prepared to encourage institutions to reflect on and analyze issues affecting instructional quality and, ultimately, accreditation. Topics addressed in the paper included public questions and institutional responses, outcomes and arts assessment traditions, components of outcomes assessments, cautions, common goals, and the role of expertise. The paper was one of the first prepared specifically for arts disciplines to assist them in making distinctions about values and proposals congruent with the nature of education and training in the arts and to encourage continuing attention to improving assessment and measurement of the growth of student knowledge. Six key interconnected elements of outcomes assessment procedures were identified: clarification of the nature of the issues being addressed; identification of logical, clear, understandable, and realistic goals; identification of common bodies of essential knowledge and skills; development of appropriate means for evaluating achievement in acquisition of the common body of essential knowledge and skills developed for each academic entity; implementation of systematic overviews as a basis for evaluation and improvement and to answer accountability questions; and follow-up of graduates.

The paper presented no universal models, since institutions and programs differ. It advised institutions that assessment does not involve a cookie-cutter approach and that no system of outcomes assessment has value in and of itself. Rather, the themes of the paper were that an assessment plan and the implementation of that plan are only as good as the "vision, will, commitment, and intellect of those who operate it" (CAAA, 1990, p. 5).

The paper also urged caution. In particular, it advised institutions and programs not to focus on assessment measures that do not consider the natures, goals, and values that distinguish education in the arts from other disciplines. For example, it suggested that multiple-choice testing in the arts probably explores student learning in a fragmented way and does not allow for the assessment of how students integrate knowledge and skills in professional work. The focus of any assessment process or program should be on results, not on technique, especially a mathematically based technique. As another caution, the paper urged that assessment and accountability be kept in appropriate proportion to the task of education; that is, accountability overkill does not allow for time to carry out the essential work at hand and resources and processes must be kept in balance. Lastly, the paper provided an appendix containing examples of student achievement goals and some indicators or evidence analysis to measure the goals.

The *Sourcebook for Futures Planning* was prepared in 1990 by NASAD (1990b) as a resource for members interested in developing action plans for the future. Although not specifically geared toward learning outcomes, the document provided a myriad of means to assist visual arts units in thinking about taking initiative rather than demonstrating accountability. Various methods were suggested that could be used as springboards for developing unique approaches to a particular situation and conducting a realistic contextual analysis to create a basis for action. As such, if used as intended, the sourcebook includes examples that units adopt to develop an assessment plan, design a new program, project the viability of a certain program, consider the impact of external forces, or find the basis for moving forward with greater enthusiasm. Throughout the sourcebook, various terms are used that are central to the assessment effort: *mission, goals, objectives,* and *action plans.*

Although not specifically directed toward student learning outcomes, two other documents prepared by NASAD in the early 1990s addressed programmatic assessment in art and design (1990a, 1991). As such, they did help to raise consciousness about the assessment movement and encouraged institutions, programs, and units to plan for the improvement of current programs, examine the viability of current programs, assess the need for new programs, and plan new programs. The documents encourage ongoing self-assessment as a vehicle for improvement. The intention of the documents is twofold: to assist units to develop a holistic view of undergraduate and/or graduate education and to aid in developing and improving the quality of education in the visual arts. A comprehensive process that takes into account various factors of the education enterprise is recommended. These documents could be used in tandem with the assessment materials prepared by NASAD outlined earlier.

Lessons learned from the assessment of student learning should not stand in isolation from the kind of programmatic assessment outlined in these documents. Both are necessary to create healthy, viable, and energized learning environments for students.

More recently, CAAA (1997) prepared a document that answered frequently asked questions about accreditation in general, *Tough Questions and Straight Answers About Arts Accreditation.*[2] The document answers a number of questions about the nature of accreditation in the arts, including the concept of assessment. A theme of the paper is that arts accrediting organizations are not special interest groups seeking benefits for their particular discipline but are focused on what students are learning, on what they know, and on what they are able to do.

Case Studies

Two institutions—a large, comprehensive, state research institution and a private, independent art school—are examined to understand how assessment is being practiced in the visual arts at this time. The two institutions afford interesting comparisons with regard to what is possible in a small visual arts college as opposed to a large public university.

University of Cincinnati, School of Art and School of Design in the College of Design, Architecture, Art, and Planning

Background   At the University of Cincinnati, a Carnegie Research I state institution that enrolls about 34,000 students, visual arts programs are located in the College of Design, Architecture, Art, and Planning (DAAP), one of 18 colleges and divisions at the university. The college has been accredited by NASAD since 1948 and is a charter member. For the purposes of this study, two schools in the college—the School of Art and the School of Design with about a thousand art majors combined—are examined. Like other institutions accredited by the North Central Association (NCA), the University of Cincinnati submitted a comprehensive assessment plan in 1994. However, it was not until preparing for the on-site visitation scheduled for the spring of 1999 that the university began to look at the progress of assessment across the institution. Thus, in the College of DAAP, discussions about assessment began to materialize in 1996, with implementation beginning during 1997–1998 (Wood, 1998). Each of the colleges in the university was responsible for developing an assessment plan. Those plans and the accompanying assessment reports were reviewed by the NCA evaluation team during its on-site visit. In the Schools of Art and Design, the faculty developed plans that were congruent with NASAD guidelines so that assessment activities would also help in meeting NASAD standards.

Methods   According to the DAAP assessment plan, outcomes activities in the college are grouped into three areas of knowledge acquisition: cognitive skills, which are assessed by the faculty via juried critiques and oral defense of theses; behavioral learning, which is assessed through observation of presentation skills, oral communication, group interaction skills, initiative, writing, and problem-solving skills; and affective learning, which is assessed through student, alumni, and employer surveys that yield important information about growth and change in attitudes from matriculation to the completion of the degree program and throughout the careers of alumni. Large-scale testing is not used in DAAP; instead, each school put in place a variety of measures to evaluate student learning and how objectives are fulfilled through a curricular plan. From the college perspective, much of the evaluation of student learning is conducted in the classroom by faculty through the comprehensive studio, which serves to integrate what students have learned across a sequence of classes. A major component of the undergraduate experience in the college is the DAAP Works exhibition that is held each year in June and features the work of graduating seniors. The show stands as a significant venue for public display of student work and provides the opportunity for outside experts to critique student effort. Each of the schools also developed a survey to be distributed to graduates at periodic stages in their careers to evaluate educational and professional experiences in light of program goals for career preparedness and other general criteria.

The schools in the college were responsible for identifying specific assessment objectives, processes, and feedback loops in order to complete the assessment process. In response to assessment outcomes, the faculty have instituted some significant programmatic changes. For example, the School of Design identified eight assessment activities to be implemented over a four-year period, consistent with the NASAD standard on Evaluation, Planning, and Projections discussed earlier. These include a first-year threshold review to assess student learning during the foundation year, a professional practice assessment to review professional practices experiences, an external educators assessment by educators outside the school, a professionals assessment by faculty and practicing designers during the senior year, a penultimate year assessment for first-year graduate students, a thesis review for master's level students, an alumni survey, and an external recognition activity to document achievements of students. As a result of initial assessment efforts, the School of Design introduced a new track of study in the fashion design program: product development and merchandising. The new program was created by the fashion design faculty in response to student concerns and to focus on product development processes in the fashion industry as opposed to apparel design. The program was recommended by school faculty and approved through the university's governance process.

In the School of Art, assessment techniques include a freshman survey, successful completion of the undergraduate review after 48 credit hours in studio work, the senior seminar and senior studio as capstone course experiences, exit interviews, and alumni surveys. The school has been collecting assessment data since 1997, and, as a result of that data, the faculty have made changes in the curriculum and the structure of a student's academic experience, reorganizing eight studio media into three major options: 3D major—ceramics, sculpture, fibers; 2D major—printmaking, painting, drawing; and media arts major—electronic art and photography. Other changes have included a new foundations curriculum, changes in credit hours for studio courses, shifting of course sequencing, and the introduction of a capstone experience for seniors. The faculty developed these changes (consistent with NASAD standards) with the view that assessment would help in meeting accreditation standards. Data gathered by the faculty revealed, in addition, that advising needed attention and the undergraduate review was not serving its intended purpose. To that end, two additional faculty were appointed as a student advisory team and more faculty were assigned to the review teams so that students receive feedback from more points of view.

This year, the university conducted its first university-wide student satisfaction survey that will provide information about student perceptions of many aspects of the university, including their academic programs and faculty.

Findings   Challenges remain as the university and its visual arts programs make the transition from a teaching to a learning paradigm. Educating faculty about this shift is critical. For the visual arts, the difficulty exists in how to take projects and courses and have them mesh with expected student learning outcomes. The university has recognized that institutional support is necessary and, in order to provide assistance for its academic units, has identified a vice provost to serve as the director of institutional effectiveness.

Center for Creative Studies, Detroit

Background   The Center for Creative Studies (CCS) in Detroit is a private, independent, not-for-profit art college with about 1,050 students. CCS offers the BFA degree in crafts, fine arts, communication design, industrial design, interior design, photography, animation, and digital media. The Center has been accredited by NASAD since 1972. It initiated an assessment program in 1994 following an accreditation site visit by NCA, which gave the school a three-year time frame in which to start an assessment program. The school was advised that locally designed initiatives should be put in place, that multiple measures would be necessary, and that the program could be implemented in phases. Studying the college's assessment plan in some detail offers insight on how all aspects of a student's educational experience, including liberal studies and studies in the visual arts major, can be linked to specific learning outcomes. The following analysis demonstrates the manner in which a small independent college has designed and implemented a plan that responds to its specialized accrediting body, NASAD, and is likewise in keeping with the expectations of its regional accrediting body, NCA.[3] The program has been in place for five years now, and annual reports for all five years were analyzed in order to prepare this case study.

As pointed out earlier, portfolio review, competitions, juried shows, and class critiques are all forms of outcomes assessment in the visual arts and already existed as essential and traditional parts of arts education at CCS. From the outset, the school had in place many components of a good assessment program. Providing feedback to students regarding their individual progress within their specific major field of study was generally done well at CCS. However, the school found that an effective assessment program according to the criteria established by NCA needed to do more than that: it needed to provide data with an institution-wide scope that could then be used to improve the BFA program and demonstrate accountability. Thus, in 1994, CCS began the journey toward developing and initiating an institution-wide assessment plan with the following strategy: develop the plan, relate the plan to the goals of the BFA program, and establish a timetable for implementation (Suczek & Foles, 1994).

Methods   The faculty at CCS began their research for the assessment plan by meeting as a whole to generate ideas about expectations of all CCS graduates regardless of the major. Concepts common to all or most of the departments were synthesized and distilled into a goals statement and presented to the faculty. Department chairs then worked with the faculty in each department to identify expectations within the department. All responses were discussed, reviewed, and organized into the assessment plan. During the year, faculty held numerous meetings to review and modify the proposed plan and to become aware of the various ways in which they would participate in the implementation phases.

Following this step, the goals of the BFA programs were reviewed in light of NCA's charge that an assessment plan must be linked to the mission, goals, and objectives of the institution for student learning and academic achievement. Three areas were identified as in need of development. First, the liberal arts component of the student's education had been assessed almost exclusively by course grades. Second, although studio department assessments had provided regular and formal feedback to the student about his or her progress, there were significant variations among departments in how this was handled; the process remained personal rather than programmatic. Third, the objectives of the different programs had not always been sufficiently well articulated or related to an evaluation of the program.

From all of these discussions, CCS identified 11 goals for its BFA program:

1. A high level of technical proficiency in the student's chosen medium or media and an in-depth knowledge of the chosen area(s) of specialization

2. Ability to make valid assessments of artistic and design quality

3. Ability to utilize both intuitive and critical thinking skills in their work and in the evaluation of the works of others

4. Ability to use words to receive and express ideas adequately

5. Ability to recognize, comprehend, and apply basic design principles, concepts, and terminology in their own work and in the analysis of the work of others

6. Skill in drawing that is sufficient to communicate visually ideas appropriate for the area of specialization

7. Broad knowledge of the history of art as a product of culture

8. Basic understanding of other major areas of human achievement and the thinking that underlies these disciplines

9. A clear understanding of the citizenship responsibilities inherent in their professions

10. Awareness of the necessity for flexibility and the desirability of continued learning and self-actualization

11. A basic knowledge of technological developments applicable to the chosen discipline(s)

Once the goals had been clarified, CCS faculty tried to link the components of an assessment plan to the aforementioned goals. It was thought that Goal 1 through Goal 7 connected nicely with different aspects of artistic competence, knowledge in art history, and basic skill in critical thinking and communication and could easily be assessed through the initial stages of the plan. The Academic Studies Department was asked to clarify the objectives of Goal 8 in an effort to identify ways to assess student knowledge beyond course grades. The faculty believed that Goal 9 and Goal 10 were important aspects of the program, although difficult to assess, and decided to wrestle with the issue of what kind of evidence substantiates the teaching of values and attitudes. For Goal 11, the faculty believed that external reviewers and employers in industry could provide good feedback.

When the goals of the CCS assessment plan are compared with the NASAD standards for all undergraduate programs in art and design, it is clear how consistent they are. For example, NASAD's general standards for undergraduate degree programs in art and design are classified in three categories: studies in art and design, general studies, and relationships between visual arts and design studies and general studies. In the first category, it is expected that undergraduate studies should prepare students to become visually literate, including competence with the nonverbal languages of art and design; to develop visual, verbal, and written responses to visual phenomena and to organize perceptions and conceptualizations both rationally and intuitively; to develop the capacity to identify and solve problems within a variety of physical, technical, social, and cultural contexts; to become familiar with major achievements in the history of art/design, including the works and intentions of leading artists/designers in the past and present; to understand and evaluate contemporary thinking about art or design; and to make valid assessments of quality and effectiveness in design projects and works of art, especially their own (NASAD, 1998, pp. 68–69). The standards further state that undergraduate studies in art and design should focus on conceptual understanding of components and processes integral to work in the visual arts and design; continued practice in creating, interpreting, presenting, analyzing, and evaluating the visual arts and design; increasing understanding across a broad range of cultures and history; acquiring capabilities to integrate art and design knowledge and skills; and accumulating capabilities for independent work in the art and design professions.

In the area of general studies, NASAD standards state that artists and designers must develop an understanding of other areas of human achievement, including the ability to think, speak, and write clearly and effectively; an ability to address culture and history from a variety of perspectives; and the capacity to explain and defend one's views effectively and rationally. The combined influence of visual arts and design studies helps to establish a foundation for students who are expected to acquire an awareness of differences and commonalities regarding work in artistic, humanistic, and scientific domains; a personal artistic/intellectual mission associated with one or more fields of art and design; and a sense of individual responsibility for cultural development as a whole and for its development in the visual arts and design in particular.

Thus, CCS faculty organized their assessment plan into 12 components that provided the mechanisms to measure student learning consistent with the goals of the school and standards identified by NASAD. The components are carried out as follows:

1. An external review of the student show is conducted by professional artists and designers to critique program effectiveness and prepare a written report.

2. A review of student portfolios is conducted following clearly stated criteria.

3. A standardized test of English usage is administered to all incoming students as a pre-test and to all second-semester sophomores as a post-test. A minimum competence level is established such that students with scores below the minimum are required to take additional writing classes and utilize the tutoring services available through the learning/study skills center.

4. Tests of writing ability are implemented at three levels: an essay required as part of the application for admission, an essay required for application to junior standing, and the senior thesis.

5. An Art History/Visual Literacy test is administered during the first week of Art History Survey I as a pre-test and during the last week of Art History Survey II as a post-test.

6. Pre- and post-tests are administered for the first year Basic Drawing program.

7. Ongoing focus groups are created for currently enrolled students.

8. Reports from apprentice and internship supervisors are gathered.

9. Participation in competitions is measured: participation in juried shows, quality of competitions entered, standing in competitions.

10. An Exit Interview and Alumni Surveys (1 year, 5 year, 10 year) are administered to collect data on percentage of applicants admitted to student's first-choice graduate school, scores on the Graduate Record Exam, percentage of alumni who receive an advanced degree, percentage

of students working in their field, and percentage of students working at an appropriate level in their field.

11. Teacher and course evaluations are administered.

12. A longitudinal student outcomes datafile is to be created.

Essentially, CCS faculty were interested in addressing the central concerns of NCA regarding assessment and, thus, organized the implementation of the plan in four stages. In Stage 1 (1994–1995), seven components were to be phased in: external review of student show, revised evaluation forms used for portfolio review, administration of a standardized test of English usage to all incoming students, administration of an art history/visual literacy test, evaluation of student performance as an apprentice or intern, establishment of a procedure to keep alumni list up to date and to formulate questionnaires, and establishment of a committee to review course/teacher evaluation methods. For Stage 2 (1995–1996), the following were to take place: administer the post-test version of the English competence test to second-semester sophomores, modify the art history/visual literacy test based on a study of results of the pilot project in the previous year, develop a senior thesis requirement for the capstone course, further refine the graduate survey, initiate focus groups with students and use data to improve course/teacher evaluation, and construct pre- and post-test versions for basic design exam. In Stage 3 (1996–1997), the following were planned: administer pre- and post-test versions of the basic design exam; initiate a thesis requirement for the capstone course with papers read by at least two instructors, one from Academic Studies and one from the studio department; and begin discussion of "values" in order to find means to measure. In Stage 4 (1997–1998), the plan called for a formal evaluation of the assessment plan and the implementation of proposals for measurement of Goal 9 and Goal 10. Following NCA guidelines, the faculty at CCS wanted to ensure that the plan was linked to the mission, goals, and objectives of the institution; that faculty remained involved in the development and implementation stages; and that the efforts would lead to institutional improvement.

Findings By the third year (1997) of the program, the school had identified an assessment coordinator, John Ganis, who was also a faculty member. His annual report (August 1, 1997) for the 1996–1997 year provides an excellent overview of the progress the school made in implementing its plan, collecting data, modifying measurement means, and revising curriculum based on assessment outcomes (Ganis, 1997). On the whole, the school believed that its assessment program was on track: Stages 1–3 had been implemented and diverse constituencies had bought into the effort and were using the assessment program as an effective vehicle for monitoring and improving the quality of education at CCS. Faculty perceptions were positive concerning the way in which the assessment measures—the capstone experience and the senior paper, the English and Art History pre- and post-tests, and the comprehensive portfolio—dovetailed with the external review program and the senior survey.

Based on student feedback, the capstone experience in the senior year was serving to facilitate the synthesis of the student's college education and to polish skills and attributes that students would need upon graduation. The accompanying senior paper was also in place. The assessment of students in English and Art History was being accomplished by the pre- and post-test designed by CCS faculty in respective areas and had been revised and updated by the faculty as necessary. After careful consideration, the faculty had decided to use scoring teams to grade the exams. Finally, a new component of the assessment plan had been introduced—the comprehensive portfolio. It was implemented as part of the Foundations Programs with the intent of documenting longitudinally a student's studio work and the ability to think critically about the work. Since 1997, each foundations student has been asked to make slides of several pieces of his/her own work and to write a brief self-evaluative essay about a major studio piece. Students continue to add slide documentation and an essay for the sophomore, junior, and senior years. The college will then have a permanent archive on each student and an accurate picture of each student's artistic and intellectual growth.

The annual report for 1996–1997 provides interesting feedback on the school's assessment efforts. The results of the first two years of the English pre- and post-test indicated that there was no improvement in student writing ability after having taken the freshman English sequence. These scores were considered alongside the writing scores on the Senior Paper, which were also judged low. Keeping in mind that a guiding principle of assessment is multiple measures, the faculty decided that the English curriculum needed to be improved, and a plan to implement a new English curriculum for 1997–1998 was developed. It was decided that the scores for the first two years could be considered a baseline measure that should improve with the new curriculum. On the other hand, the results of the first two years of the Art History pre- and post-test showed significant improvement in student knowledge after completion of two semesters of "survey" classes. Despite these results, some concern remained that the mean of the scores remained too low. To that end, curriculum changes were planned for the coming year so that a new humanities class would touch on some art history in order to provide a context for the survey courses, which would follow later in the curriculum.

The year 1997 also marked the third year of the external review of student work in each department in the annual student exhibition. For this assessment technique, each department selects an outside reviewer who comes to campus to view the student show and then prepares a report that is shared with the faculty when they return in the fall. The faculty found that the activity was working well and seemed to confirm their understanding of departmental strengths and concerns. On the whole, reviewers were positive about the creative work students were producing.

As cited previously, mean scores for the senior paper/capstone experience indicated a need for improvement in the writing of the papers. It was noted that in two areas—Fine Art and Photography, where a senior paper had been a requirement prior to the implementation of the assessment program—the scores were higher and there was less resistance on the part of students to write the paper. In these areas, critical thinking had also been emphasized as part of the departmental culture. In the design areas—Communication Design and Industrial Design—there was more resistance to writing the paper and the scores were lower. The papers were scored by the assessment coordinator and liberal arts faculty using seven criteria: coherence of thesis statement; clarity of supporting statements and or materials; attention to art and design issues; grammar, syntax, and spelling; summary conclusion; documentation; and overall evaluation. A goal was set to raise the mean scores for the senior paper, with the understanding that it might take several years to see improvements since incoming students were only now being exposed to the changes in the liberal arts curriculum and time was needed for this cohort of students to move through to the senior year. It was thought that studio faculty needed to encourage students to take writing seriously and to engage in it regularly.

It is instructive to look at the capstone course guidelines that were prepared and to see how closely they are allied with the NASAD standards discussed earlier. For example, some of the intended outcomes of the course were to include assignments, projects, and discussions that provide curricular linkages and connections; preparation of a portfolio that integrates studio skills and critical thinking skills in a group setting; and writing and speaking abilities essential to real work situations such as the job search or gallery search. Guidelines for the senior capstone paper required that the paper provide evidence of the student's ability to place his or her work and ideas within the context of relevant historical and or contemporary developments in the field of art or design, to demonstrate the student's ability to analyze and think critically about his or her own work, and to show points of inspiration as well as origins of concept development.

Responses to the Graduating Senior Survey for 1997 were in general positive. Overall, the results showed that students responded much more positively on those questions relating to their personal creativity than on general understanding of broad educational topics. In analyzing the scores, students were separated into four different cohorts: resident working half-time or more, resident not working half-time, nonresident working half-time or more, and nonresident not working half-time. One of the patterns that emerged was that lower scores were given by students who did not work and were nonresidents, suggesting that the educational experiences of the nonresident student needed to be enhanced or improved. Other questions that received less than desirable outcomes included those about "education contained adequate breadth," confirming what was perceived to be a weakness in the Liberal Arts component; and "good internship opportunities" and "one-on-one contact with highly able faculty members," suggesting that students were less satisfied with internship opportunities and the amount of contact with CCS faculty.

By the fifth year of the program (1999), all components of the original plan were fully implemented and continued to center around five essential outcomes measures: pre- and post-tests of competence in English and Art History, the capstone experience for seniors and the senior paper, the comprehensive portfolio project, external review of the student exhibition, and the graduating senior survey (Ganis, 1999). Furthermore, the school had created an Assessment Committee, a full standing committee of the college's Faculty Assembly and fully recognized by the CCS Board of Trustees.

The results of assessment activities for the 1998–1999 academic year reinforced patterns and trends that had emerged during the past two years, with some positive changes in responses concerning students' educational experiences at CCS. For the art history post-test, an identifier page was introduced in order to track transfer and nontransfer students. The art history post-test scores rose significantly, particularly in students' ability to define historical names and terms in art. The English post-test showed that students who had taken the English sequence within CCS performed better on the exam than those who had transferred credits to CCS. The third year of the capstone experience and the senior paper requirement began in 1999. Assessment of this activity showed that certain areas of the capstone course still needed attention: Faculty needed to do a better job of working with students on the paper; faculty needed to communicate more clearly about guidelines and due dates; and the scoring system needed to be reevaluated so that scoring could be compared from one year to the next. This was also the first full year of the comprehensive portfolio project, with work from freshman through junior year collected. For this activity, students did a better job of preparing their reflective essays, although not all students participated fully in the project. The external review of the annual student exhibition remained a cornerstone of the school's assessment plan. It continued to provide each department with an evaluation of outcomes in the form of student work in art and design and examined how well the department's educational objectives are being met based on stated goals and BFA standards shared by other colleges throughout the country. A goal for the coming year was to make sure that NASAD's measurable objectives are reflected in the questions asked of the reviewers and incorporated into the review formats. The senior survey has now been given for four years and continues to provide feedback from graduates on how well the school is meeting its stated goals and purposes. Similar to previous years, students tended to give higher ratings to questions that had to do with their own art and design work and learning skill in the art/design disciplines. Those questions that deal with breadth of education and liberal arts study were rated slightly lower, but the art history questions received more favorable ratings. The survey continued to show that nonresident students were less satisfied with their educational experience than resident students. Based on an analysis of student responses, it was clear that the capstone course was having a positive effect on the educational climate at CCS.

During the 1999–2000 academic year, the school conducted an alumni survey (results not known) and planned to have the assessment program evaluated by an outside evaluator. Additionally, the school plans to prepare an assessment publication for 2000–2001 that can be used as a public relations piece by the college community to improve communication with students, faculty advisors, and other college constituents about student learning at CCS.

Lessons Learned

What can be learned from the preceding discussion? It seems apparent that visual arts schools already have in place key components that can be incorporated into a comprehensive and integrated assessment plan. NASAD has provided useful materials that can assist institutions in developing an understanding of the outcomes movement and in designing plans unique to their institutions. A critical problem that persists is how to take efforts that are individually based and focus on self-reflection and make these programmatically centered. Central for schools of art and design is that assessment must focus on applying appropriate measures of student learning in the visual arts and that, to be truly successful with this kind of initiative, institutional support is necessary and faculty and administrators must support the effort.

So, where are visual arts schools today with regard to assessment? Faculty in art and design schools are and always have been consumed with assessment in terms of the field itself, as I pointed out in my introductory remarks. If our programs are to be effective and our students capable, this commitment is essential; but art and design schools are not into doing assessment for its own sake, or as a bureaucratic exercise, or because it might be driven by external forces and processes. Field-based, content-centered assessment is integral and always welcome. For art and design schools, assessment works best when outcomes are well defined and tied to improving student learning in the discipline and to enhancing the value of the degrees awarded and when the process is in control of local classroom faculty. Under the right conditions and for the right reasons, art and design schools engaged in assessment, as demonstrated here, have found that it works and is meaningful.

Notes

1. The Council is a joint ad hoc effort of the National Association of Schools of Art and Design, the National Association of Schools of Dance, the National Association of Schools of Music, and the National Association of Schools of Theatre.

2. This document includes material that originally appeared in *A Philosophy for Accreditation in the Arts Disciplines,* a statement of the National Association of Schools of Art and Design, the National Association of Schools of Dance, the National Association of Schools of Music, and the National Association of Schools of Theatre, published in May 1996.

3. I would like to thank Roger Williams, Dean, and John Ganis, Assessment Coordinator, for graciously sharing their assessment materials with me.

References

Council of Arts Accrediting Associations. (1990, April). *Outcomes assessment and arts programs in higher education* (Briefing Paper). Reston, VA: Author.

Council of Arts Accrediting Associations. (1997). *Tough questions and straight answers about arts accreditation.* Reston, VA: Author.

Cox, J. W. (1995, Spring). Assessment from the inside out. *Issues and Inquiry in College Learning and Teaching,* 19–28.

Cox, J. W. (1993, Winter). In search of the perfect instructional model. *Issues and Inquiry in College Learning and Teaching, 20–32.*

Ganis, J. (1997, 1998, 1999). *The assessment program at the Center for Creative Studies.* Final Reports to the College Community, Detroit, MI.

National Association of Schools of Art and Design. (1990a, second printing 1992). *The assessment of graduate programs in art and design.* Reston, VA: Author.

National Association of Schools of Art and Design. (1990b). *Sourcebook for futures planning.* Reston, VA: Author.

National Association of Schools of Art and Design. (1991, second printing 1997). *The assessment of undergraduate programs in art and design.* Reston, VA: Author.

National Association of Schools of Art and Design. (1998). *National Association of Schools of Art and Design handbook 1999–2000.* Reston, VA: Author.

National Association of Schools of Art and Design [On-line]. Available: http://www.arts-accredit.org/.

Suczek, M., & Foles, C. (1994). *The Center for Creative Studies institutional assessment plan.* Detroit, MI.

University of Cincinnati Provost's Office. (2000). *University of Cincinnati student satisfaction survey.* Cincinnati, OH: Author.

Wood, M. (1998). *College of Design, Architecture, Art, and Planning reports on assessment of student learning,* University of Cincinnati, Cincinnati, OH.

II

ACCREDITED PROGRAMS AND AUTHENTIC ASSESSMENT

Douglas J. Eder

Professional Education and the Baccalaureate Promise

Overall, when one reads contemporary educational literature in even a cursory way, one senses wide agreement that baccalaureate education has a large task to do. Among the cognitive skills, it should develop "critical thinking and conceptualizing, accompanied by high-level written and oral communication. . . . These abilities—not the knowledge acquired, for it becomes quickly obsolete—distinguish persons who have outstanding careers. Helping students recognize this is key" (Chickering, 1994). Nearly as important are interpersonal skills such as the ability to work within a group, to negotiate, and to accept people with diverse backgrounds and opinions. Stated another way, the holder of a baccalaureate education should possess

- Excellence in communications skills such as reading, writing, speaking, and listening

- Understanding of foreign language and culture

- Skills in critical thinking and problem solving

- Flexibility and tolerance of ambiguity in situations and people

- A sense of personal responsibility and ethics (Marchese & Hersh, 1994)

When asked to rank in importance the traits sought in prospective employees, a panel of upper management representatives from four corporations, ranging in scope from local to global, stated:

1. Written communication

2. Oral communication, both personal and public

3. A sense of ethics and etiquette

4. Disciplinary or technical knowledge (Corporate Managers Panel, 1994)

The question of whether American higher education is delivering these goods is beyond the scope of this paper, but there is a significant—occasionally loud—opinion out there that says it is not. This paper chronicles the experience of Southern Illinois University Edwardsville (SIUE) in developing a teaching-embedded program of authentic assessment (Wiggins, 1993) to enhance delivery of the baccalaureate promise and, simultaneously, to monitor the degree to which that promise is being fulfilled.

Authentic Assessment Embedded in Teaching

Consider for a moment your most recent flight on a commercial airliner. Suppose you had been informed that the pilot and copilot graduated numbers one and two in their class. Moreover, their extraordinary class rank—in fact, their qualifications to fly at all—were based solely on achieving high scores on four standardized written tests: airframe mechanics, flight dynamics, navigation, and U.S. flight regulations. In short, this was how they became cockpit qualified. How would you feel about flying with such a crew? Most people respond by mentioning that pilot qualifications should go way beyond written exams and include a large amount of actually taking off and landing an airplane. Furthermore, pilots should train extensively, perhaps in a cockpit simulator, for emergencies such as cabin depressurization, tire blowouts, engine fires, electrical malfunctions, and loss of power on takeoff, all circumstances that are too dangerous to practice in a real airplane. In short, pilots should practice real flight situations under supervision before they are turned loose on the public.

The cockpit simulator is an excellent device for simultaneously teaching and assessing. The assessment part ("Can you, the pilot, manage this simulated emergency?") is embedded in and even indistinguishable from the teaching part ("Here are the steps for how to handle this emergency. You crashed last time and need to try it again"). What we need in college and university education are teaching- and learning-embedded assessment devices that help us ask the right kinds of questions. We need the equivalent of the cockpit flight simulator. We need an *academic simulator* (Ehrmann, 1997).

The Senior Assignment, or SRA, is a type of authentic assessment—at its best, an academic simulator—that is embedded in teaching and learning, makes student achievement visible in context, and is a valid indicator of student learning. SIUE defines the SRA as a scholarly engagement by the baccalaureate student, under the supervision of a professor, that results in a product. Because the product is visible, it, and the curriculum that produced it, can be assessed. Depending on the goals of the discipline, the product can be a thesis, poster, composition, exposition, performance, design, or a combination of these with other forms of expression. A Senior Assignment may be almost entirely student-designed (a critical investigation of the economic theories of Nobel Laureate Paul Samuelson) or professor-designed with student contributions (ongoing clinical research on new diagnoses and drug therapies for Alzheimer's disease). The student pursues the project—lab research, field study, institutional analysis, clinical investigation, whatever—and subsequently presents the product to members of the faculty, university community, outside specialists, or the general public. Accordingly, the student may be examined or asked to defend or explain the product. This means that the SRA is not an abstract intellectual exercise but, instead, is a concrete integrative revelation to the faculty of student learning and the curriculum behind it all. Assessment with this in mind seems particularly important for accredited and professional programs, where students are asked necessarily to integrate content, structure, and professional process in a way that strictly liberal arts students usually are not.

Two local conditions were critical for assessment success at SIUE. First, beginning with its earliest assessment conversations in 1986, SIUE acknowledged the need for flexibility and diversity. In the same way that flight simulators are not the same for MD-80s and 727s, neither are academic simulators the same for assessing, say, business and engineering. SIUE's Senior Assignments might assess for common themes—written communication, analytical thinking, global perspective—but this is not required. Their structures and practices are flexible. They celebrate the diversity of our university culture, something that has been a source of their strength. Second, the university believed in the advice of national leaders in assessment and backed the installation of assessment with substantial and continuing new money. Most of the backing remains identified as the Senior Assignment Fund, whose major purpose is to foster and enhance student-faculty academic relationships. This squarely embeds assessment activities in teaching and learning.

Authentic Assessment in Practice
The Senior Assignment in SIUE's School of Business

With the benefit of hindsight, construction of assessment in the School of Business appears today more organized than it did when it was being conceived. Fundamentally, business faculty cobbled together three separate items, each of which had its champions but all of which taken together satisfied requirements for continued reaccreditation from AACSB—The International Association for Management Education. The three items are (a) a curriculum mapping project that is akin to what Driscoll, Toth, Pacheco, and Davidson (1999) have developed into *course alignment*; (b) two courses, one at the sophomore and one at the senior level that specifically assess baccalaureate skills; and (c) an international business competition that requires complex disciplinary and extradisciplinary performance over several months.

The School of Business agreed that exiting baccalaureate students should be able to

1. Demonstrate skills acquisition.
   - Express ideas effectively through written communication.
   - Present ideas and arguments effectively in oral communication.
   - Understand and evaluate written and oral information.
   - Develop an understanding of alternative systems of reasoning and problem solving.
   - Develop basic competences in the foundation of quantitative analytic technique.

2. Demonstrate liberal knowledge.
   - Develop an appreciation of the cultural value of the arts and broaden their understanding of the creative arts.
   - Experience philosophical and imaginative literature and develop an appreciation of its contribution to cultural development.
   - Develop an understanding of the historical context, particularly of the United States, within which social, political, and business systems have developed and currently operate.
   - Understand fundamental principles in the natural sciences.
   - Develop an understanding of the social and political institutions, domestic and worldwide, which provide the contemporary context for human behavior.

3. Possess business goals.
   - Understand why a liberal education is the foundation of business knowledge.

- Understand the moral and ethical context of managerial and corporate decisions and the social responsibilities of managers.
- Appreciate the reciprocal interaction between business organizations and their cultural context.
- Possess the ability to cope with uncertainty.
- Show an awareness of how the areas of business are interrelated.

4. Possess business skills.
   - Maintain personal, interpersonal, and leadership skills.
   - Demonstrate communication skills.
   - Develop and apply an analytical and systematic approach to problem solving and decision making.
   - Develop skills in information acquisition and evaluation and use them in decision making.
   - Show the ability to use relevant technology for making business decisions.

Having agreed on these things, how does one know whether exiting students actually possess these traits? The first step was to ascertain just where in the curriculum these items were taught. This became a curriculum-mapping exercise. Conceptually, professors who taught required courses within the business curriculum were independently asked, both through conversation and through their syllabi, which of the preceding items were part of their courses. A grid of the sort shown in Table 11.1 was developed to reveal which courses taught what items.

Table 11.1. Conceptual Curriculum Map of Outcome Items and the Courses Where They Are Taught

	Item 1	Item 2	Item 3	Item 4	Item 5	Item 6
Course 1	x			x	x	x
Course 2	x	x			x	x
Course 3	x	x	x	x	x	
Course 4		x		x		x
Course 5						
Course 6	x	x			x	x
Course 7	x			x	x	
Course 8		x		x	x	
Course 9				x	x	
Course 10	x				x	x

Examination of the map revealed that some items were heavily emphasized in the curriculum (e.g., Item 5) while others received little emphasis (e.g., Item 3). Similarly, some courses seemed to be organized around the agreed-upon baccalaureate goals (e.g., Course 3) while others were not (e.g., Course 5). The discussion that resulted from this kind of map required (and continues to require) care and sensitivity, because neither blame nor praise should be attached to the findings. The assessment objective at SIUE was to assess whether the business curriculum was actually teaching the things that the faculty as a whole said were important. Necessarily, some courses focus on areas that may not have discipline-wide importance. The mapping exercise made the curriculum visible in order to facilitate an intelligent conversation.

Assessment of student achievement takes place in the Business School Senior Assignment, which is contained in the second of two specially designed assessment courses known, respectively, as GBA 300 and GBA 490. The actual Senior Assignment is a formal, complex memorandum addressed to a [fictional] corporate departmental manager. The purpose of the memorandum is to review a major business case study and an accompanying published article that encompasses such things as technology, court decisions, international markets, accounting rules, tax laws, and labor relations. Each student presents and defends his/her memorandum orally in class with members of the faculty present. The analysis reflected in the memorandum must include contents, implications, and recommendations that reflect the student's subdiscipline. Rules of appropriate business communication apply. Each memorandum is assessed by members of the faculty in four areas: writing mechanics and grammar, application of appropriate concepts and principles, analytical reasoning, and effectiveness of writing. A modified Primary Trait Analysis (Walvoord & Anderson, 1998) is used for the assessment.

School of Business faculty found that the curriculum was producing students who satisfactorily controlled disciplinary and technical knowledge, critical thinking skills, and oral and written communication. Despite overall satisfaction with student performance, however, the faculty decided to continue its emphasis on thinking and communication skills, encouraging students throughout the curriculum to attain higher than merely "satisfactory" levels in these skills. The faculty aimed to achieve this goal by changing the curriculum, which now includes a research course and more case studies. Such changes were made not on the basis of faculty whim but, rather, on findings from assessment of student performance. Altogether, the benefit of the Senior Assignment has been to engage, as a group, faculty members with diverse interests to examine how their curriculum works and then to change it so that it works better.

A third assessment mechanism has been implemented through support of multidisciplinary student teams to engage annually in the International Business Policy Competition, an authentic assessment of business knowledge and skills. Initial competition between student teams begins on campus and is handled through the Internet; final competition has been held at San Jose State University. Organizers of the competition synthesize several rounds of quarterly reports for idealized companies, each with its own set of problems and opportunities. Student teams around the world examine the reports and, for each round, generate analyses and recommendations. Survivors of the rounds are invited to San Jose for final, on-site competition. SIUE students participating in the 1999 competition finished in second place.

As an assessment tool, this competition reveals student abilities in technical knowledge, analytical thinking, and communication skills. It asks students to undertake as a simulation that which they actually will do later as professionals. Thus, as an authentic assessment, the competition separates the curriculum into component parts; by analyzing student performance, one can examine it for strengths and weaknesses. This has been far more revealing than holistically comparing the place at which one's team finishes. Authentic assessment looks at the differential abilities of a school's curriculum to produce desired business behaviors in its students.

SIUE's assessment program evolves, and its evolution includes the components in the School of Business initiative. The school is presently considering a change in the structure of GBA 490 to permit a more intense, one-day, business simulation. This authentic assessment would revolve around a case study to be analyzed during the weeks prior to the one-day simulation. Students would work in teams to unravel a problem designed to have content-specific as well as ethical and communication dimensions. Student presentations would have written and oral components, the latter being scored through Primary Trait Analysis of videotapes. The reason for considering the shift of formats is to streamline the faculty workload, which can become large with authentic assessments. Simulations of this sort have been or are being considered at Indiana University, Kennesaw State University, and Texas Tech, among others.

The Senior Assignment in SIUE's School of Education

The School of Education consists of four departments: Curriculum and Instruction, Kinesiology and Health Education, Special Education and Communicative Disorders, and Psychology. Each of these departments has its own mission, and, in keeping with SIUE's overall celebration of diversity in all its forms, each department has its own authentic assessment. The written goals and assessment processes of the first three departments are organized around educating future teachers. Because the goals and processes in Psychology differ significantly, that department's assessment is discussed separately.

Authentic assessment in education revolves around building a professional portfolio that serves simultaneously to document student learning and also to build a device that reinforces an application for professional employment. Thus, the activities and products represented in the portfolio are those of the emerging student-as-school-teacher. SIUE subscribes to the Professional Development School model of education, which immerses students in professional development during their tenure as upper division students. In general, that means they spend a major portion of their last two years of college in supervised practice in the clinical or professional setting—their future working environment. By doing so, SIUE students simultaneously fulfill the graduation requirements of a baccalaureate education; all expectations of the professional accrediting agency, the National Council for Accreditation of Teacher Education (NCATE); all expectations of specialized accrediting agencies (e.g., National Association for Speech, Language, and Hearing Association— ASHE); and the requirements for teacher certification in the State of Illinois.

A composite list of goals for the departments in the School of Education follows. Baccalaureate students in Education will

1. Exhibit general education knowledge and skills to serve as a foundation for professional study and practice.

2. Demonstrate control of professional study in the areas of child growth and development; learning theory; philosophy and organization of American education; and content, structure, and methodology of the curriculum in [special education/speech pathology/elementary education . . .].

3. Identify and use instructional methods and curricula that are appropriate to specific areas of professional practice in meeting the needs of individual learners.

4. Participate judiciously in the selection and use of appropriate instructional materials, equipment, supplies, and other resources needed in the effective practice of teaching in [special education/speech pathology/elementary education . . .].

5. Use individual and group diagnostic and assessment instruments that do not discriminate against persons on the basis of race, color, sex, creed, national origin, political practice, family and social background, sexual orientation, or disability.

6. Promote learning among children with differing cultural and social/class backgrounds.

7. Demonstrate competence to teach effectively in a variety of settings.

8. Develop effective communication with parents based on mutual respect for their roles in achieving benefits for learners of all kinds.

9. Maintain confidentiality and ethical standards of behavior with all individuals.

The kind of student portfolios produced for Senior Assignments in Education are authentic means for students to assemble crucial, profession-related performance indicators for faculty review. The portfolios make visible the learning achievements—some mandatory, others voluntary—that the curriculum is supposed to promote. Assessment asks, To what extent and at what level of quality do indicators of student performance in the professional/clinical setting show up in the portfolio? Monitoring the extent to which this occurs is central to the School of Education's assessment process.

Some departments structure the portfolios more stringently than others. For example, the Department of Curriculum & Instruction, the Program in Special Education, and the Program in Health Education all expect student portfolios to exhibit lesson plans that visibly reflect analytical and problem-solving skills, communication skills, foundation in the liberal arts, appreciation of cultures, scientific literacy, and a sense of ethics. Students are guided toward situations in their clinical experiences where these elements are encountered. They are expected to deal with them and present them, with reflection, in the portfolio. Materials also include a statement of teaching philosophy as honed by clinical experience, a videotape of a teaching experience with analysis, and products of the teaching-learning encounters. The Program in Special Education additionally requires a written in-depth case study for which the student assisted in the intervention. The Program in Communicative Disorders expects additional analysis of a complex, hypothetical problem that yields evidence of research.

Portfolios are not limited only to student-generated information. Also included are such things as evaluations by both the cooperating teacher and the supervising professor, a checkoff of state standards, products of the student's students, and performance indicators of the student's students. Viewed collectively, portfolios in the School of Education have revealed overall student understanding of disciplinary content, such as the theoretical background that accompanies teaching skills and methods, professional behavior, and ethical responsibility. The portfolios have also suggested that the curriculum could be improved through a greater emphasis on practicing classroom management techniques, such as how to use active learning and how to promote an atmosphere of classroom civility and diversity.

Evolution of the School of Education toward portfolio assessment was overall relatively rapid and easy. Attuned as they are to proceedings in primary and secondary schools, the school's faculty members gravitated toward portfolio assessment as flexible, embedded in what they were already doing—and in what students *should* already be doing—and intruding only minimally upon faculty time. Completed portfolios are put on display for review well before final exams and for a duration of two weeks. Professors read at their leisure, comment in writing, and meet as a faculty once a year to discuss intensely what the curriculum has wrought.

The Psychology Department has a much different story. The department is populated by research-oriented individuals who initially saw assessment as an unwelcome intrusion. Numerous external indicators such as research awards, a number one national ranking of the local Psi Chi chapter, faculty productivity, popularity of several of the professors, and popularity of the program with students—none of which went to the heart of outcomes assessment—reinforced the notion that assessment was something to be finessed, not embraced. The initial assessment plan, assembled in haste but presented with flair, centered on something less than a term paper. As an assessment, it failed to address outcomes the department said mattered; competence in oral communication was the most obvious of these. Psychology was one of the very few departments that the University Committee on Assessment (COA) called on to testify regarding its assessment plan. In response, the department sent a young, untenured assistant professor to deliver the testimony. It was with clear signals of impatience that the COA eventually accepted the modified plan that Psychology submitted for approval.

Learning goals in the modified plan stated that baccalaureate students in Psychology will

1. Have acquired a basic overview of psychological knowledge and techniques.

2. Have acquired specialized knowledge in the areas of social psychology, developmental psychology, applied/clinical/counseling psychology, industrial/organizational psychology, and experimental psychology.

3. Have demonstrated supporting knowledge in statistical analysis and data interpretation, computer applications, the use of laboratory and field research techniques, and the use of psychological tests.

4. Be able to satisfy requirements for admission to area graduate programs and possess knowledge and skills necessary for successful application to graduate school.

5. Be able to communicate effectively both orally and in writing.

6. Be aware of the cultural, social, historical, ethical, and economic impacts of psychological knowledge and techniques.

COA regarded these goals as acceptable but, despite its displeasure, resisted the impulse to force Psychology to rewrite its entire plan. Had COA coerced Psychology immediately to submit a plan that more closely approximated everything it wanted, Psychology may never have become the university's flagship example of good assessment practice. Instead, with COA's blessing, the assessment office began working quietly with the department through the assistant professor. After one year's experience, the department itself became dissatisfied with its assessment efforts and was open to suggestion. It was then that the assessment office reinforced the idea that the university maintains a substantial Senior Assignment Fund, the primary purpose of which is to foster and enhance student-faculty academic relationships. This notion appealed to a research-oriented department and elicited a response that amounted to a dare: "We'll give you a plan for authentic assessment built around student research, but we want our students to go all the way and present their findings at the Midwest Psychological Association annual meeting in downtown Chicago. That way we get external peer review of the products of our curriculum. And we want the trips for students and attending professors paid for. Moreover, if we're going to commit to reorganizing our curriculum to do this, we want a reciprocal commitment of multiyear support." Psychology is successful in its endeavors, and here was a dare that had earned the right to serious consideration. The request for multiyear funding was negotiated on the basis that a guarantee was not possible; but, if results were forthcoming as predicted, then Psychology would certainly be first in line for the next year's funding. On that basis, 13 students presented in Chicago the first year. Some seven years later, the most recent group contained 47 students, all supported by the Senior Assignment Fund. As pedagogy, the chance for students to do research and receive rewards for it is unparalleled. As assessment, the experience is embedded in the department's best teaching and learning practices. Psychology procedures in assessment are now modeled throughout the campus.

In preparation for the Chicago trip, students present and defend their work at a local, whole-department poster symposium. University administrators are specifically invited to witness the event. Students are questioned deeply, yet there is a celebratory air due to the presence of ample refreshments. A most memorable session occurred one year when the Psychology faculty suspected a weakness in its departmental statistics program and specifically assessed the statistical content of the research posters. Indeed, students could answer questions about the methods they used but were much less able to describe why they picked one particular method as appropriate over another. This singular finding precipitated a substantial curricular change and led to improved student understanding of statistics beginning the very next year—as revealed on the assessment posters!

Psychology is a flagship example of how assessment can work well. The university has learned many lessons from the Psychology example, not the least of which are these two: (a) The enemy of the Good is the Perfect. If one waits for the perfect plan to come along, one never gets a good plan operating. Imperfect plans can always be improved if they are aiming at the right thing. If they are aiming at the wrong thing, no amount of improvement will compensate for that fact. (b) Sometimes it takes a champion to get a good idea operating. The assistant professor mentioned in this story was a champion for assessment and remains so to this day. By treating seriously the dare she conveyed from her department, assessment validated her credibility as well as its own. That made her a more effective champion. Such a circumstance is recognized as a win-win situation, and it is something worth pursuing. Interestingly, the so-called "term paper option" has fallen from favor with the faculty but it remains available as a Senior Assignment. It is not favored by the students either, who overwhelmingly select the more rigorous—and more substantive—authentic assessment option.

The Senior Assignment in SIUE's School of Engineering

The School of Engineering consists of five departments: Civil Engineering, Construction, Computer Science, Electrical and Computer Engineering, and Mechanical and Industrial Engineering. Programs in this school are accredited by ABET, the Accreditation Board for Engineering and Technology. The foundation of assessment in Engineering is the Senior Design Project, which fulfills all university expectations for an authentic Senior Assignment and all expectations of ABET as well.

Announced goals for all departments within the school are similar but not identical. The example of Civil Engineering is representative. Baccalaureate students in that discipline will

1. Be able to recognize problems that can be solved with civil engineering methods and apply the knowledge and tools necessary to design appropriate systems to solve those problems.

2. Understand current civil engineering issues, recognize the need to remain informed about civil engineering issues throughout their careers, and engage in lifelong learning.

3. Include ethical, societal, and global considerations when making decisions regarding engineering solutions.

4. Be able to function on multidisciplinary teams.

5. Be able to express ideas effectively in both oral and written communication.

6. Be able to conduct laboratory experiments and critically analyze and interpret data pertinent to civil engineering applications.

7. For the majority, have had civil engineering–related work experience.

Throughout the school, all students are required to complete a major design project in a design course that, depending on the department, may last one or two semesters. The design project is comprehensive and focuses on professional practice, requires the use of information and insights from past course work, and includes a variety of nontechnical issues such as safety, reliability, aesthetics, ethics, and social impact. The student must draw on his/her undergraduate experiences in writing, speaking, critical thinking, analytical and mathematical knowledge, computer literacy, physical science, aesthetic awareness, ethics, and economics. Successful completion of the project consists of a written report together with an oral presentation of its central features. In some departments, team projects are encouraged. The report contains both a description of the strictly engineering features of the project as well as an analysis of the manner in which the nontechnical questions have been addressed. Reports and presentations are often reviewed by experts from outside the university who are invited to campus for this purpose.

By reading reports and observing oral presentations, faculty are able to assess students' abilities to express ideas effectively in these modes. By examining the proposed designs described in the reports, faculty can assess students' abilities to make use of analytic and quantitative problem-solving skills. By considering the scope and depth of students' treatments of nontechnical issues, faculty can assess students' abilities to consider wider societal issues that often accompany engineering practice.

What sorts of things constitute authentic assessment for Senior Assignments in Engineering? First example: The university exists about 100 miles from the New Madrid fault, an infrequent but violent source of earthquakes. Teams of six civil engineering students were assigned to undertake seismic analyses of existing and planned buildings by using the technical perspectives and tools that a good baccalaureate engineering education should have given them. Could they do the blueprint study, soil analysis, structural examination, and kinetic calculations to do the job? Yes, they could, and they discovered a design error in the plans for a new campus building! Second example: Modern rock concerts often require very rapid and highly choreographed spotlight movements in order to put on the light show that accompanies the music. High-intensity spotlights are heavy and have great inertia; thus, they pose a loading problem for the motors that move the lights. One electrical engineering student's solution to the problem employed low inertia, easily movable mirrors so that the spotlights could remain fixed, yet the beams could be moved quickly and precisely by computer-controlled stepping motors. Third example: The university wishes to convert to a more user-friendly computerized system suitable for advising, registration, and maintaining student records. Several systems are commercially available, but deep inspection of these systems consumes much time. In addition, tailoring them to specific, local needs is difficult, and trying them out involves significant costs. Teams of computer science students consulted with the faculty and developed a PC-based records and advisement system, complete with security protection. Having developed it and presented it for inspection, they then established it for pilot use in volunteer departments.

Other examples abound. The key property of them all is that students engage, under supervision, in building solutions to the sort of real problems they will face as professional engineers. Moreover, technical solutions themselves do not comprise the entire Senior Assignment; problems of oral and written communication, client expectations, ethics, confidentiality, and other nontechnical aspects are also open to assessment by the supervising faculty. And, of course, it is with respect to the faculty's own standards of performance that the curriculum is subsequently judged. Amazingly, everyone benefits from such exercises. Students exit with evidence of achievement and not merely with aptitude and hope, the curriculum improves as the faculty closes the feedback loop from assessment findings, and the university itself gains incalculably.

Across all Engineering departments, the number one finding has been a strength in critical thinking and problem analysis. Students have been able to reach across the curriculum to apply components in novel and appropriate ways to solve problems. Group collaboration and ability to work in teams have also been seen as strengths. The top thing that the School of Engineering wishes to continue improving is student performance in written and oral communication. As the curriculum comes to include even more writing and speaking practice—some of it by means of enhanced video technology, some through a collaboration with the Department of Speech Communication—student performance inevitably will be monitored in the authentic assessments provided by the Senior Assignment.

The Senior Assignment in SIUE's School of Nursing

More than many other disciplines, the nursing profession has experienced assessment and incorporated it into its culture, language, and practices. The school and its programs are accredited by both the National League for Nursing (NLN) and the Commission on Collegiate Nursing Education. These agencies, as is true for the other professional accrediting associations, expect to see assessment as an integral component of the educational enterprise. Therefore, assessment plays a role in satisfying external as well as internal purposes. Nowhere is this seen more vividly at SIUE than in the School of Nursing.

According to the written goals of the school, baccalaureate students in nursing will, in order to optimize health maintenance, health restoration, and health promotion for individuals, families, and communities,

1. Synthesize concepts from general education, nursing, and biopsychosocial sciences.

2. Use professional process, including problem solving, decision making, and critical thinking.

3. Evaluate the effect of communication and interpersonal skills.

4. Perform psychomotor skills at precision level with ability to adapt to a variety of settings.

5. Collaborate with members of interdisciplinary health teams.

6. Perform nursing activities with diverse populations in a responsible, accountable, and sensible manner.

7. Assume the role of the licensed professional nurse in accordance with the provisions of the Illinois Nursing Act and the Rules and Regulations.

8. Evaluate the impact of professional nursing in the delivery of health care.

9. Participate in change that contributes to the effectiveness of health care services.

10. Use knowledge of ethical, social, political, and health issues to benefit society, while being sensitive to issues of human diversity.

11. Use principles of scientific inquiry and findings of nursing research.

12. Develop professional competence through self-directed learning.

The Senior Assignment consists of a written evaluation (25–30 pages) of a client and family, including elements that demonstrate the preceding departmental objectives. The assignment requires each student to identify and discuss economic, social, political, cultural, and historical factors as well as ethical considerations related to the client. To achieve such an evaluation, the student is expected to draw on his/her entire baccalaureate education. The student then uses the identification and analysis of the impact of these factors to develop a nursing plan of care specific to the client. Students present and defend their care plans in both written and oral forms. The curriculum committee and the full faculty of the School of Nursing are responsible for the quality assurance process of the Senior Assignment. Results of the Senior Assignment are reviewed by the full nursing faculty.

The most effective assessment is that which is embedded in learning and teaching. Assessment pervades the Nursing curriculum; the Senior Assignment is merely a student's last encounter. Evidence of how deeply the academic simulator and authentic assessment are embedded in the Nursing curriculum is visible in the new psychomotor nursing skills laboratory. The School of Nursing describes its simulation laboratory as a 3,000-square-foot area with realistic settings in which students gain mastery of their psychomotor skills for nursing practice in the real world (SIUE School of Nursing Faculty, n.d.). The laboratory is divided into three hospital patient rooms, three clinic rooms, two psychiatric interview rooms, one intensive care room, one operating room, one room for computer instruction, and one room for clinical laboratory work, including use of the microscope. All of these rooms occupy the perimeter of the laboratory. In the middle is a mock nursing station. The lab is scheduled for class use during the day with practice times available during evening hours. The hospital, clinic, operating, and psychiatric interview rooms are supplied with equipment and materials needed to simulate the real setting. Students apply their knowledge from the classroom, and they practice technical and communication skills with classmates during laboratory hours. Video cameras on movable tripods allow for videotaping and subsequent discussion and evaluation. The microscope has a teaching lens that allows several individuals to share the microscopic view. In the computer room, students have access to videodiscs, computer-assisted instructional programs, videotapes, Web-based instruction, and other information on topics covered in their course work.

Within the laboratory are adult and pediatric human patient simulators. The simulators are state-of-the-art computerized mannequins that can simulate real-life patients with a variety of chronic and acute health conditions. They also provide nursing students with physiological and pharmacological information so that students can apply knowledge to critically assess, ponder, consult, intervene using technical skills, and evaluate actions depending on how the simulator reacts. Television monitors, hanging from the ceiling, are placed throughout the laboratory so that a full class may view simulated scenarios in real time or on videotape. The human patient simulators are seen as particularly useful for nurse-anesthesia and medical-surgical training (SIUE School of Nursing Faculty, n.d.).

The decision to build this kind of intense active learning into the curriculum resulted from the reasoned consideration of prior years' assessment results in combination with good faculty judgment. The School of Nursing faculty tend to phrase questions about their curriculum not in terms of, "What do we teach?" but, rather, "What do students learn?" Through Primary Trait Analysis and other devices that make curriculum performance visible, the school has been able to uncover areas where students are not learning up to faculty standards, despite very high quality teaching efforts by the faculty. By judiciously applying feedback from assessment findings about student *learning,* new *teaching* approaches are being identified so that both the standards of excellence and curriculum performance rise together.

Summary

Unifying statements for assessment at SIUE are difficult to compose. The university acknowledges and celebrates diversity in its students and in its academic programs. The same is true for assessment. There is no university-wide assessment device, nor is one intended. Schools and departments experiment with plans that match their teaching and learning goals and, as they evolve, so do their assessments. It seems, therefore, that the following keys are the most that can be offered prudently:

- Assessment devices in SIUE's professional schools have been designed sincerely for internal purposes; they ask questions about what matters to *us*. External agencies are welcome, invited participants in our assessment processes.

- SIUE's professional schools are proactive in assessment and consult with professional accreditors regularly without prompting.

- The assessment program at SIUE matches *our* institutional culture, one that values diversity and shared student-faculty scholarship.

- Assessment tools presently in use involve many other methods not described in this chapter, but the ones most attended to by the faculty and students are the ones deeply embedded in the normal course of teaching and learning. These are the authentic assessments of the Senior Assignment, the ones that subscribe to the concept of the academic simulator.

References

Chickering, A. (1994, December). Empowering lifelong self-development. *American Association of Higher Education Bulletin*, 3–5.

Corporate Managers Panel. (1994, March). *Opening remarks*. Presentation at the Senior Year Experience Conference, Orlando, FL.

Driscoll, A., Toth, M., Pacheco, S., & Davidson, S. (1999, June). *Alignment: A critical process in assessment design*. Paper presented at the American Association for Higher Education Assessment Conference, Denver, CO.

Ehrmann, S. C. (1997, July–August). The Flashlight Project: Spotting an elephant in the dark. *Assessment Update*, 9(4), 3–13.

Marchese, T., & Hersh, R. (1994, November). What our publics want, but think they don't get, from a liberal arts education. *American Association of Higher Education Bulletin*, 8–10.

Southern Illinois University Edwardsville School of Nursing Faculty. (n.d.). *School of Nursing psychomotor skills lab brochure*. Edwardsville, IL: Author.

Walvoord, B. E., & Anderson, V. J. (1998). *Effective grading*. San Francisco: Jossey-Bass.

Wiggins, G. (1993, November). Assessment: Authenticity, context, and validity. *Phi Delta Kappan*, 200–214.

12

THE BRITISH EXPERIENCE IN ASSESSING COMPETENCE

Lee Harvey

Competence is not a term much associated with higher education in the United Kingdom, especially at the undergraduate degree level. Competence implicitly relates to technical proficiency and, as such, is a concept that has its main currency at the subdegree or post-degree levels rather than the undergraduate experience.

In one use, competence relates to the technical ability to perform specific tasks such as plumbing or motor vehicle maintenance. This is encapsulated in the development of National Vocational Qualifications in the United Kingdom (see, for example, Flude & Sieminski, 1999). Competence in this sense is closely linked to employability and has been "officially" defined as "the ability to apply knowledge and understanding in performing to the standards required in employment, including solving problems and meeting changing demands" (DfEE, 1996). This technical, competence-based education "tends to be a form of education that derives a curriculum from an analysis of prospective or actual role in modern society and that attempts to certify student progress on the basis of demonstrated performance in some or all aspects of that role" (Grant et al., 1979, p. 102). Theoretically, such demonstrations of competence are independent of time served in formal educational settings. A competence-based curriculum specifies in detail the required outcomes of learning and leaves students complete liberty as to the learning process by which they acquire the capacity to demonstrate those outcomes (Jessup, 1991). The result in technical subdegree education has been the fragmentation of the curriculum into bite-sized units and the reductionistic approach to learning. Competence also is used in the holistic professional context to imply someone who can be let loose to serve the public in professional roles such as solicitor, accountant, medic, architect, or engineer. It is this element of competence that engages higher education that is addressed in this chapter.

The impact of addressing the issue of "competence" in the United Kingdom seems to be rather different than in the United States. Its real impact so far in British higher education has only been in the professional sphere, and university staff who teach in those areas are very much used to complying with requirements of professional or regulatory bodies. They may not always agree with the requirements but are aware that, for the sake of their students who want access to the professions, they need to ensure that the program of study enables students to obtain the desired credential. Professional competence may be seen as intrusive, but there is not the same concern about academic freedom as may be felt in the United States. In the last resort, the standards of most professional education, as in all higher education in the United Kingdom, are mediated by the long-established external examiner system, which tends to be much better respected than the newer forms of external monitoring and evaluation, such as that imposed on the sector in the United Kingdom by the national Quality Assurance Agency (QAA).

The issue, as this chapter goes on to explore, is the intrusion of the national quality agency into issues of standards, with its accompanying promotion of competence issues. This intrusion, which is at its early stages, is resented both by those in the professions and by those outside. The former consider the QAA to be far less competent than their professional body in this respect. The latter see the agency's intrusion as an assault on academic freedom primarily through taking emphasis away from scholarship and replacing it with burdensome bureaucratic demands.

> Everything has to be documented. All the marking has to be moderated with written reports. We spend a lot of time remarking other people's stuff and all for the sake of a QAA visit. Every new initiative has to be seen in terms of how it will be seen at the next QAA visit. We have to keep attendance registers to show that we are trying to monitor non-attendance. All this adds to the administrative burden and creates systems that don't make a hoot of difference to what the students get. No money comes in to improve things, it's just pressure to make us do more bureaucracy. I haven't seen any real changes since the last visit: it's all cosmetic. (Comments from a lecturer in social science, 9/28/2000, name withheld)

Professional and Regulatory Bodies

Professional education and training are important aspects of post-compulsory educational provision in Britain. A significant proportion of higher education provision is linked, in one way or another, to professional education and training, and more than 100 professional or regulatory bodies (PRBs) are involved in monitoring course provision in U.K. universities.

A survey of 92 of these PRBs revealed that 74 award professional qualifications (Harvey & Mason, 1995b). The growth of professional education is perhaps the most significant feature of the development of higher education in the United Kingdom over the past 30 years (Barnett, 1992, p. 185). Furthermore, the number of jobs in professional occupations is rising faster than in other occupations (Connor, 1997).

In the United Kingdom, the certification of professional competence is, in the last resort, the province of PRBs. The PRBs determine professional competence either directly or via delegated responsibility but essentially through processes that are ancillary to the undergraduate experience. Undergraduate education involves little direct attempt to engage or assess professional competence except in medical, health, and teaching. In these areas, assessment is based on work-based practice in real settings—hospitals and schools. In other areas, such as engineering, law, and architecture, undergraduate education involves a rigorous theoretical grounding and some practical work or problem solving but no real attempt to engage the issues of specific professional competence. Although PRBs control professional education in the United Kingdom, their organization and powers vary considerably.

Regulatory Bodies

A regulatory body is created by government to regulate qualifications and/or training for a particular occupation, for example, the Engineering Council for the United Kingdom, the General Medical Council (GMC), the U.K. Central Council for Nursing, Midwifery and Health Visiting (UKCC), and the Teacher Training Agency (TTA). Regulatory bodies do not offer membership to practitioners and do not see themselves, in the first instance, as serving practitioners.

Regulatory bodies exercise control over the profession in various ways. They are "external" watchdogs at one step removed from the profession. Most, but not all, regulatory bodies are established by statute, have their powers defined by statute, and thus operate with the force of law. Regulatory bodies usually

- Control entry to the profession by specifying the required knowledge and competence

- Maintain a register of practitioners, inclusion on which is required for continued practice (although this is not the case in social work or teaching, for example)

- Enforce a code of practice determined to be in the public interest

Some regulatory bodies (for example, British Acupuncture Accreditation Board, General Council and Register of Naturopaths, General Council and Register of Osteopaths Ltd., National Council for Drama Training), although keeping an oversight of the professional area, have no statutory powers, and registration with these bodies is not required in order to practice.

Professional Bodies

Professional bodies are entrusted with ensuring the public interest in the absence of any effective checks on the activities of the professional through the operation of the market (Ormrod, 1968). A professional body is a formally recognized organization having jurisdiction over a profession or a section of a profession. In some cases, formal recognition is based on charter or statute.

Professional bodies have individuals as members; and criteria for full membership usually, but not always, comprise passing professional examinations and undertaking a minimum period of assessed professional practice. In essence, professional bodies control the profession by

- Controlling entry to the profession

- Specifying ongoing requirements to practice

- Providing and enforcing a code of practice based on acceptable professional values

There are two types of professional bodies based on this role definition: those for which membership is *compulsory* for practice within the profession (such as solicitors) and a much larger group where membership is advantageous but where it is possible to practice (albeit in restricted settings in some cases) without being a member of the professional body (such as electrical engineers).

Entry requirements to a professional body include one or more of the following:

- A suitable undergraduate qualification

- A postgraduate qualification

- Obtaining a qualification provided by the professional body

- A period of time as a practitioner (which may or may not be supervised or assessed)

- Being sponsored

The requirements for continuing membership might be the payment of an annual fee, continued employment within the profession, or some form of continuing professional development.

Initial and Professional Education

Although professional bodies vary enormously in the requirements they place on entry to the profession and the specification of the necessary education and training, there is a broad tendency among many professions for a two-tier approach. The first tier of education is often referred to as *initial* education and frequently consists of a specified type of undergraduate degree program or diploma in a college or university.

The second tier is the specific *professional* training and takes a variety of forms. Sometimes these are based in a wide range of universities and colleges. Sometimes provision is limited to a number of regional centers, as in the case of the Chartered Institute of Bankers, and occasionally restricted to a single specialist training establishment as, for example, in the training of barristers. Professional bodies tend to be less directly involved in curriculum design, standards setting, and quality monitoring in initial education and rather more involved at the professional stage. However, the power of the professional or regulatory body does not correlate exactly with the degree to which they directly assess or evaluate the competence of students seeking professional accreditation.

Ensuring Professional Competence

Professional bodies seek to control student competence in four ways:

- By defining the content of the program of study

- By determining the suitability of institutions or parts of the institution to deliver the program

- By assessment of student competence, knowledge, and values, either directly or via delegated responsibility

- By specifying the ongoing education and training required for continued practice within the profession[1]

Course Content

PRBs are concerned with the content of both initial and professional education and training. They need to satisfy themselves that the program of study equips successful students with the knowledge and ability to progress into the profession. For example:

> Our role is to assess the programme as suitable for an aspiring member of the Institute of Electrical Engineering. . . . For example, every course should culminate in a final year project. We prescribe the need for sufficient mathematics but we don't say what that is, we let the department decide. (IEE, 1995)

The Law Society, for example, is clear that certain minimum knowledge and skills are required before a candidate can proceed into professional education and training:

> What we are saying is: take what you want but you do need these basics if you wish to come to us for the professional education and if you haven't got them or some of them, you may have to take a refresher course, or take another course which gives you those basic building blocks. (Law Society, 1995)

In a survey of 92 PRBs, 42 claimed to have a *direct input* into higher education curricula and a total of 81 bodies think that they *influence* curricula (Harvey & Mason, 1995b). Of the 74 bodies that indicated they offered a professional qualification, nearly half (35) indicated that some element of their syllabus is compulsory.

There are various approaches to specifying syllabus content. The General Dental Council (GDC) issues recommendations concerning the dental curriculum and requires institutions to provide information about the courses of study and examinations for its degrees and licenses. Similarly, The General Medical Council's (GMC) Education Committee's *Recommendations on Undergraduate Medical Education* determine the general form and content of undergraduate curricula. However, within these broad guidelines, each medical school is expected to develop its own individual curriculum and arrangements for assessment, although major changes must be communicated to the committee for comment.

In some cases, the professional body "owns" the syllabus, and universities and colleges provide courses, based on these syllabuses, with the blessing of the professional body. For example, the Chartered Institute of Bankers (CIB, 1995) is unequivocal in considering that they own the courses and syllabus and that universities and colleges teach toward its examinations. Some professional bodies have expectations of content based on a model syllabus but encourage local variations. Many PRBs do not specify a syllabus as such but indicate the kind of things that ought to be included in an institution-designed syllabus.

Typically, a program team will produce a program of study comprising the required number of units. Individuals or subgroups of the course team will produce unit syllabi that include objectives, content, descriptions of learning and teaching process, and indications of how students will be assessed. These will take into account university regulations and professional-body requirements. The composite will normally be overseen by a program director who will produce a definitive program document that contextualizes the proposed program. The course team will discuss the content at different stages in the production, which normally lasts about 18 months. External advisors from other institutions may be involved. The finished product will be subject to review by an internal university panel that may include external invited members or those nominated by the professional body. The outcome is a team-constructed program within which individuals have areas of "ownership." Ensuring that they fulfill minimum external requirements, the individuals are more or less free to "experiment," or not, as they consider appropriate.

Determining Suitability

Professional and regulatory bodies also control professional competence by determining whether an institution or part of an institution is a suitable professional education provider and that the program is devised in an appropriate manner that leads, or is likely to lead, to the desired professional outcomes. It does this through accreditation and validation procedures.

Accreditation   *Accreditation* is official approval and recognition awarded to academic and vocational awards. Accreditation is vital if a higher education institution wishes to run courses that offer awards controlled by PRBs. Accreditation may be of specific courses or, less often, of entire institutions. The approach and extent of accreditation varies from the recognition of courses as representing industry standards of training (such as those accredited by the National Council for the Training of Broadcast Journalists [NCTBJ]) to the complex and tightly constrained inspectorial procedures of the General Medical Council (GMC, 1995):

> The Education Committee of the GMC, which is ultimately responsible to the Privy Council, has power to petition the Privy Council to

add to the list of universities entitled to award registerable primary degrees in medicine and surgery in the event that new medical schools are established. The Committee would only proceed in this way if it were satisfied that the arrangements for teaching/learning and assessment met the requirements laid down in its *Recommendations on Undergraduate Medical Education*. It would satisfy itself by means of appointing a team to carry out a formal "visit" (to assess the teaching) and "inspection" (of the examinations/assessments) over a five-year period, and would only reach a final decision when the first cohort of students had completed the five-year course and the qualifying examinations. (GMC, 1995)

Validation   *Validation,* applied to higher education courses, is the process that ensures that the intentions and purpose are reflected in the content, organization, available resources, delivery, assessment, and outcomes of the course being proposed or under review.

In the Harvey and Mason (1995b) survey, 51 of the 92 bodies indicated that they *validate* courses in higher education institutions. Validation is closely linked to review, and nearly all PRBs who are involved in approval undertake reviews of approved courses and re-visit whenever significant changes are made to such courses. However, reviews are more likely to be periodic, and few organizations undertake annual monitoring of approved courses. Reliance is often placed on their formal committee structure, professional networks, and branch meetings to alert them to actual or potential problems (Brown, 1994). Although validation and review procedures could theoretically lead to withdrawal of approval, this occurs very rarely in practice. Instead, bodies prefer to emphasize the positive developmental and enhancement role of approval and review mechanisms.

Approval procedures   Accreditation and validation, which will be referred to jointly as "approval" (Brown, 1994), involves a variety of procedures, but the vast majority of PRBs use a mixture of the following:

- Exchange of correspondence
- Scrutiny of documentation
- Special on-site visits
- Attendance at internal validation events

Most procedures requiring visits make use of peer-review procedures, and peers are often involved in scrutiny of documentation. Approval of *initial* education varies from a very "hands-off" approach based on receipt of documentation through participation in internal validation and review events to a very close scrutiny involving specially arranged visits following the receipt of specified documentation.

Approval of *professional* education is similarly varied, but PRBs tend to get more closely involved than when validating initial education and to have more closely specified validation processes. For example, in nursing, midwifery, and health visiting, validation is undertaken by national boards in each of these disciplines and processes are minutely documented.

The Law Society, similarly, adopts a much more rigorous approach in its validation of the professional course than for undergraduate degrees. The Society approval of courses is dependent on acceptable levels of resourcing, closely specified student numbers, and clearly specified curricula that contain the prescribed elements. Once approved, annual assessment visits are mandatory for continued validation. The assessment visit involves between two and eight assessors (depending on the size of the course) visiting an institution for a minimum of three days. The assessment teams include academic peers and practicing professional solicitors. The visit includes direct observation of teaching and evaluation of resources. The assessment visit results in the production of a report that goes to the Legal Practice Course Board and to every institution offering the Legal Practice Course. The aim is not to withdraw validation (although this can happen) but to ensure that problems are overcome.

Assessment

The third strand of professional control of competence comes through the assessment of students seeking professional status. At the undergraduate level (initial education) on most programs, competence (as opposed to academic ability) is not directly assessed. Where competence to perform is most closely assessed, in such areas as nursing, teacher training, medicine, dentistry, and social work, it is the result of close supervision and evaluation of practice in real settings such as hospitals, schools, and social services departments. Nursing undergraduates, for example, have a 46-week academic year and spend half of it as trainees in hospitals. Trainee teachers also spend up to 50 percent of their academic year in school settings. The supervisor in the practice setting evaluates the day-to-day competence of the student, and, in some cases, the student will be subject to a formal practice assessment, as, for example, when trainee teachers are observed teaching a class of students.

For professional and regulatory bodies, assessment is closely tied to concerns with standards that are at the heart of professional body involvement in higher education. Most professional and regulatory bodies have maintenance of standards as part of their basic rationale; indeed, this is often a statutory responsibility. The UKCC, for example,

> exists in the context of the *Nurses, Midwives and Health Visitors Act* of 1979 and 1992. . . . our function under the Act is to establish and maintain standards of education and training for nurses, midwives and health visitors both leading to and beyond registration. (UKCC, 1995)

Standards as a concept used in the context of professional education has three different meanings:

- Service standards
- Academic standards
- Standards of competence

Service standards are measures devised to assess identified elements of the service or facilities provided (that is, what the student can reasonably expect from their higher education institution). Such standards may include the professional status of teachers, turnaround times for assessing student work; maximum class sizes; frequency of personal tutorials; availability of information on complaints procedures; time lag on introducing recommended reading into libraries; and so on. Benchmarks are often specified in "contracts" such as student charters. They tend to be quantifiable and restricted to measurable items, including the presence or absence of an element of service or a facility. *Post hoc* measurements of customer opinions (satisfaction) are used as indicators of service provision. Thus, service standards in higher education parallel consumer standards.

Academic standards measure ability to meet specified levels of academic attainment. In relation to teaching and learning, this refers to the ability of students to fulfill the requirements of the program of study, through whatever mode of assessment is required. This usually involves demonstration of *knowledge* and *understanding*. Implicitly, other skills are assessed, such as communication skills. Sometimes "higher level" skills, such as analysis, comprehension, interpretation, synthesis, and critique, are explicitly assessed.

Standards of competence measure specified levels of ability on a range of "competences." Competences may include general "transferable skills" required by employers or specific skills required for induction into a profession. The latter usually relate to the ability of the practitioner to *apply specific skills* and abilities according to occupational or professional criteria. Professional competence may also include exhibiting the values and ethics of the profession and ensuring that procedures and practices conform to British Standards and European Directives (Brown, 1994).

As noted earlier, professional and regulatory bodies address such service standards through the accreditation and validation procedures. Assessment of academic standards and, particularly, standards of competence is the third means for professional and regulatory bodies to control competence.

It is necessary for professional education to set *academic standards* and ensure that candidates achieve them if the public is to be reassured that the practitioner has attained a level of knowledge sufficient to ensure that they can act effectively. Usually, professional bodies set minimum levels of academic standards (or benchmarks) that have to be achieved by students to gain recognition, although these are often not much more than the award of a degree or other required qualification. This is usually the focus of initial education, and, in the main, PRBs do not directly assess this academic standard but leave it to the institutions to assess via the long-established external examiner system. What PRBs are concerned with is the identification of minimum standards required from initial education to allow a student to enter the professional stage of education and training. In effect, at the initial education level, PRBs delegate monitoring of academic standards to external examiners whom, in some cases, they have formally approved.

However, in some areas, such as medical education, control over standards of initial education remains very tight. The Education Committee of the GMC may make written enquiries of the universities with medical schools whenever it sees fit, in order to satisfy itself that standards that it sets are being maintained. It normally exercises that power on an annual basis. Furthermore, the Committee may use its statutory powers to visit courses or inspect assessment whenever it chooses, and its report, along with any reply by the university, is sent to the Privy Council. A similar procedure operates for the General Dental Council, whose leaders may periodically appoint visitors to be present at examinations of dental students:

> The Council has power, if it considers that the course of study or examinations of a particular body are not such to ensure that graduates of licentiates possess the requisite knowledge and skill for the efficient practice of dentistry, to make representations to the Privy Council, who may order that the degree or licence shall cease to confer the right to be registered in the Dentists' Register. (GDC, 1994)

Professional and regulatory bodies usually encapsulate specific *competence* requirements within the *professional,* as opposed to initial, level of education. These are benchmarked through such things as pass grades on professional examinations and satisfactory performance of a specified period of practice. In the case of professional level competence, the PRBs may be more directly involved in assessment. A number of approaches have been adopted by PRBs for assessing and monitoring standards of professional education. In the survey by Harvey and Mason (1995b), 34 of the 74 bodies offering professional qualifications had compulsory examinations and 41 included a compulsory work experience element.

At one end of the continuum is the singular focus on candidate abilities as determined through a centrally set and assessed professional examination independent of the student learning experience. This effectively substitutes the *assessment* of standards for the *setting* of standards. In such cases, there is often no attempt to define the required standards in advance nor even to specify the nature of programs. Potential recruits to the profession are required to pass an examination that the professional body sets and marks. For example, the National Association of Goldsmiths of Great Britain and Ireland has a compulsory syllabus and examination but does not require enrollment in a higher education course.

The other end of the continuum involves an integrated partnership between a professional body and higher education, which involves joint development of curricula, work experience, and continuing education. Often, the process is something in between these extremes. The Chartered Institute of Bankers (CIB), for example, assesses standards by two means: monitoring examination results and using a network of education officers in regional centers supported by a central Tuition Services Manager. The education officer is a part-timer, normally a banker whose job is to make sure the students know what provision is available and who acts as a conduit for local needs. Education officers also keep an eye on standards and monitor performance. Pass and failure rates at each regional center are compared to the national average. If there appears to be a problem, the regional education officer is expected to investigate the causes (CIB, 1995).

Increasingly, assessment of standards in professional education is being delegated to the provider institutions, using the external examiner system to mediate the process. Despite retaining strict control over the professional Legal Practice qualification, the Law Society delegates the setting and marking of examinations to higher education institutions. This is subject to the scrutiny of the monitoring assessment visits and the external examiners, who are nominated by the institution but actually appointed and paid for by the Law Society (Law Society, 1995).

In summary, although professional bodies have a determining role in issues of competence and standards, in the main they work closely in partnership with higher education. In most cases, professional bodies tend to be a bit conservative in their views on teaching and on outcomes. However, the situation continues to evolve, and, especially at the undergraduate level, the delegation of responsibility means that academics are able to develop innovative approaches.

Teacher Training

Teacher training, though, provides an example of an area of competence assessment where, at the initial level, control remains very tight. In the UK, initial teacher training is not controlled by a professional body but by a government agency—the Teacher Training Agency (TTA). It is mandated to ensure that teacher training is of a high standard and operates within guidelines prescribed by the Department for Education and Employment (DfEE). The agency does not refer to "competences" of students but, rather, refers to "standards" to be achieved.

> The TTA standards ("competencies" finished in 1998) are a set of standards that all trainees (as we now have to call them) must complete. There are generic ones about teaching, assessing, planning and class management and then there are specific ones related to ICT, English, Maths and Science in the Primary and Secondary curriculums. So, they do have to spend time doing these in school but also, some of them are included in our under- and postgraduate programmes. For example, ensuring that trainees understand the legal requirements upon teachers and are familiar with a range of DfEE circulars. (Hoskyns, 2000a)

A central feature of the requirements is that students spend a significant proportion of their time actually teaching in schools:

> The time in schools is also laid down 32 weeks for all 4-year full-time undergraduate programmes, 24 weeks for all full-time secondary postgraduate certificate in education (PGCE), and 18 weeks for all full-time primary PGCEs. The school experience is then woven into the courses in order to allow the trainees to be assessed against the standards towards the end of their last school experience. The school experience and the university-based study inform each other in a continuously rotating pattern. (Hoskyns, 2000a)

Staff get together as a team to identify what is required, taking into account the Agency requirements, when drawing up the program outline for each training pathway. Furthermore, teacher training is constructed as a partnership between the higher education provider (the university) and the practitioner environment (the schools).

> The "standards" for teacher training are dictated by the TTA so we have to ensure that all our students, when assessed reach at least a reasonable standard. However, the assumption is that the majority of trainees will be not merely competent, but good! . . . The pathway staff do get together to decide what standards shall mean, but the issue of Partnership means that schools have to be involved in this as well. (Hoskyns, 2000b)

In teacher training, the guarantee that students obtain the required learning comes as a result of normal academic processes. Students are assessed using an array of devices including essays, examinations, oral presentations, and projects. Professional-specific skills are developed and assessed through observation of performance.

> Assessment of trainees against the standards does take place in school and is assessed through:
> (a) a profile of evidence; and
> (b) formal observation conducted by mentors (school teachers trained for the job).
> In some Primary schools, they ask University tutors to do this assessment, where they haven't yet been trained or for other reasons are not able to do the assessment. (Hoskyns, 2000a)

The standards are assessed initially by students, their school mentors, and academic staff; moderated by university tutors; and then further moderated by external examiners, as in any other degree subject in the United Kingdom. However, a further external scrutiny operates in teacher training. The Office of Standards in Education (OFSTED) undertakes periodic inspections of training provision alongside its ongoing inspection of the United Kingdom's schools.

> We do have to guarantee that students obtain the required standards, both in practical teaching and in academic assignments. To do this we have to provide our own assessment to external inspectors (OFSTED) and they then crawl all over us to demonstrate whether we are "Good, with outstanding features" (Grade 1) "Good" (Grade 2) "Compliant,

but needs substantial improvement" (Grade 3) "Non-compliant with the Secretary of State's standards" (Grade 4). (Hoskyns, 2000b)

Indeed, teacher training in universities is about as far as one can get from the traditional model of academic freedom and autonomy. Not only are outcomes inspected, the assessment instruments are also scrutinized. The assessment process is constantly reviewed through the periodic review and validation procedures, the external examiner system, the internal scrutiny of Boards of Studies, and via student and staff evaluations; and it is also inspected externally by OFSTED.

One of the main OFSTED inspection objectives is to identify whether or not our assessment procedures are rigorous, fair, reveal major weaknesses, etc. (Hoskyns, 2000b)

In the United Kingdom, there is an extensive system of quality control and continuous improvement prompted by internal mechanisms and external evaluations, which tend to be more "intrusive" and "directive" than, for example, U.S. accreditation mechanisms. There are, therefore, numerous ways in which the results of external evaluations and internal reviews of student progress and abilities are fed back into the development of programs of study, details of which are beyond the scope of this chapter. In the case of teacher training at UCE, for example, a key document, produced annually, is the Annual Report of each pathway leader (equivalent to a program director).

Pathway leaders have to collate and examine that which has occurred in the previous academic year, analyse the statistics, analyse and respond to external examiners' reports, answer to some kind of peer or other evaluation [including the university-wide Student Satisfaction survey] and then the whole is reported on to Senate [via collation and synthesis through the Faculty Academic Board]. Pathway and Faculty quality assurance procedures are crucial to ensuring that students are fairly and reasonably assessed. (Hoskyns, 2000b)

On the basis of the program Annual Report, changes will be implemented in practices and procedures for the following academic year. The aim is constantly to identify the optimum way of producing good graduates. Although there is intense external scrutiny in teacher education, the system still relies heavily on the external examiner system, which has been pivotal to maintaining standards in U.K. universities and, in professional areas, ensuring appropriate levels of competence.

Quality Assurance Agency (QAA) Benchmarks

Despite the long-standing and well-respected external examiner system, higher education in the United Kingdom has not been particularly good at explicitly specifying how it sets standards. Historically, standards have been established *post hoc* through the mediation of esteemed colleagues at other universities who provided legitimation and mutual support for their endeavors (Silver, 1995). This basic principle of esteemed peer mutual support has changed little over two centuries. The approach has allowed standards to remain largely implicit rather than explicit. This was in clear contrast to approaches in other European countries, such as Denmark, where the aims and focus and forms of assessment on university courses were set centrally by the education ministry, on advice taken from the higher education sector.

Following protracted debates and readjustment of the complex external quality monitoring procedures in the United Kingdom during the 1990s (HEQC, 1995), there has been an attempt to establish explicit national "threshold standards" for all undergraduate degrees on a subject-by-subject basis. This process is ongoing. The development of standards in three subject areas was piloted, and subject benchmarks (of enormous variability) have been established for 22 subjects (QAA, 2000c).[2] These benchmark standards attempt to specify in the form of outcome statements the minimum knowledge and abilities that graduating students will possess. The use of these benchmarks in external assessments by the new Quality Assurance Agency for Higher Education (QAA) will not apply until later in 2001 in Wales and Scotland and not until January 2002 in England.

The specification of threshold minimum standards by the QAA rather than gradations of standards reflects the approach of professional bodies (Brown, 1994) and of academics who teach professional courses (Harvey & Mason, 1995a).

Law

The benchmark standards in law "set out what an employer, student or funder can reasonably expect to be the *minimum* achievement of a graduate with an honours [sic] Bachelors degree in Law or Legal Studies" (QAA, 2000a). The standards do not specify the mode of study nor the learning methods by which a student is able to achieve these outcomes. Currently, there is no attempt directly to examine the competences of students undertaking a degree in law (LLB).

> Although students are given the opportunity to practice various skills they are not assessed on them. The demonstration of "Skills and Other Attributes" will become a requirement of all Honours level

undergraduate law programmes in the near future, because it is required by the Law Benchmark Standards and most undergraduate programmes are working on ensuring the standards are complied with. (Humphreys, 2000)

The law benchmark standards, for example, require that any student graduating in Law must show achievement in *all* of the following seven areas of performance, "demonstrating substantially all of the abilities and competencies identified in each area of performance" (QAA, 2000a):

Knowledge. Students should be able to
- Demonstrate knowledge of a substantial range of major concepts, values, principles, and rules of the legal system
- Explain the main legal institutions and procedures of that system
- Demonstrate the study in depth and in context of some substantive areas of the legal system

Application and problem solving. Students should demonstrate a basic ability to apply knowledge to a situation of limited complexity in order to provide arguable conclusions for concrete problems (actual or hypothetical).

Sources and research. Students should demonstrate a basic ability to
- Identify accurately the issue(s) that require researching
- Identify and retrieve up-to-date legal information, using paper and electronic sources
- Use primary and secondary legal sources relevant to the topic under study

General transferable intellectual skills—analysis, synthesis, critical judgment, and evaluation. Students should demonstrate a basic ability to
- Recognize and rank items and issues in terms of relevance and importance
- Bring together information and materials from a variety of different sources
- Produce a synthesis of relevant doctrinal and policy issues in relation to a topic
- Make a critical judgment of the merits of particular arguments
- Present and make a reasoned choice between alternative solutions

Autonomy and ability to learn. Students should demonstrate a basic ability, with limited guidance, to
- Act independently in planning and undertaking tasks in areas of law that they have already studied

- Be able to undertake independent research in areas of law that have not been studied
- Reflect on their own learning and to seek and make use of feedback

Communication and literacy. Both orally and in writing, students should demonstrate a basic ability to

- Understand and use the English language (or, where appropriate, Welsh language) proficiently in relation to legal matters
- Present knowledge or an argument in a way that is comprehensible to others and that is directed at their concerns
- Read and discuss legal materials that are written in technical and complex language

Numeracy, information technology, and teamwork. Students should demonstrate a basic ability to

- Use, present, and evaluate information provided in numerical or statistical form
- Produce a word-processed essay or other text and to present such work in an appropriate form
- Use the World Wide Web and E-mail
- Use some electronic information retrieval systems
- Work in groups as a participant who contributes effectively to the group's task
  (Adapted from QAA, 2000a)

The benchmark statements are expanded, and the law benchmark descriptors run to 30 pages. The detailed text for law schools indicates that the purpose of the benchmark standards is threefold: (a) to "guide institutions in reporting clearly and accurately to the wider public the nature of their provision in a standard way"; (b) to "provide a basis for institutions to devise their own learning outcome statements compatible with these benchmark statements" These two purposes reflect service standards: clear information and output requirements; and (c) "to set as a minimum certain achievements in areas of performance that a student must demonstrate to be awarded an undergraduate degree in law" (QAA, 2000a). However, despite their scope, the "benchmarks" are mainly so vague that they cannot be used as benchmarks in the sense of clearly defining minimum levels of achievement. At best, they are suggestive. There is considerable variation in specificity *within* the law benchmarks.

For example, the section on "Application and problem solving" in the law benchmarks is expanded as follows:

An ability to apply knowledge and to solve problems need not be demonstrated in relation to each subject studied. It is sufficient that a student can demonstrate with sufficient frequency an ability to apply knowledge. A student might demonstrate application through moots, law clinic, tutorial work as well as though conventional problem questions in unseen examinations. (QAA, 2000a)

For illustrative purposes, the following are used as descriptors of proficiency in the area of application:

Very proficient: Able to apply knowledge to difficult situations of significant legal complexity, to analyze facts, and to produce well-supported conclusions in relation to them.

Proficient: Able to apply knowledge to complex situations, able to recognize potential alternative conclusions for particular situations, and to provide supporting reasons for them.

Pass: Able to apply knowledge to situations of limited complexity and to produce arguable conclusions treating the situation as an exemplification of established rules and lacking an awareness of more sophisticated issues. (QAA, 2000a)

The additional detail on proficiency in the use of computer and information technology is as follows:

Given the background of many students, many aspects of performance may well have been achieved before they arrive in university. The requirement is fairly limited. In terms of word processing, the essential skills required are to be able to produce a word-processed essay or other text and to present such work in an appropriate form. Information retrieval systems may, but need not, include LEXIS. Standard information retrieval systems would include electronic library catalogues. (QAA, 2000a)

The associated proficiency statements relating specifically to the Internet follow:

Very proficient: Able to create a WWW home page and produce HTML documents; able to set up and manage E-mail discussion groups.

Proficient:	Able to conduct efficient searches of websites to collect relevant information; able to exchange documents by E-mail and to manage information exchanged by E-mail.
Pass:	Able to locate WWW sites from given Web addresses and retrieve information from them; able to send and receive E-mail messages. (QAA, 2000a)

Thus, the law benchmarks are not clear-cut measures but, rather, are indicative of the areas of proficiency and the range of ability that might be expected. Furthermore, there is no prescription about the form or nature of assessment. Each institution will develop their own assessment criteria that provide them with "the appropriate form of evidence" they require that a student has met the minimum standards. Indeed, all that is necessary is "a statement that the student has passed a requisite standard in that area" rather than that they achieve some form of pre-specified academic or skill *level*. The satisfying of the standards remains the province of the external examiner system.

Although a new departure for the external monitoring agency, specification of outcomes is not new to the sector. Apart from professional-body output requirements, it is indicative of the expressed outcomes that were encouraged in the old polytechnic sector (now the post-1992 universities in the United Kingdom) by the Council for National Academic Awards (CNAA). Ironically, broad outcome statements were considered to be too general to be feasible by the QAA's precursor, the Higher Education Quality Council (Brown, 1998).

This generality is also evident in the further attempt to provide criteria for grading included in an Appendix to the law benchmarks (QAA, 2000a). For example:

First-class answers are ones that are exceptionally good for an undergraduate and that excel in at least one and probably several of the following criteria:
• Comprehensiveness and accuracy
• Clarity of argument and expression
• Integration of a range of materials
• Evidence of wider reading
• Insight into the theoretical issues

At the other end of the scale, third-class answers demonstrate some knowledge or understanding of the general area, but a third-class answer tends to be weak in the following ways:

- Descriptive only
- Does not answer the question directly
- Misses key points
- Contains important inaccuracies
- Covers material sparsely, possibly in note form
- Assertions not supported by authority or evidence

This type of generic grading descriptor was embedded in course documents drawn up under CNAA auspices. Furthermore, this type of generic descriptor clearly has written essay or examination answers in mind. At root, they are vague and ambiguous when applied, in practice, to a specific course work task.

The QAA benchmarks express no preference as to the form of evidence, but an institution "must have in place mechanisms which provide it with reliable evidence that students have reached the minimum standard in each area of performance" (QAA, 2000a). External examiners and QAA academic reviewers will expect to be informed of these mechanisms and to make judgments about their sufficiency. However, as the benchmarks do not require that all the skills associated with each benchmark area are directly assessed, the extent to which these QAA subject benchmarks become a vehicle for assessing competence will depend on the approach adopted by programs. As one tutor noted:

> There is no requirement that we "assess" the skills in the sense that we would normally use that word, but we have to demonstrate not only that our students have the opportunity to achieve them, but also that they do in fact do so. Therefore, incorporating them into at least some of our assessments is the way we have chosen to go. (Humphreys, 2000)

Output statements, because of their generality (Yorke, 1999), are unlikely, in the long run, to provide anything but minimum assurance to professional bodies of the integrity of undergraduate degrees. Indeed, these standards are not meant to be directly linked to professional body requirements—they are also drawn up in nonprofessional subjects.

Sociology   In areas outside the sway of professional bodies, the benchmarks tend to be very vague, indeed. For example, the sociology benchmarks are very much more "academic" with virtually no references to "skills." The sociology benchmark statement is only nine pages long. It expects that

> All programmes will address the following areas of sociological knowledge and understanding:
>
> - Key concepts and theoretical approaches that have been developed and are developing within sociology
> - An awareness of social context, of the nature of social processes, and of social diversity and inequality
> - An understanding of the value of comparative analysis
> - An understanding of the relationship between individuals, groups, and social institutions
> - An understanding of the role of culture in social life
> - An understanding of the social processes underpinning social change
> - An understanding of the nature and appropriate use of diverse research strategies and methods in gaining sociological knowledge
> - An understanding of the relationship between sociological argument and evidence
> - An awareness of the distinctive character of sociology in relation to other forms of understanding, such as its relation to other disciplines and to everyday explanations (QAA, 2000b)

The proficiency descriptors operate at two levels, threshold and typical (Table 12.1).

There is no mention of information technology, teamworking, presentation skills, or any other "transferable" skills not directly related to the academic pursuit of sociology. Yet, this is an area where many students go into employment *because* of the transferability of their skills. Ironically, it is within sociology at UCE that considerable effort is being put in identifying transferable skills and enabling students to develop them through work placements and varied types of assessed assignments. Indeed, it is in sociology that the most effective advance in targeted assessment has been made. Rather than vague generic assessment criteria, some sociology staff have adopted standard specifications for individual assignments.

Individual assignment standard specification (IASS).   Individual assignment standard specifications clearly specify, in advance, the assessment criteria *and* weighting for each individual piece of assessed work against a predetermined set of knowledge, skills, and abilities that the assignment is

Table 12.1. Example of Proficiency Descriptors in Sociology

Benchmark	Threshold Achievement	Typical Achievement
An understanding of key concepts and theoretical approaches that have developed and are developing within Sociology.	Able to describe a range of key concepts and theoretical approaches within Sociology.	Able to describe and examine a range of key concepts and theoretical approaches within Sociology and evaluate their application.
An awareness of social diversity and inequality and of their impact on the lives of individuals and groups.	Able to recognize patterns of social diversity and inequality.	Able to provide an analytical account of social diversity and inequality and their effects.
An understanding of the value of comparative analysis.	Able to recognize and illustrate the use of comparison in Sociology.	Able to evaluate strengths and weaknesses in the use of comparison in Sociology.
An understanding of the nature and appropriate use of research strategies and methods in gaining sociological knowledge.	Able to identify diverse research strategies and methods and illustrate their use in gaining sociological knowledge.	Able to examine a range of research strategies and methods and assess the appropriateness of their use.

Note From Quality Assurance Agency for Higher Education (QAA), *Benchmark Standards for Sociology*. [On-line May 2000]. Available: http:www.qaa.ac.uk/. Adapted with permission.

attempting to evaluate. Instead of vague generic criteria such as "excelling in comprehensiveness and accuracy," the IASS breaks down the assessment into several dimensions relating to the assignment. For example, an assignment requiring the student to produce a costed research outline might include the following dimensions: clarity of research aims, appropriateness of proposed methodology, feasibility of timetable, realism of the indicative costing, inclusion of appropriate theoretical context, general layout and readability, production of proposal against deadline. The dimensions are weighted in proportion to their importance in the assignment. Under each dimension, specific criteria are provided as a guide to what is needed. Students are given a grade against each dimension and, thus, can easily see where they need to improve.

In general, IASSs can be constructed to ensure that, within a program of study, all the elements of the professional-body requirements or QAA benchmark standards have been covered adequately. Such an approach would reduce ambiguity and ensure transparency to both learner and external evaluator and go well beyond the vague approach of the proposed benchmarks.

Conclusions and Recommendations

Quality assessment of subject areas used to take a broader view of the learning experience of students, addressing the quality of the provision rather than the standard of outcomes. The new approach places far more emphasis on standards and, thus, at the undergraduate level, overlaps somewhat with the traditional role of external examiners and the oversight role of professional bodies.

The external examining system has been the traditional way that the standard and outcomes of courses has been monitored and compared. The close scrutiny of student work by invited external peers has been the means of assuring providers that their output is comparable with others in the same field.

The change in emphasis in national quality monitoring with the emphasis on benchmark standards at the undergraduate level, although identifying outcomes, does so in a generalist manner that falls short of prescriptive competence statements. Although there will be pressure to take account of the benchmarks, there is little evident enthusiasm among academic staff. The feeling at this early stage is that requirements will be complied with in the usual cosmetic manner and that, no doubt, in time the whole thing will fall into abeyance as it becomes evident that the approach is flawed and unworkable. Although the QAA is energetically trying to encourage other national agencies to adopt a similar benchmarking approach, the academic community will weather the bureaucratic storm.

To date, in the United Kingdom, competence statements are most closely associated with national vocational qualifications rather than degrees (Bates, 1999). Competence statements are resisted by academics in higher education and, to a degree, by employers who, at the graduate level, want rounded, critical, reflective, and flexible employees rather than narrowly competent ones.

Given the changes in the quality monitoring processes, it seems likely that professional bodies will increasingly concentrate on professional-level accreditation and standards and adopt a more hands-off approach at the undergraduate or initial level. However, as there are so many different professional and regulatory bodies involved in higher education in the United Kingdom, it is unlikely that there will be a uniform approach to the specification and monitoring of professional competence at any level. Nonetheless, it is contingent on all professional and regulatory bodies that they define the specific competences, including underpinning knowledge, that are required of graduates in order for them to be effective practitioners.

For teachers, the single biggest step that can be taken in the face of the QAA benchmarks, specific requirements to identify skills and abilities, and professional-body expectations is to adopt the IASS model. This has been done successfully in some areas. The IASS model involves clearly identifying the dimensions of subject standards that each individual assessed assignment is addressing, making explicit the weighting given to each and the criteria of success for the particular assignment.

Notes

1. Continuing professional development (CPD) is too extensive to cover in this chapter. As it suggests, it is about the ongoing development of higher-level knowledge and competences among established practitioners.

2. The subject areas are Accounting, Archaeology, Architecture, General Business and Management, Chemistry, Classics and Ancient History, Computing, Earth Science, Environmental Sciences and Environmental Studies, Economics, Education Studies, Engineering, Geography, History, Hospitality, Leisure, Sport and Tourism, Law, Librarianship and Information Management, Philosophy, Politics and International Relations, Social Policy and Administration and Social Work, Sociology, Theology and Religious Studies.

References

Bates, I. (1999). The competence and outcomes movement: The landscape of research. In M. Flude & S. Sieminski (Eds.), *Education, training and the future of work II: Developments in vocational education and training* (pp. 98–123). London: Routledge and the Open University Press.

Barnett, R. (1992). *Improving higher education: Total quality care.* Buckingham: The Society for Research into Higher Education and Open University Press.

Brown, R. (1994). Quality and standards: the HEQC perspective. In L. Harvey & S. Mason (Eds.), 1995a, *Proceedings of the third QHE 24-hour seminar, quality and standards: The role of the professions,* December 15–16, 1994. Birmingham, QHE, pp. 22–30.

Brown, R. (1998). Co-operation or compliance? The National Committee of Inquiry proposals on quality and standards. *Quality in Higher Education,* 4(1), 85–96.

Chartered Institute of Bankers (CIB). (1995). Interview between Mr. Brian Rawle, Director of Studies, and Selena Mason, Centre for Research into Quality, April 20, 1995.

Connor, H. Graduate employment trends: Key issues in the labour market of the late 1990s and beyond. In R. Burgess (Ed.), *Beyond the first degree: Graduate education, lifelong learning and careers* (pp. 168–185). Buckingham: The Society for Research into Higher Education and Open University Press.

Department for Education and Employment (DfEE). (1996). *Building the framework: A consultation paper on bringing together the work of NCVQ and SCAA.* London: Author.

Flude, M., & Sieminski, S. (Eds.). *Education, training and the future of work II: Developments in vocational education and training.* London: Routledge and the Open University Press.

General Dental Council (GDC). (1994). Letter from Mrs. J. M. Gordon to Professor Lee Harvey, December 20, 1994.

General Medical Council (GMC). (1995). Letter from Miss H. M. Burke to Professor Lee Harvey, December 8, 1994.

Grant, G., et al. (1979). *On competence: A critical analysis of competence-based reforms in higher education.* San Francisco: Jossey-Bass.

Harvey, L., & Mason, S. (1995a). *Proceedings of the third QHE 24-hour seminar, quality and standards: The role of the professions,* December 15–16, 1994. Birmingham: QHE.

Harvey, L., & Mason, S. (with Ward, R.). (1995b). *The role of professional bodies in higher education quality monitoring.* Birmingham: QHE.

Higher Education Quality Council (HEQC). (1995, June). *The future development of the external examiner system.* HEQC consultative document. London: Author.

Hoskyns, J. (2000a). E-mail correspondence from Janet Hoskyns to Lee Harvey, April 3, 2000, 15:45.

Hoskyns, J. (2000b). E-mail correspondence from Janet Hoskyns to Lee Harvey, April 5, 2000, 12:59

Humphreys, V. (2000). E-mail correspondence from Valerie Humphreys to Lee Harvey, April 5, 2000, 13:22.

Institution of Electrical Engineers (IEE). (1995). Interview between Mr. Clive Holtham, Director of Qualifications, and Selena Mason. Centre for Research into Quality, April 6, 1995.

Jessup, G. (1991). *Outcomes. NVQs and the emerging model of education and training.* London: Falmer.

Law Society. (1995). Interview between Mr. Paul Bradbury, Senior Inspector of Legal Education, and Professor Lee Harvey, Centre for Research into Quality, April 11, 1995.)

Ormrod, R. (1968, April). Medical ethics. *British Medical Journal.*

Parsons, T. (1954). *Essays in sociological theory pure and applied* (2nd rev. ed.). Glencoe: Free Press.

Quality Assurance Agency for Higher Education (QAA). (2000a). *Benchmark standards for law.* [On-line May 2000]. Available: http:www.qaa.ac.uk/crntwork/benchmark/law.pdf

Quality Assurance Agency for Higher Education (QAA). (2000b). *Benchmark standards for sociology.* [On-line May 2000]. Available: http:www.qaa.ac.uk/crntwork/benchmark/sociology.pdf

Quality Assurance Agency for Higher Education (QAA). (2000c). *Benchmarking academic standards.* [On-line June 2000]. Available: http://www.qaa.ac.uk/crntwork/benchmark/benchmarking.htm

Silver, H. (1995). *History of the external examiner system.* Draft pre-publication paper.

Teacher Training Agency (TTA). (1995). Interview between Mr. Phil Holden, Quality Team Leader, and Selena Mason, Centre for Research into Quality, March 30, 1995.

United Kingdom Central Council (UKCC) for Nursing, Midwifery and Health Visiting. 1995. Interview between Mrs. Margaret J. Wallace, Assistant Registrar Education, and Sue Moon, Centre for Research into Quality, March 3, 1995.

Yorke, M. (1999). Benchmarking academic standards in the UK. *Tertiary Education and Management, 5* (1), 81–96.

I3

ASSESSMENT EXPERIENCES IN ACCREDITED DISCIPLINES

Catherine A. Palomba

As the preceding chapters indicate, numerous faculty, administrators, and staff in accredited disciplines have committed themselves to improving student learning. Often with encouragement and support from relevant accrediting bodies, these individuals have developed assessment programs that provide valuable evidence about student achievement—evidence that can be used to guide improvement efforts. Based in part on their experiences, we now raise a series of questions: What is the state of assessment in accredited disciplines? How have accrediting bodies influenced assessment of student learning in these disciplines? What assessment-related lessons, challenges, and issues do faculty in these disciplines have in common? We conclude that, although each discipline's assessment story is clearly unique, enough similarities exist to make sharing of assessment experiences across disciplines meaningful and productive.

Assessment in the Disciplines

Attendance at disciplinary, regional, and national assessment conferences demonstrates that many faculty in applied fields have made great strides with assessment, but many are still eager to learn. Tom Zlatic notes in Chapter 4 that a large number of pharmacy schools are "still experimenting and sometimes struggling" to implement coherent assessment plans. Zlatic concludes that his review of assessment in pharmacy schools is "probably both overstated and under-reported." This conclusion can be extended to other chapters in this book. Self-reports sometimes describe only the best that is occurring and fail to report problems and challenges. At the same time, since the disciplinary reviews we commissioned were not exhaustive, many programs in these fields may be doing exemplary assessment work that is not included in the chapters. Yet, on a very positive note, the chapters contain examples of assessment programs that are models for their disciplines. Kristi Nelson writes about a thorough assessment program at the Center for Creative Studies, a private art college in Detroit. Zlatic describes a thoughtful program in the Division of Pharmacy Practice at the St. Louis College of Pharmacy. Based on the assessment programs they have developed, social work faculty at Columbia College and Virginia Commonwealth University (VCU) are considered campus leaders in assessment.

As the following review shows, assessment programs developed by faculty in professional fields contain all of the elements necessary for successful assessment (described in Chapter 2). These programs include explicit statements of expected competences, useful assessment methods, and widespread involvement of faculty and other stakeholders. The review also shows that faculty in applied disciplines have drawn on their natural advantages in conducting assessment, such as close ties with external stakeholders and opportunities for active learning experiences.

Multiple Approaches

The chapters reveal a rich variety of assessment practices, both across disciplines and within disciplines. Even within particular colleges or divisions, programs in related areas may approach assessment differently. Each program in the Pamplin College of Business at Virginia Polytechnic Institute and State University (Virginia Tech) has implemented its own assessment processes, as has each program in the School of Education at Southern Illinois University Edwardsville. Allowing variation within a college or division provides a strong advantage in that each program's faculty can choose the methods and approaches that are most appealing to them. However, the practical result is that the level of success with assessment can vary within the college or division. Faculty in one program may implement effective assessment methods, while those in another may fail to approach assessment in a meaningful way. While eliminating variation should not be a goal, additional oversight for program-level activities may be helpful. An institution-wide committee, a college- (or division-) level committee, or both, can provide oversight for unit programs.

Multiple Influences

Disciplinary accrediting bodies are only one of several external influences on assessment in professional fields. On some campuses, the shape of assessment reflects requirements that come from the state legislature or higher education commission. All departments at Virginia Tech are subject to a state-level process that requires them to submit assessment reports every five years. In Indiana, teacher education programs must develop unit assessment systems that utilize performance assessment to address standards endorsed by the Indiana Professional Standards Board (Weisenbach, Mack, Scannel, & Steffel, 1998). Regional accreditation requirements fostered assessment in the social work program at the College of St. Catherine and the University of St. Thomas and were prominent in the visual arts programs described by Kristi Nelson. The Center for Creative Studies began its assessment program in 1994 following a site visit by NCA. Similar to other art programs, the Center had many elements of performance evaluation and feedback in place, but faculty needed to develop a more explicit, coordinated assessment plan that could be used for program improvement. Regional accrediting bodies influence disciplinary assessment primarily through the impact they have on institution-wide assessment requirements. Once in place, institution-wide requirements can influence many aspects of assessment in the major. In Chapter 11, Douglas Eder describes how departments at Southern Illinois University Edwardsville are expected to design Senior Assignments for their majors.

Fortunately, institutional resources often are available to support assessment in the disciplines. At the Georgia Institute of Technology, the university assessment coordinator conducts focus groups with seniors from various departments; and, at Virginia Tech, faculty participate in campus-wide workshops that address issues of student learning. When faculty from the Department of Management at Central Missouri State University were developing outcomes statements for the major, they were able to adapt the university's general education outcomes statements to reflect their own expectations. Thus, faculty involved in assessment of professional programs draw on a variety of resources as they balance competing pressures for assessment information.

Expectations for Competence

In their 1998 book, *The Bases of Competence,* Evers, Rush, and Berdrow assert that "The debate as to whether college graduates should be specialists or generalists is over; they need to be both" (p. 3). Evidence provided in the preceding chapters indicates that faculty in applied disciplines agree with this assertion. Although perhaps not to the satisfaction of higher education critics, every discipline examined in this book addresses both types of skills. The 11 learning goals for graduates of the Center for Creative Studies in Detroit include (a) the ability to utilize intuition and critical thinking skills in their work and in the evaluation of others' work, and (b) awareness of the desirability of continued learning and self-actualization (Chapter 10). Teacher education faculty at Ashland University capture the essence of their program in eight tenets that describe their collective view of the professional educator. Among other skills, graduates of their program are expected to

1. Work cooperatively and collaboratively with members of the educational community

2. Communicate clearly and effectively

3. Assume lifelong responsibility to grow academically, professionally, and personally (Chapter 3)

Expected competences for graduates of Winthrop University's College of Business Administration include communication, teamwork, adaptability, problem solving, and ethics. Computer science students at Brigham Young University (BYU) must be well grounded in ethical and moral values related to their personal and professional lives. They are required to formulate and write a personal code of ethics. Faculty from the Department of Management at CMSU expect their majors to be competent in valuing, that is, "applying a value system that will enable him/her to act in an ethical, moral, socially responsible way in business situations, while retaining personal integrity" (Andrews & Neal, 1999, p. 7). Faculty in applied disciplines require their graduates to develop many of the competences expected by employers, including communication, critical thinking, and lifelong learning skills, as well as appropriate attitudes and values.

Faculty in a number of professional programs have articulated expectations for competence that allow students to build their skills over time. Alverno College expects its teaching majors to progressively develop skills as they first work one-on-one with K–12 students, then move to small group projects, and finally manage a whole class. Asbury College uses a Continuous Improvement Model that makes use of on-demand performance tasks, exhibitions, and projects to evaluate teacher education candidates. The model includes developmental expectations for candidates' growth at key points in the curriculum. All programs in King's College have developed competency growth plans that embed assessment into every course. Faculty at Indiana University School of Nursing have developed a competency-based model that identifies a set of attributes for each competence that graduates must possess when they begin nursing practice. For example, critical thinking includes the attributes of intellectual curiosity, rational inquiry, problem framing, information validation, and evaluation of judgment. Faculty have developed statements of expected competences for each year that students are in the program and have based expectations for succeeding years on those from the prior year.

Assessment Methods

The use of locally developed techniques dominates the examples described in the chapters. Some measures have been developed in reaction to new requirements for assessment, but faculty also have drawn on instruments and methods that were already in place. In particular, many faculty have used existing classroom activities from capstone or other courses as bases for programmatic assessment. Rather than relying on a single test or survey, faculty typically use multiple methods to assess their programs, often including both quantitative and qualitative approaches. For example, nursing faculty on some campuses use narratives to evaluate students' abilities in problem identification and clinical judgment. Faculty use both direct measures that demonstrate learning and indirect measures that provide reflections about learning. In several instances, college-wide activities are used in conjunction with department or program activities. In business colleges, the core curriculum often is assessed through college-wide tests, surveys, or common capstone projects.

As might be expected, performance assessment is used extensively by faculty in professional fields. Alverno College has pioneered the use of performance assessments that make outcomes visible. These are used not only for those in teacher education but for all Alverno students (Mentkowski & Associates, 2000). Kristi Nelson writes that the use of student portfolios, critiques to provide feedback, and public exhibitions of student work, as well as an emphasis on self-assessment skills, are "part and parcel of every art program in the country" (Chapter 10). As Nelson describes, the College of Design, Architecture, Art, and Planning (DAAP) at the University of Cincinnati uses juried critiques and oral defense of theses to evaluate cognitive skills. Student learning also is evaluated in the classroom during the comprehensive studio, when students are required to integrate what they have learned across a sequence of classes. BYU computer science students complete programming projects in computer laboratories. After the projects are completed initially, teaching assistants deliberately insert errors into the computer programs, then return them to students to correct within a limited amount of time. All students in the School of Engineering at SIUE are required to complete major design projects that result in both written reports and oral presentations. At Rose-Hulman Institute of Technology, engineering students participate in portfolio assessment.

Although performance methods are favored by faculty in applied fields, some faculty do use objective tests for assessment. The Center for Creative Studies in Detroit uses a pre-post standardized test as well as writing samples to evaluate English skills. Faculty in some nursing programs use the Watson-Glaser Critical Thinking Appraisal and/or the California Critical Thinking Skills Test. Ball State University (BSU)'s College of Business uses an objective pre-post test to evaluate students midway through the business core. Winthrop's College of Business includes a capstone test for all majors. In fact, discussion at AACSB conferences reveals that many business faculty still favor this traditional quantitative approach to evaluating students.

Faculty in professional fields, not unlike those in other disciplines, appear more comfortable assessing knowledge and skills than attitudes and values. Chapter authors did share some examples of how faculty assess the latter competences. Faculty in the College of DAAP use student, alumni, and employer surveys to evaluate growth and change in attitudes from matriculation through graduation and careers. Faculty in pharmacy employ attitude surveys, preceptor evaluations, and the California Critical Thinking Dispositions Inventory to assess attitudes and values. Nevertheless, Zlatic notes that assessment in these areas remains "elusive" (Chapter 4), and Muffo notes the discomfort of engineers in dealing with "soft" subjects such as lifelong learning (Chapter 9).

Stakeholder Involvement

As the chapters demonstrate, thoughtful strategies have been used to involve faculty, students, and external stakeholders in assessment. Some interesting examples are reviewed here.

Faculty   Tom Zlatic describes how faculty from the Division of Pharmacy Practice at the St. Louis College of Pharmacy used division meetings, development workshops, and retreats to help faculty understand the rationale for curricular reform in pharmacy education. Teams of faculty also attended Alverno College's week-long assessment workshop. Once seven abilities were identified for all courses, division faculty were assigned to ability subcommittees to develop criteria for three levels of student performance; to create self-, peer-, and expert-assessment forms; and to map abilities across courses. Social work faculty at VCU attended bi-weekly meetings and participated in content teaching groups when they were developing program goals, course objectives, and student outcome statements prior to a reaccreditation visit from their disciplinary accreditor. In the Center for Creative Studies, faculty met as a whole to generate ideas, synthesize concepts, and create goal statements that were common to all graduates of the Center. After faculty responses were organized into a proposed assessment plan, numerous meetings were held to review the plan and establish responsibilities for participating in it.

Students   Faculty in several programs have developed materials to help students become familiar with assessment. The student manual developed by Seton Hall's business faculty describes the purpose for assessment, as well as all expected competences. Seton Hall's business faculty also hold workshops to prepare students to participate in assessment panels. Students, of course, are the source of most assessment information. Through various assessment projects, students both demonstrate their learning and provide their opinions and self-reflections about learning. For example, social work faculty at VCU conduct exit interviews with their students using a focus group approach. However, the examples in the chapters here do not provide much evidence that students participate directly in the design of assessment procedures or in the development of outcomes statements; both are areas where students could contribute more.

As the chapters illustrate, assessment influences students in various ways. Often it is used for developmental purposes—to improve the learning of individual students. As Mary Diez describes, faculty at Alverno College employ feedback to help teacher education candidates understand the outcomes and criteria that are used to evaluate their performances. Feedback also helps candidates set goals for future performance and conveys the message that "assessment is a learning opportunity." At Alverno, self-assessment is used to help candidates become their own "coaches and critics" (Chapter 3). Assessment also is used for high-stakes decisions that determine students' standing in their programs. The University of Mississippi School of Pharmacy evaluates performance in problem-based learning experiences in order to determine if students are ready to advance into their sixth year. In one assessment conducted during the weekend, students complete novel cases that are evaluated for clinical reasoning and self-learning skills. As Diez notes, both approaches have a role to play in assessment of student learning.

Other Stakeholders   Higher education is frequently criticized for failing to respond to public needs. The American Council on Education (ACE) has noted that "a chasm separates the academic and corporate worlds." Academic leaders believe that corporations have little respect for campuses. Corporate leaders believe that university faculty and administrators "do not understand the requirements of the private sector and the need for students to be better prepared for the demands of a changing global economy" (1997, p. 3). In contrast to this conclusion, several chapter authors report examples of close collaboration between faculty and external stakeholders. Alverno College faculty invite teachers and principals to review teacher education candidates' portfolios. When faculty from the University of Indianapolis design assessment procedures, they involve teachers from affiliated community schools. Business faculty from King's College gather feedback from internship supervisors. Faculty in Ohio University's human resource management program work closely with their advisory board of practitioners. The board not only helped faculty articulate expected competences for their majors; it also helped them design projects to assess these competences. Engineering faculty typically draw on industrial advisory committees and alumni committees for assistance with assessment. As Boland and Laidig write, nursing faculty use surveys, focus groups, and other approaches to actively seek input from several interest groups, including colleagues, employers, community leaders, and recent alumni (Chapter 5).

Organizing for Assessment and Using Results

Several chapter authors describe assessment processes that are based on thoughtful assessment plans—plans that identify key committees and processes. In the Division of Pharmacy Practice at the St. Louis College of Pharmacy, the curriculum committee is responsible for reviewing the syllabus for each course to make sure it is structured along ability-based lines and includes outcomes, practice, criteria, and feedback. Assessment responsibilities for undergraduate programs in BSU's College of Business were assumed by an existing (although renamed) curriculum and assessment committee. Committees such as these play an important role in providing what Hutchings and Marchese call a "home for assessment" within existing structures (1990, p. 34).

Explicit timelines and/or regular reports also benefit assessment. Social work faculty from Columbia College annually review an assessment report prepared by the program director. Then the social work advisory committee makes recommendations to the faculty for action. The assessment coordinator at the Center for Creative Studies writes an annual report discussing progress and next steps for that assessment program. Business faculty in both King's College and Virginia Tech participate in institution-wide assessment programs that require regular assessment reports. The business dean and the associate dean for undergraduate business programs at Virginia Tech recommend that such reports be very candid and include negative as well as positive results. As they point out, sometimes negative results need to be shared for change to occur.

Reflecting good assessment practice, the chapters in this volume contain many examples of faculty who have used assessment evidence to improve their programs. The School of Art at the University of Cincinnati reorganized eight studio media options into three majors, shifted course sequences, and changed the credit hours assigned to studios. At SIUE, the School of Nursing created a psychomotor skills laboratory to allow students more opportunities to practice their skills. Faculty in SIUE's engineering departments are collaborating with the Department of Speech Communication and using video technology to incorporate more writing and speech practice into the curriculum. Based on very positive assessment results, a writing program initially offered in only one department of Virginia Tech's College of Engineering was extended to all departments in the college.

Influence of Disciplinary Accreditors and Professional Associations

Accrediting bodies have several characteristics in common. They evaluate programs using standards that have been endorsed by members, require self-evaluations conducted by program faculty, and facilitate campus site visits by peers. As William Dill points out, "most are creatures of their member campuses" (1998b, p. 21) with deans and professors serving on committees, setting policies, and conducting evaluations. A new item can be added to the list of commonalities—accreditors foster campus assessment efforts. They provide resources to facilitate assessment, identify competences that should be addressed, and expect faculty to use assessment results to improve student learning. Through these expectations, accreditors encourage their members to implement good assessment practice.

Embracing Assessment

Several factors have influenced disciplinary accreditors to require that their members develop meaningful assessment processes. Prominent among these is the federal government expectation, first introduced in 1988, that accreditors must focus on program outcomes as a condition of their own recognition; but other factors have encouraged assessment. In the disciplines of pharmacy, nursing, computer science, and teacher education, profound changes in expectations for graduates have made it increasingly important to assess student learning. In the discipline of business, leaders of AACSB—The International Association for Management Education, having observed competitive pressures forcing corporations to evaluate their own performances intensively, have asked members to be equally introspective.

In response to the various influences, disciplinary accrediting bodies have shifted their emphasis from input to outcomes measures when evaluating programs for accreditation. Although clearly pushed by external forces, and perhaps slower to respond than some critics would have liked, several accreditors have embraced the assessment movement and, in fact, have become advocates for assessment.

Assessment in applied fields has been fostered by professional bodies as well as accreditors. Since as early as 1989, the American Association of Colleges of Pharmacy (AACP) has provided vision for pharmacy schools as they rethink their educational missions. In that year, the AACP created a commission that affirmed pharmaceutical care as the new mission of pharmacy practice and recognized the importance of developing outcomes as the basis for assessing student achievement. The AACP established an advisory panel that proposed a set of general and professional outcomes for the practice of pharmaceutical care. The accrediting body in pharmacy, the American Council on Pharmaceutical Education (ACPE), later endorsed this work. In computer science, professional societies actually existed before the academic discipline was developed. In Chapter 8, Gordon Stokes writes that the Association for Computing Machinery (ACM) facilitated debate about the body of knowledge that now serves as the foundation of the discipline. The ACM fostered the birth of the Computer Science Accreditation Commission that began accrediting programs in 1987. The American Association of Colleges of Nursing (AACN) issued competence statements for baccalaureate and master's prepared nurses in 1998 and 1996, respectively. This group created an independent agency in 1997 that, along with the National League for Nursing Accreditation Commission (NLNAC), now accredits nursing programs. Regional and state associations also have fostered assessment in nursing.

Not every accreditor has been quick to embrace all aspects of assessment. Kristi Nelson describes how the National Association of Schools of Art and Design (NASAD) initially took a conservative attitude toward assessment, carefully studying its meaning and relevance for the visual arts. Because performance assessment concepts were already embedded in visual arts accreditation standards, NASAD urged its members to resist any push to adopt methods that were inappropriate. By 1990, the accrediting bodies in the arts, through the Council of Arts Accrediting Associations, had prepared a paper, *Outcomes Assessment and Arts Programs in Higher Education,* that explored outcomes assessment issues and encouraged attention to assessment. The paper argued that assessment should be "carried out within a context defined by the nature of the discipline" (p. 2) and that, because evaluation activities in the arts are typically more comprehensive and targeted than those in other disciplines, arts units should be able to "defend the unit's outcomes assessment effort against benighted and unwarranted intrusion" (pp. 2–3). These statements clearly reflect an attitude of caution. Note, however, that the reservations expressed by NASAD and the Council of Arts Accrediting Associations about the inappropriate use of mandated methods such as objective tests were similar to those national assessment leaders were expressing at that time (Hutchings & Marchese, 1990).

Resources to Support Assessment

Accreditors and professional organizations typically support assessment efforts of their members through conferences and written materials. Each summer, the AACP offers an Institute on Pedagogical and Curricular Change, a five-day conference that promotes the development of strategies that enhance teaching, learning, and assessment in pharmacy schools. Twenty to twenty-five schools send faculty teams to attend workshops and develop plans that they can use on campus to facilitate educational improvement. AACSB has now held three conferences devoted entirely to assessment and also features assessment in its annual *Continuous Improvement Symposium*. Beginning in the late 1980s, NASAD used a series of sessions at its annual meetings to encourage its membership to, as Nelson writes, "debate the pros and cons of outcomes assessment and how it might be applied to art and design programs" (Chapter 10). The Commission on Accreditation (COA) of the Council on Social Work Education introduced a faculty development program in 1999 to help faculty learn how to develop mission statements, program goals, and student outcomes assessment plans. Accreditors in dentistry and dietetics have published handbooks on outcomes assessment. AACSB, the Computing Sciences Accreditation Board (CSAB), the Accrediting Board for Engineering and Technology (ABET), and many other accreditors have developed helpful websites.

Expectations About Competences

Accrediting bodies expect their members to assess particular competences, including both general education and discipline-specific skills. Thus, accreditors implicitly encourage their members to respond to the workforce needs of employers. ABET criteria state that engineering graduates should be able to function on multidisciplinary teams and possess an understanding of ethical responsibility. The social work COA has issued 12 educational outcomes for baccalaureate graduates, including critical thinking and understanding the positive value of diversity. NASAD expects artists and designers to develop the abilities to think, speak, and write clearly. In addition to therapeutic nursing interventions, NLNAC expects nurses to be competent in critical thinking and communication. AACN has issued a longer list of expected competences, but Boland and Laidig lament that the lack of a national model has forced nursing faculty to devote a great deal of time to developing institution-specific competence statements (Chapter 5).

Most accreditors do expect their members to create statements of expected outcomes that are campus specific, giving campus meaning to the outcomes that accreditors have endorsed. For example, NASAD's 1991 document, *The Assessment of Undergraduate Programs in Art and Design,* "supports the need for a variety of missions among institutions offering undergraduate degrees in art/design" (p. 1). Rather than providing specific answers, the document poses a series of questions to assist institutions in clarifying their own goals and objectives for learning.

In the field of teacher education, the National Board for Professional Teacher Standards has developed standards and assessments for the certification of accomplished teachers. Similarly, the Interstate New Teacher Assessment and Support Consortium (INTASC) has developed standards and assessments for beginning teacher licensure. Following their lead, the National Council for Accreditation of Teacher Education (NCATE) requires links between standards and performance assessment. Rather than identifying an additional set of standards, NCATE expects teacher education programs to develop clear statements that demonstrate that candidates meet professional, state, and institutional standards. As they develop these statements, Diez urges teacher education faculty to focus on broad outcomes rather than on "bits" of information (Chapter 3).

Expectations About Assessment Methods

Although accreditors expect their members to select and/or design their own assessment activities, some have endorsed the use of performance assessment—without necessarily using that label. The 1990 paper written by the Council of Arts Accrediting Associations urges educators to focus assessment on students' "ability to integrate knowledge and skills comprehensively on professional work" (p. 6). Zlatic describes the expectations of ACPE, the pharmacy accreditor. Its guidelines state that "evaluation should extend beyond the acquisition of knowledge by students to the application of knowledge and skills in the care of patients" (Chapter 4). Further, ACPE advises that assessment procedures should encourage students to integrate and apply their skills rather than encourage memorization of details and facts. ACPE's endorsement of performance assessment is similar to NASAD's. However, ACPE's advice is aimed at changing the practice of members (who, Zlatic writes, often rely on objective tests) rather than at resisting public pressure for inappropriate measures (as NASAD was attempting to do.)

Based on her review of the standards, Mary Diez concludes, "NCATE 2000 represents a major shift to performance assessment of outcomes" (Chapter 3). NCATE 2000 expects teacher education faculty to use multiple methods over time to demonstrate that teacher education students (candidates) know the content of their fields and can apply what they know so that their own students learn. AACSB asks members to review placement rates for graduates and obtain information from stakeholders but is otherwise silent about particular methods. Nevertheless, in the early 1990s, AACSB participated in the development of a standardized objective examination that has since been abandoned and, more recently, has worked with Educational Benchmarking, Inc., as they pilot benchmarking surveys.

Expectations About Stakeholders

Several accreditors explicitly encourage their members to include various stakeholders in their assessment processes. As noted by Zlatic, guidance from ACPE about assessment in pharmacy schools asks for systematic evidence from "sources such as students, alumni, state boards of pharmacy and other publics, professional staff of affiliated practice facilities, and a variety of other practitioners" (Chapter 4). The guidelines specifically mention student exit interviews, alumni surveys, and preceptor evaluations as appropriate means to collect evidence. The COA for social work encourages faculty to collect assessment information from employers of graduates, field instructors, clients, consumers, and others. ABET visiting teams typically include a large percentage of individuals drawn from industry rather than academe.

With respect to impact on students, some accreditors have drawn attention to the important role of feedback in improving student learning. As Mary Diez points out, NCATE expects not only assessment over time, but "ongoing feedback to individual candidates" so that assessment is used to support and develop learning. However, NCATE does not rule out the use of assessment for high-stakes decisions such as advancement in a program (Chapter 3).

Requirements About Reporting and Using Evidence

Accrediting bodies emphasize the role that assessment can play in fostering improvement of student learning and view assessment as a process that encourages change. ACPE expects its members to engage in "data-driven continuous improvement." In its standards document, AACSB states that it "promotes continuous quality improvement in collegiate schools of business"

(2000, p. v.). To be accredited, business schools must demonstrate that they have processes in place to monitor their curriculums and that these processes "have resulted in new or revised curriculums" (p. 20). NASAD encourages faculty to ask if they have "a specific concept of excellence for that curriculum beyond its current status" (1991, p. 4).

The Commission on Collegiate Nursing Education (CCNE), the new accreditation body created in 1997 as an autonomous agency of the AACN, looks for continuous quality improvement within a framework of program effectiveness and efficiency. Rather than repackaging traditional expectations and methods, this agency is encouraging assessment as a "conversation" focused on the knowledge and skills nurses need for the new century. For example, nurses are encouraged to debate the role of technology in creating innovative teaching techniques.

Because accreditors now evaluate members with respect to their own unique missions, they have an opportunity to move away from requiring rigid templates for collecting information. Just as performance assessment allows students to choose how they will demonstrate proficiency, so too the new emphasis on program performance and improvement should allow faculty this choice. Indeed, several accreditors have become less prescriptive. AACSB standards no longer include any templates or charts that must be submitted. Instead, each standard includes a section titled *Basis for Judgment* that lists types of information business schools must provide (AACSB, 2000). Dill points out that "schools gripe about what accreditors expect, but are often grateful for templates to be reviewed against" (1998a, p. 15). Zlatic also makes this point. The challenge for accreditors is to provide sufficient direction without taking away the initiative for faculty to tell their own stories.

Lessons, Challenges, Issues

Chapter authors describe many successful assessment programs but also are candid about issues and challenges that faculty and administrators face regardless of their best intentions in carrying out meaningful assessment. Several of these lessons and challenges are reviewed here.

Assessment Should Support the Learning Process

Perhaps most important, for assessment to succeed, it must support the point of view of learning that has been adopted in the discipline and within the larger institution. Faculty who believe in active learning and feedback for students need to reflect this in the assessment processes they develop. Some accreditors explicitly encourage their members to link assessment to an over-all view of teaching and learning. As part of the move to professionalize teacher education, in 1987, NCATE began requiring its member institutions to build their programs on conceptual frameworks and to spell out the philoso-phy, purpose, and critical knowledge bases that guide all aspects of their cur-riculums. The outcome statements now required by NCATE 2000 are typically incorporated in the conceptual framework.

As in teacher education, innovations that have occurred in the assessment of pharmacy students are part of a larger set of changes that affect the way stu-dents are taught and evaluated. Tom Zlatic describes how the mission of pharmicists has shifted away from providing products toward providing patient care. In implementing the new mission, educational leaders recom-mended the adoption of an ability-based curricular plan. This meant that fac-ulty would articulate outcome goals for students expressed at three levels of progress, provide learning experiences to help students develop these abilities, and design assessment methods to provide feedback that enables students to gauge their progress. In advocating this approach, pharmacy leaders were endorsing the assessment-as-learning principles and practices that originated at Alverno College. It is unclear whether all pharmacy schools will adopt this model, but several have implemented aspects of it with great success. Mary Diez also describes the use of this approach with education students at Alverno College and recommends that others adopt its principles as they respond to the new accreditation standards developed by NCATE.

Assessment Requires Flexibility and Patience

Because things do not always turn out quite the way that was expected, assess-ment plans often have to be modified. In some cases, additional time is needed to allow faculty to become more comfortable with the process. According to Neil Palomba, assessment leaders should focus on making annual progress rather than sticking to a rigid timetable. In fact, the schedule for the assess-ment program in BSU's College of Business was changed after assessment lead-ers observed that faculty needed more time to complete their curriculum review and to develop program-level assessment plans. After some initial expe-riences with their senior seminar, business faculty at SIUE changed their approach to the course. They now ask students to create rather than revise papers, and they have added a letter grade to the course in order to increase student motivation to do well. Faculty in the Center for Creative Studies cur-rently are reworking the scoring system for their senior papers. For assessment to have its greatest impact, faculty must be willing to reevaluate regularly and make adjustments to their assessment processes and activities. Accreditors too can benefit from introspection as the COA for social work has done with its Quality Assurance Research Project.

Assessment Requires Faculty Involvement and Administrative Leadership

The examples contained in the foregoing chapters make it quite clear that faculty involvement is crucial for effective assessment. Social work faculty at the College of St. Catherine and the University of St. Thomas have learned that assessment is a collective responsibility that cannot be "taken care of" by one member of the faculty (Chapter 6). It is also clear that faculty roles can differ. Faculty can serve on key assessment committees, collect assessment information in their classes, participate in assessment discussions, and critique assessment results. Not everyone needs to lead, but it is important that each individual have an opportunity to contribute. Clarity about roles is necessary, and, as faculty in BSU's Master of Business Administration program have done, it may be helpful to write out an explicit statement of responsibilities. It is also important that assessment leaders seek input and approval of the faculty as a whole at several points in the process. At NAU and Seton Hall, the work of small groups of faculty was eventually endorsed by the entire department.

Several chapters make it clear that meeting internal and external expectations for assessment of student learning has not been an easy challenge for faculty or administrators. Boland and Laidig indicate that responding to outcome criteria posed by NLNAC "posed an overwhelming struggle to faculty groups" who looked for existing models from colleagues in nursing and other disciplines (Chapter 5). Muffo writes that changes in the ABET accreditation process left engineering faculty in "a world somewhat alien to them" and notes their "apparent lack of support for the new criteria" (Chapter 9). Lee Harvey describes how faculty in the United Kingdom are concerned about the requirements for "threshold standards" for undergraduate degrees that are being created by the Quality Assurance Agency in Higher Education (Chapter 12).

On many campuses, faculty across disciplines have been encouraged not only to voice their concerns about assessment but also to take advantage of opportunities to learn more about how to meet their assessment responsibilities. Chapter authors indicate that numerous faculty have attended conferences and participated in on-campus training with respect to assessment. At Southern Illinois University Edwardsville, business faculty participate in writing-through-the-curriculum workshops that are facilitated by faculty from English and speech. Learning about performance assessment and the process of creating scoring rubrics or guides has been particularly important for faculty in applied disciplines.

The issue of faculty rewards for assessment continues to be discussed on many campuses. BSU has had great success with summer assessment grants; and, at Ohio University, departments have received awards for educational improvement, funded by the provost based on reported assessment activities (Williford, 1997). The real challenge is to reflect assessment activities in the traditional reward structure. Contributions to assessment are considered an important element of teaching activities in BSU's College of Business and are considered in merit pay decisions. Boland and Laidig point out that in nursing, faculty research has refocused on assessment-related issues.

Although faculty involvement is a key aspect of assessment, assessment also needs to have leadership and oversight. In several cases, division- and/or program-level curriculum or assessment committees have played important roles in sustaining assessment efforts, typically providing encouragement, guidance, and coordination for the process. As assessment develops, some programs find they need to provide additional leadership. In the third year of the Center for Creative Studies assessment program, an assessment coordinator was appointed, and two years later a standing assessment committee was created and approved by the Board of Trustees.

Assessment Should Reflect and Enhance Existing Faculty Culture

Muffo argues that the "culture of the discipline must drive the assessment process," and he advises faculty to draw on curriculum methods that are traditional to the discipline such as senior design courses in engineering (Chapter 9). The previous chapters indicate that, in a number of programs, assessment has not only drawn on the existing faculty culture but it has succeeded in changing that culture. It has encouraged faculty to place more value on evidence of learning other than course grades and to think collectively about how student learning can be improved. But what makes this happen? In programs that succeed in changing their cultures, faculty devote not just weeks or months but years to developing successful assessment programs. Faculty in Indiana University's School of Nursing began developing their curriculum revision and assessment process in 1994 and implemented it in 1998. Faculty like these see assessment as a "work in progress" rather than a collection of reports to be sent to an accreditor every few years. Assessment leaders in these programs create opportunities for faculty discussion and foster a sense of shared purpose. In addition to shared purpose, faculty culture involves shared language, values, and traditions, all of which can be influenced by assessment.

The chapters demonstrate some differences in assessment-related language across disciplines. Teacher educators both in the United States and the United Kingdom tend to speak about standards rather than outcomes when describing what students should know and be able to do, while faculty in other disciplines refer to competences, learning objectives, or expectations for students. Accreditors also differ in the way they use terms. NLNAC defines "outcomes" as performance indicators that illustrate how well a program has accomplished its mission. In addition to critical thinking and communication, NLNAC outcomes include graduation rates and patterns of employment. Several accreditors use the term "assessment of outcomes" for all of the areas they examine rather than just for assessment of student learning. With so many possibilities, faculty need to agree on the meaning of these terms within their own programs. Discussing and agreeing on a definition for the word "assessment" can be particularly helpful for faculty. Also important, faculty need to operationalize the statements of expected competences that come from accreditors or for that matter from the institution. This gives local meaning to what are often very broad concepts. As Boland and Laidig write, in nursing, educators and practitioners "grapple with common language to explain what comprises discipline-specific nursing knowledge." Further, they observe that critical thinking has been a particularly difficult outcome to define and assess (Chapter 5).

Sorensen and Spencer from Virginia Tech note the importance of relating assessment to what is valued in the department. Faculty who value teaching and learning can be reminded of the important role assessment plays in fostering learning. Baskind, Shank, and Ferraro tell us that in the social work program at Columbia College, "assessment has become a way of thinking." It has made faculty "better teachers" (Chapter 6). Faculty who emphasize research in their careers can be encouraged to view assessment as an opportunity to study student learning, as nursing faculty have done. Because faculty in many programs value accreditation, the pressure from accreditors to undertake assessment is sometimes viewed as helpful. An important question is, "How much value is placed on improvement?" For assessment to succeed, faculty have to be willing to change what they do and to think differently. The culture in NAU's College of Business began to change when faculty were able to move beyond course boundaries and think about the business core as a joint venture. In Chapter 3, Diez references Weisenbach (2000) who points out the importance of replacing pronouns like "I" and "mine" with ones like "we" and "ours."

To continue tradition, the value of assessment must be shared with new-comers to the faculty or the profession. At King's College, all new faculty participate in workshops to help them understand the importance of their competency growth model. Faculty at the St. Louis College of Pharmacy conduct teaching seminars to provide their residents with experience in designing and carrying out assessment projects.

Assessment Benefits From Communication and Collaboration

Successful assessment requires communication and collaboration both across programs and within programs. Boland and Laidig lament "limited avenues for sharing" particularly in "real-time" forums (Chapter 5), and Tom Zlatic writes that "more sharing needs to be established between schools, honest sharing that extends beyond public relations documents" (Chapter 4). Assessment in pharmacy schools benefited greatly from the AACP-appointed focus group that brought representatives from several schools together to think about the future of pharmacy education. Three schools represented on the group later received a grant from the Fund for the Improvement of Postsecondary Education (FIPSE) to develop a common approach to student assessment. Then, with a follow-up FIPSE grant, faculty from these schools served as consultants to eight additional schools that were adapting ability-based learning and formative assessment. Although accreditors are unlikely to fund curriculum development projects directly, they can continue to appoint special committees, hold conference sessions, and distribute written materials in ways that allow programs to share their experiences.

Increased communication between accreditors and their members also benefits assessment. Dill argues that accreditors should be more aggressive in seeking input, perhaps visiting campuses to seek feedback on new initiatives; and members need to be more eager in providing their input on draft standards and other documents prepared by accrediting agency staff. Dill also challenges accreditors to "share more of the results of accreditation" (1998b, p. 25) through reports that contain general descriptions of the state of the field and are distributed to employers and other interested parties. Although the theme here is collaboration, Dill believes that having more than one accrediting agency in a field, as in nursing and teacher education, can be "a potent weapon for reform" (1998b, p. 23). For example, the Teacher Education Accreditation Council has introduced an innovative audit process to examine the capacity of their member institutions to self-assess and improve (Dill, 1998a).

Not to be overlooked, colleagues from abroad can help faculty and administrators learn more about assessment. In Chapter 12, Lee Harvey describes the context for assessing student competence in the United Kingdom. In that country, professional and regulatory bodies are heavily involved in the provision of professional education and training. The International Conference on Assessing Quality in Higher Education, which is held each year at an international site, offers a valuable opportunity to learn about assessment in other countries.

Internal communication is also important. Many faculty have been able to use assessment results to improve their programs, but this does not happen automatically. To facilitate programmatic assessment, leaders must provide opportunities for collective review and discussion of assessment evidence. These can be ad hoc opportunities such as brown bag lunches or faculty retreats, but planned opportunities, such as regular faculty or committee meetings, also need to be in place. Students, too, can add to this dialogue, perhaps helping to define outcomes, as well as to evaluate findings.

Kristi Nelson writes that in the visual arts, "a critical problem that persists is how to take efforts that are individually based and focus on self-reflection and make these programmatically centered" (Chapter 10). She describes how faculty in the Center for Creative Studies were able to work together to organize their efforts into a coherent assessment plan. Nelson believes that faculty expertise in assessing individual students should not be isolated from programmatic assessment; both are needed to "create healthy, viable, and energized learning environments for students" (Chapter 10). Nelson's point applies equally well to disciplines other than fine arts.

Accreditors Need to Ensure That Visiting Teams Are Well Prepared

The importance of development efforts in preparing faculty to engage in assessment has already been noted. But faculty are not the only ones who should be prepared. Because the focus of accreditation has shifted so greatly, it is extremely important that visiting teams be familiar with the new emphasis on assessing student learning. The good work of accreditors in alerting their members to assessment expectations and responsibilities will not be successful if teams cannot effectively evaluate the assessment programs they observe on college and university campuses. Good assessment practices need to be recognized and encouraged; poor practices need to be challenged. Tom Zlatic notes that faculty in some pharmacy schools privately hope that visiting teams will probe beneath the surface to "force substantive change that will make assessment more meaningful." Zlatic concludes, "Accrediting teams that confuse paper with reality will slow the assessment movement" (Chapter 4). Dill points out that "good reviewers are gems" but reviewers can also be unprepared, ill-informed, or unrealistic. As Dill urges, accrediting bodies should focus training of reviewers on "enlarged expectations about planning and assessment" (1998b, p. 21).

Disciplinary accreditors have recognized the importance of sending well-prepared teams to college and university campuses. John Muffo notes ABET's concern that reviewers be able to evaluate schools according to their new standards. In January 2000, the Council for Higher Education Accreditation (CHEA) adopted a *Statement of Good Practices and Shared Responsibility in the Conduct of Specialized and Professional Accreditation Review.* According to the statement, specialized accreditors need to ensure that accrediting teams are well-informed and prepared for review and that standards and policies are applied consistently. Similarly, the Association for Specialized and Professional Accreditors (ASPA) has had a *Member Code of Good Practice* in place since March 1995. The code sets forth expectations for member organizations including the need to work with institutions to ensure that the collective experience and expertise of site team members is appropriate.

Accreditors Need to Emphasize Improvement in Educational Programs

The ultimate reward from assessment occurs when faculty use assessment evidence to improve their programs. Accreditors need to help make this happen. Dill (1998a, 1998b) believes that, rather than protecting special interests in the fight for larger budgets, accreditation should help programs develop distinctive offerings and respond to the needs of the public. Clearly, many external challenges exist. Boland and Laidig detail numerous pressures in the field of nursing, including changing population demographics, the technology explosion, and a decreasing workforce. Mary Diez writes about the impact public policy might have on future teachers as Title II regulations begin to require states to rank teacher education programs. Accreditors should help programs meet these challenges. Dill praises agencies that "try to mobilize their members' experience and their links to practitioners and the public to help open windows on where the world is heading" (p. 24), and he urges accreditors to take the role of "missionaries dedicated to improving academic programs" (1998b, p. 20).

Conclusions

Due at least in part to encouragement from accrediting bodies, faculty in professional fields have become campus leaders in assessment. Accreditors can feel justified in having insisted that their members not only undertake assessment but also implement good assessment practice. For example, accreditors have urged their members to articulate expected competences including both general education and discipline-specific skills, involve a wide network of stakeholders, engage in performance assessment, and use assessment evidence to improve learning. Through their actions, accreditors have recognized that assessment is a process that needs to engage faculty and yield results if it is to thrive.

Although passage of the 1998 amendments to the Higher Education Act served as an additional spur to action, many disciplinary accreditors were already heavily engaged in assessment. AACSB, for instance, rewrote its guidelines in 1991 to encourage continuous quality improvement and assessment; and accreditors, similar to faculty, have learned through experience how to encourage assessment most effectively. For example, the Commission on Accreditation for Social Work recently introduced a faculty development program for assessment in response to the needs of its members.

Can or should accreditors do more? It is very important that accreditors permit faculty to shape their own assessment programs. An advantage in implementing assessment in accredited programs is the consensus that often exists in the profession about the knowledge, skills, and values that graduates in the field should possess. Yet the preparation of a business graduate from, for example, Miami University might be different in some important respects from that of one who graduates from Ohio University. Accreditors need to resist the impulse to make things too prescribed or too uniform. The chapters in this book contain evidence that faculty have often struggled to determine what accreditors want, a process that can be a distraction from more important questions such as: What should our own graduates be like? And how will we know if they have achieved that?

With this caution in mind, what more can accreditors do? As already stated, the need to have well-trained reviewers who emphasize assessment in their reviews is imperative. Although not mentioned frequently in the foregoing chapters, in some instances, faculty have been disappointed when their hard work in assessment has gone unrecognized. Disciplinary accreditors should make special efforts to celebrate the assessment successes of their members. Newsletters, conferences, recognition programs, and websites can be used for this purpose. Developing an inventory of successful assessment practices, such as universities and colleges create for their academic units, is another possible strategy.

To enhance the positive effects they have on assessment, disciplinary accreditors should leverage their influence beyond intermittent five- or ten-year visits. How can they do this? The preceding suggestions may help. In addition, during their reviews, accreditors need to focus on the assessment processes that are in place at their member institutions, paying attention to whether or not appropriate structures exist to sustain assessment efforts past accreditation visits. Accreditors also can attempt to continue assessment conversations between visits, perhaps through occasional roundtable discussions of members selected at random. Although no one would welcome elaborate annual reports, regular updates about assessment progress could be exchanged for less frequent or less burdensome self-study reports. Whatever strategies are adopted, accreditors do need to find ways to ensure that assessment efforts are continuing.

Both CHEA and ASPA have taken strong stands on the need for assessment of student learning and appropriate conduct for accreditors. As this and other chapters demonstrate, accrediting bodies and their members have responded. Now may be an opportune time for CHEA or ASPA to bring together representatives of disciplinary accrediting bodies and their members to discuss "best practices" in assessment. A major theme of this book is that faculty from different disciplines have much in common and thus much to share with each other about assessment practices. The same can be said for accrediting bodies as they work with their members and each other to encourage assessment.

Although more can always be done, the evidence in this book indicates that disciplinary accreditors have taken up the challenge to encourage assessment and improvement of student learning, and faculty in professional fields have risen to this challenge. We admire their efforts.

References

AACSB—The International Association for Management Education. (2000). *Achieving quality and continuous improvement through self-evaluation and peer review: Standards for accreditation.* St. Louis, MO: Author.

American Council on Education. (1997). *Spanning the chasm: Corporate and academic cooperation to improve work-force preparation.* Washington, DC: Author.

Andrews, K., & Neal, J. C. (1999, February). *The basics of outcomes and assessment.* Paper presented at the AACSB Outcome Assessment Seminar, Clearwater Beach, FL.

Association for Specialized and Professional Accreditors (ASPA). (1995, March). *Member code of good practice.* Chicago, IL: Author.

Council of Arts Accrediting Associations. (1990, April). *Outcomes assessment and arts programs in higher education.* Briefing paper, Reston, VA: Author.

Council for Higher Education Accreditation (CHEA). (2000, January). *Statement of good practices and shared responsibility in the conduct of specialized and professional accreditation review.* Washington, DC: Author.

Dill, W. R. (1998a, November/December). Guard dogs or guide dogs? Adequacy vs. quality in the accreditation of teacher education. *Change: The Magazine of Higher Learning,* 30 (6), 12–17.

Dill, W. R. (1998b, July/August). Specialized accreditation: An idea whose time has come? Or gone? *Change: The Magazine of Higher Learning,* 30 (4), 18–25.

Evers, T. E., Rush, J. C., & Berdrow, I. (1998). *The bases of competence: Skills for lifelong learning and employability.* San Francisco: Jossey-Bass.

Hutchings, P., and Marchese, T. (1990). Watching assessment: Questions, stories, prospects. *Change: The Magazine of Higher Learning,* 22(5), 12–38.

Mentkowski, M., & Associates. (2000). *Learning that lasts: Integrating learning, development, and performance in college and beyond.* San Francisco: Jossey-Bass.

National Association of Schools of Art and Design. (1991, second printing, 1997). *The assessment of undergraduate programs in art and design.* Reston, VA: Author.

Weisenbach, E. L. (2000). *Standards based accountability as a tool for making a difference in student learning.* Paper presented at the American Association of Colleges for Teacher Education Annual Meeting, Chicago, IL.

Weisenbach, E. L., Mack, K., Scannell, M., & Steffel, N. (1998). *Multiple voices: A shared vision.* Paper presented at the American Association of Colleges for Teacher Education Annual Meeting, New Orleans, LA.

Williford, A. M. (1997). Ohio University's multidimensional institutional impact and assessment plan. In P. J. Gray & T. W. Banta (Eds.), *The campus-level impact of assessment: Progress, problems, and possibilities.* (New Directions for Institutional Research, No. 100.) San Francisco: Jossey-Bass.